There Goes English Teacher

Also by Karin Cronje:

This Protracted Birth, short story, in
Lyfspel/Body Play (1994)

Vir 'n pers huis (1998)

Aah, short story, in *40 is g'n vloekwoord* (1999)

Alles mooi weer (2008)

There Goes English Teacher

A memoir

Karin Cronje

Published in 2018 by Modjaji Books
Cape Town, South Africa
www.modjajibooks.co.za

© Karin Cronje
Karin Cronje has asserted her right to be
identified as the author of this work.
All rights reserved. No part of this book may be
reproduced or transmitted in any form or by any
means, mechanical or electronic, including photocopying
or recording, or be stored in any information storage or
retrieval system without permission from the publisher.

Some names of people and places have been changed
to protect the privacy of those involved.

Edited by Alison Lowry
Cover text and artwork by Gretchen van der Byl
Book layout by Andy Thesen
Set in Stone

Printed and bound by RSA Litho, Cape Town
ISBN print: 978-1-928215-61-5
ISBN ebook: 978-1-928215-62-2

NATIONAL ARTS COUNCIL
OF SOUTH AFRICA

*For Marko Coetzee and Karen Trudel
for your warm hearts and unshakeable
presence in my life*

When we are young, the words are scattered all around us. As they are assembled by experience, so also are we, sentence by sentence, until the story takes shape.

– Louise Erdrich

GWENG-SONG

"VICTORIA I'M GOING to Korea!"

"Where's that?"

"Above us somewhere."

Victoria and I are crouched on the loo in my son's bathroom, squashed between a window and the shower wall in an effort to read the world map stuck on the shower wall. I go up Africa's west coast. She takes the right side of the world.

"I'm lost in America. I'll come over to your side."

"Here it is," she says. "This spot near Japan."

"It's not very big, hey?"

"It's far, Karin."

"It's bloody far. But that's where I'm going."

Victoria seems worried. "What are you going to do there?"

"Teach English."

"Why do you want to go away?"

"I can't sit under the oak tree looking at the mountain and wondering where the hell I am in my life for another moment. Besides, my money is running out."

"You should not have given up those contracts with the publishers."

"I want to dedicate my life to something, do an ethical, moral kind of thing. I don't want to promote authors and their books any longer."

"You did that coaching course."

"Yes, but the training was really bad. And I suspect coaching is a new bandwagon full of poorly equipped people."

Silence.

"You're not a teacher."

"I'll make it up as I go along."

"I don't know."

I don't know either. And how is teaching going to be moral?

"You write, all these years. Ag no, man, Karin."

"Oh yes, the writing."

That's a never-ending saga.

Perhaps I should reconsider. The list of pros is strong, though:

I'll have time to write.

I'll build a pension for myself and save Victoria's.

I'll get my son through architecture; he's not even half way.

I'll hopefully make a drastic mind-shift and change the tone of my novel. Perhaps then my main character will be more palatable.

I'll be giving up Victoria, the house, my friends. And what about my country? I suspect I love this land. I'll be giving all this up to go and make Korea my home. To go and emigrate.

My son! Though mother and son should separate now. It's natural. But my heart, my beautiful Marko boy!

Best not to get into this now.

How will my leaving affect my father? And Jasper, my deepest love, Sir Jasper the schnauzer.

Stop now! These are things for cons.

Never mind pros and cons, they are window dressing. I suppose I could get those contracts back. Still.

To hell, I'm going.

Since working out the pros and cons six weeks have passed, in which I have re-arranged my entire life, thrown away my son, my dog and everything dear.

The house has been let to wonderful people who will build on a bathroom. The rent will go straight from them to the builder, who has been commissioned. The plans are to be supplied by Marko, who will liaise with the architect, who will give him sketches. For a few hundred rand the builder's draftsman will draw up the plans. Victoria will work for the wonderful people.

Marko, in the small cottage, is stocked with pots and pans and stuff from the kitchen he's been eyeing forever.

Clothes have been bought since Korean sizes are for the tiniest in the West. I have the most awful Clarks practical sandals and great knee-high boots.

Farewells have been said with a party duly held. Jasper is at my very best friends, Hazel and Ernst (can't think about the last hairy kiss between his eyes); Marko has been farewelled (definitely can't think about this); my jewellery is in Brian's safe – my friend cum kind of lover who is now promptly not a lover anymore. All other valuables are not so neatly in boxes and parked at good friend Adel's. My paintings are under a bed in friend Thea's house. Brian sat for days and copied my discs and now my music's on iTunes. It was a hell of a job. And he's given me a *Lonely Planet* ("You know nothing about Korea, you did no research"). He's also got me on Yahoo.

I stopped over in Joburg, saw my friend Helena, who came to the airport to say goodbye. I have my family's well wishes. I have five sleeping tablets from my dad and he knows not to die soon.

And here I am in Economy class with at least 15 kg of luggage hung around my neck under the snazzy new jersey. Economy class is horribly cramped. How could plane designers make you walk through Business class to here, where individuals become a horde, with mixed body odour and limbs and heads and sighs and longings and hopes stuck together into oneness?

There's something wrong with me. I'm forty-eight and I'm leaving all that's good behind. Life is a lot like a bangle. Kind of solid and devoid of definition. Until the love of friends does its thing and a gossamer filigree emerges. Perhaps this whole Korea thing is a bit of a mistake. Ag no, man, Karin, said Victoria. Ag yes, man, Victoria, it was all meant to be. The way it happened was a sign.

There I was, sitting under the oak tree, catatonic with anxiety after the contracts with the publishers had been given up, and realising that life contemplation brings no income. And then I heard about someone who was teaching in Korea and I just knew that was what I was going to do. But how to get a job? So I sat some more. Until I spoke to a colleague from my employment days whose South African friend Leona was visiting from Korea, at which the catatonia lifted and I rushed over to see her.

Yes, Leona said, it's a financial paradise, but you'll have to apply.

God help me, I can't apply for things.

But in stepped another South African, a nephew of Leona's,

Paul, and his Korean girlfriend Mae, bound together in throbbing new love. Mae got on to her little Korean phone and spoke to her friend Sarah, a hagwon owner, and right there and then I had a job, together with the hagwon owner's telephone number and email address, which are now in the new Yahoo account.

"What is a hagwon, Mae?" I asked.

"It's a private school for after government school."

"Will my contract stipulate my working hours? I'm also going there to write, you see."

"We don't make contracts. No worry. You can trust."

Yes, said Leona, it's how it works. She taught at hagwons before teaching at the university in the town next to where I'm going to be. I was still sceptical, but Paul, who is at the same university as Leona, confirmed it.

And now I must sit back, eat the Economy class food and forget my father's sensible question whether I know anything about teaching English to foreigners. And never mind that under home language – if Sarah had ever asked – I would truthfully not have been able to put down anything other than Afrikaans.

"EXCUSE ME? EXCUSE me?"

But no smallest of persons at Seoul airport understands. I need help urgently, because Sarah is not at the airport and her email address, together with cell phone number, are banged shut in the Yahoo account, of which I can't remember either address or password. I am an ever-growing frantic ball of concern. I'll have to make my way to Sarah's hagwon on my own. How could I be so disorganised? Who exactly is 'Sarah from Korea'? And 'Mae from Korea'?

Born from extreme franticness, I have the presence of mind to flip open the new Moleskine notebook. But there's nothing in it, except the filigree nonsense written on the plane.

I'll try the name of the town I'm going to, which is not on *Lonely Planet*'s map.

"Excuse me!" I have planted myself firmly in the way of an oncoming small person. "Gweng-song?"

She looks up: bewilderment, but I have her attention and to keep it I now search my bulging handbag. And as sure as the coming to Korea was a sign there is a piece of paper with an overly long telephone number on it.

The woman phones. She frowns, phones again, looks up and crosses her wrists into an X.

"Gweng-song?"

She looks at my ticket. Again the X. She looks around. A man approaches, to whom she speaks very sweetly. They phone the number, they consult the ticket. Another X and off they go.

The ticket shudders between my fingers as I put it back in its folder. My God, I have only myself. But there, oh heavens holy, is another ticket.

Gweng-song? No, Gwong-soon! I had the wrong town.

"Gwong-soon!"

7

I wave the ticket like a peace flag. People come to the rescue, check the second ticket, and someone takes me by the bent elbow and points to a bus outside. He writes down a 17 on his business card and nudges me off urgently. I realise I'm late, but where am I heading? The bus starts moving. I shout, I wave, the 15 kg around my neck flap under the designer jersey. I stumble on, I show the driver my ticket and hand him a handful of dollars. Another wristed X. What's wrong with these people? But a man from deeper in the bus comes up and pays in Korean won and says: "Please, come sit with me."

The angel Gabriel.

"This bus takes you to other airport. There you get the plane to Gwang-soon. But you. You must hurry. You are late."

Indeed. Late. The bus stops at a smaller airport. I'm rushed onto a plane and before I can register where I am we land at the smallest airport ever. Gwang-soon!

A woman with see-through eyes walks up to me.

"Karin?"

"Sarah?"

She nods. Bull's eye!

"It is only luggage you have?"

"I could only bring 30 kg."

She seems very suspicious that a mere 30 kg accompanies a settler. I don't show her the stash under the jersey.

As we drive from Gwang-soon to Gweng-song, my new town, we make pleasantries, which aren't pleasant. There are a million hills and trees, but everything is bare.

"It's winter," Sarah says.

Hell, she reads thoughts.

"A little problem. Lesley ... the apartment ... Lesley is teacher before you. But she, she leaves soon. Very soon." Then: "I can hear you are not American. You have South African accent."

Bless the ear that knows nothing about the dreaded Afrikaans accent. Here I am just South African.

"Yes, like all nations we do our own thing with English."

The towns get smaller. The roads remain excellent.

"Good roads you have."

"My husband is flop."

"A flop?!"

"He did *not* succeed at the university. He can*not* be a lecturer. Now he teaches at school."

"Oh."

"He can*not*." There's a definite pause between 'can' and the emphasised 'not'.

Silence.

"You must meet school." Meet the school? It must be close to midnight and I've been travelling for days. Surely Sarah doesn't mean right now?

We park outside a low, square building, stretched between two corners with an open piece of land, on the corner of which is a bus stop. The school is entered by way of a dirty double glass door. Inside is an orange plastic couch and odd bits of furniture that form a corner in which sits a secretary. She bows her head and smiles. There is a buzz of tired kids. Left is a staircase. Right are glassed rooms and passages. A man – the flop husband, I suppose – emerges from a passage.

"This is Mister Park, my husband."

Mister Park doesn't shake my hand. He just grumbles. "What you need?"

"Perhaps I can phone my father? I've come so far …" Not to say that he must be mad with concern, having clearly witnessed that his youngest child was not well prepared for her new life, for which she couldn't quite remember her reasons for embarking on.

"I phone. Here."

And here's my father's voice. I assure him that all went smoothly and I'm in the hands of really nice people.

"You speak other language?"

I forgot to hide Afrikaans!

"Oh, that. We speak many languages in South Africa."

"Aprica."

If ever there was a more loaded way of saying Africa. "But English … English is the main language. Yes, English."

Off Sarah and I go again. We drive up a hill and into a maze of apartment blocks. We park at the furthest block. We take the lift up to the seventh floor in silence.

"Lesley is out very soon," Sarah explains again as she opens an apartment door. No knocking. Lesley appears. Boss and newly former teacher glance silently at each other. Now Sarah smiles almost broadly. "Your apartment. But Lesley –"

"I'll be out soon," cuts in Lesley as she turns around and walks back inside. In a sec we've gone past the smallest bedroom, which is the length of a Western human being, and the width of not much more, through the kitchen, which is really a short passage, and into the living room/bedroom, which is open to some sort of enclosed balcony where washing is hanging from the ceiling.

"I washed the floors," offers Lesley.

"You'll be happy?"

"I'm sure I'll be happy, Sarah, don't worry." For by now I've spotted her concern and feverish hope that the said here Lesley causes no glitches.

The ducks in a row turn back and follow the leader. At the front door she bends down and puts on her shoes. Without another word she opens the door and out she goes.

"Oh sorry, I didn't think of my shoes. Let me take them off before I forget."

"I washed the floors," Lesley says again.

"They look great, Lesley. It's so nice and warm here."

"It's the ondol."

"Yes?"

"Heated water pipes run under the floor. The water is centrally heated for the whole block. When do you start?"

"In two days."

"You're lucky. Some people start teaching the day they arrive. Have you eaten?"

"It's midnight."

"The shops are open. I'll take you tomorrow. You must be finished."

I sleep solidly for two days on a double bed that was shipped here straight from Liberace himself. It's a monstrously kitsch thing with a carved headboard of fancy loops and curlicues with gold paint swooped around the edges. In between is stuffed and studded orange plastic. To top this, Lesley, who is in the throes of enjoying her sexuality and not at the waning end of it, has draped fairy lights all around the orange cloud.

"Perhaps I'm just overcome by this bed."

"It's jetlag. But come, you start in a while, let me show you how to get to school."

Outside are hills and vegetable patches to the right. Behind my block, low down, is a school with a soccer field without grass. In the parking lot in front of the building there are some small trees. I'm not in a concrete jungle. I can breathe.

Ten minutes downhill and we've reached the school for my first day of teaching, passed through reception with its orange couch and walked up the stairs to the staffroom. The room is divided in two: on the left are four rows of desks, each with five desks slap-bang against each other. On the right is the same set-up. The teachers are packed so tightly together they look like sardines in a tin. In the far front corner is a big free-standing desk, which houses the owner and her computer. It is dead quiet.

Suddenly all the teachers turn to me, bow, and turn back. Lesley hands me over to Diane, my co-teacher. Diane gives me the textbooks for the primary school and books with space for notes, though no notes have been made. In here one also has to write the syllabus for the day, the syllabus I find neatly printed in the syllabus book. These books are pointless and very neat with the three colours Diane uses to complete her syllabus. She hands me another book, a much-handled book – for the middle school. But for the senior classes there are no books. I have to make it up as I go along, it seems.

I take a breath and descend the stairs to the classroom, where the kids are waiting for their new teacher, who has had no time to prepare.

The first class begins and ends. The next class begins and ends. Begins and ends. It's a mayhem of a day. So many kids in the cramped hagwon, so much going on. Will every day be like this? Thank God for the rewritten syllabus. I must just follow the syllabus. And then the afternoon is done, meaning it's seven o'clock and now it's the older kids. I'm in the clapped-out book and I can't make any sense of it. It's eleven o'clock and I go home and sleep.

I wake up to a strange smell. It's cabbage, fermented fish and old garlic, says Lesley, who swears you don't smell it after a while. It drives me to the bathroom where the smell comes up through the drain in the floor, which is next to a bucket for used toilet paper. Not the soiled stuff. Lesley assures me the bucket is necessary. The plumbing in parts of Korea is suspect. The pipes are too narrow for lots of paper. I turn around and flee to the enclosed veranda where I come to a frozen standstill. It has the dirtiest windows, which can't be washed, what with the outside railings tight against them. They go from ceiling to floor, but it's better than being bricked in.

From somewhere far off in the hills I hear dogs barking, then suddenly the barking grows frantic. I'll go and check it out. But first I'm going downtown to where the shops apparently are, after which I'll teach, and then I'll go to Mae's bar, Goldfinger, although by then it will be midnight.

Dear hell. I can't find my way back from the downtown shops. I checked landmarks as I went, but I realise now that everything ahead and behind looks the same. It's no use taking a neon sign as a landmark. Every building sports ten of the things. There aren't any street names and anyway I can't read the few that have them. They are in Hangul. This would still have been okay, but it's not our alphabet. The strange marks look like hieroglyphs. And it's also not as if there's a big shopping centre or an office block. No, man. Small little cubicles on top of, behind, next to other such stuff. I'm lost forever. The tiniest story in the most unimportant newspaper in South Africa will just mention that a woman vanished in the East. As did my sense of direction.

First you must have a feeling of geographical setting, like: I'm in Africa. Then jump and widen into Europe; then America, up into a point, which feels too shiny. Veer right and down into Russia, which just feels very wide. The East is vague energy wafting to the right. And now I'm in this wafting zone where I don't even feel my continent, let alone my country, province, city, suburb. I might as well be on the moon. As for gravity, all a con, I suspect. Soon the earth will move a little more upside down and I'll simply fall off. What if billions of people regularly vanish this way? Who will be left to report it?

"What's your name? Where are you from?" a kid on the opposite side of the street shouts at the top of his voice at the only Westerner around.

"Excuse me?"

What the hell? You don't just shout at a stranger.

"What's your name?"

I walk on.

"Where are you from?"

I bow. I bow to a kid with no manners! When does one bow and when not?

I've reached the school and struggle to get in through the door. No kid makes way for a teacher, it seems. One has a large stack of what look like dried rice cakes. They all share freely. I go up the stairs with a trail of kids behind me and escape into the toilets. There are toothbrushes perched around the basin. Whose are they? A woman is mopping in the toilet and out around the seat. Then she places the mop, mop side up, next to the basin.

In the staffroom Diane hands me a piece of paper on which the day's classes are neatly written.

Is every day the same, or part of every day? Must be part of it, because now, like yesterday, there are four classes with the primary school downstairs in the fish-tank glass cages and then upstairs with the middle school, which really has no clue and wants no clue. But unlike yesterday there's an 11 pm with the high school. Please may this class come along only once a week. But on a Friday! Why can't they just give me a roster for the week?

And teacher starts, soon drop-dead exhausted trying to get uninterested kids interested, silent kids talking, and exhausted kids awake. Jacketed, gloved and hooded teacher acts her hungry and nauseated guts out, while Park's voice booms into the classrooms through the intercom system, spooking teacher to hell and gone.

The teaching's done and, although it's only the second day, I take the plunge and approach Sarah, the hagwon owner.

It's about the phone and the internet, which the contractless contract promises.

"We do *not* have contracts in Korea."

Last year apparently she broke the code of honour and gave her teachers contracts. There was a quiet uproar. They wanted to know whether she didn't trust them anymore. But foreigners, she knows, we want contracts. "You will have contract."

And now it is past midnight. I walk out into a freezer and two blocks down to the taxis. I stuff Mae's telephone number into the driver's hand and mime a telephone to an ear and a moving mouth.

"Gamsamnida." Thank you. I should get the word for please. Thank you together with a bow can't get you through a country. I should also get hello. Anyong something. But there's hello for when you enter, and another hello if someone else enters and you are already there. Or is that with the goodbye? Rather stick to thank you. One word in the hand is better than ten in the bush.

It is a short warren-like drive to a built-up deserted area. I follow a faint light up the narrowest stairs to the strong smell of urinal cleanser. I enter the toilet, I squat, I pee straight into a hole. Oh God, I don't feel so good, but I drag myself into the bar.

"Karin! You are here! Come, come!"

It's Mae and she's still as nice as when I met her in Cape Town when she got me the job.

"I make you special drink. You are too quiet."

To tell the truth my eyes won't see so well, my ears won't hear so well. I have no sense of a brain. Everything goes whiz-whiz past.

"You miss Marko? I phone, I phone."

Goldfinger is intimate, with lovely dark wood lining the walls. There is a curved counter behind which glasses are washed, drinks mixed, money taken, fruit peeled and arranged into pieces of art on big plates, and above all, Mae and Soo-mi, Mae's assistant, busy as hell. They are glittering stars, dazzling. Mae is the most enigmatic person on earth.

"Karin! You like the bar? It was design."

On the bar are ashtrays lined with wet toilet paper. Also some with dried coffee grindings. It's a great place, it sticks out like a sore thumb between all the other non-designed places.

"Karin, I show you. See, space in the middle for everyone.

Most everyone. See, there, wall, and wood, like a little house, what is that?"

"Oh, like a cubicle."

"Yes, yes, that. You see a small one, for a small party, and next to it, a big one. Round table for more people. And this one, this is biggest one. Foreigners like this one."

"Foreigners?"

And there they are, fresh from university.

"Come, I give you drink."

"No, Mae, no drink."

I have only dollars and I can't change them until I have a bank account. And it transpires that you're paid only six weeks after you start. That is so that they can get six weeks' work out of you to cover the cost of the plane ticket should you do a midnight run. People are so shocked and overwhelmed when they get here that they secretly disappear from one day to the next, back on the plane home. If the authorities are alerted you can apparently be detained at the airport.

"Mae, I have only dollars."

"No problem, I give you money, I give you drink. Come, phone Marko."

"Marko!"

"Mams!"

"It's bloody horrible. It's dirty, but also not. The buildings are not buildings. Just rooms or stuff packed onto and next to one another. The ceilings are low. Everything is small. I'm in a doll's house. There's a disproportion to me and everything else, I'm a giant."

Sobbing. Heart-out sobbing. He, on the other hand, sounds upbeat.

"Where are you?"

"In Dorrian's car. We're going to Bain's Kloof for the weekend."

More sobbing, because they're on their way to a wooden house on a river. They're going to have wine and swim and perhaps take a lilo, like Dorrian and I did for the farewell-saying, and float into the river to the small island in the middle and drink French champagne.

"Please phone Hazel and ask her how Jasper is doing. And ask Brian what my Yahoo address is."

"I'll SMS you."

"No! You can't SMS your country from here or even receive an SMS."

"That's impossible."

"Please. It's true. I don't know why. I'll phone again. Just keep your phone on."

"Mams?"

"It's bloody awful."

Whiz-whiz. Talking, laughing, black hole, hush hush we all fall down.

So desperate was I that I ended up literally hanging from a rafter. Above Mae's curved bar counter. If ever there was a mensch, it is Mae.

LESLEY HAS AT last figured out her very immediate future and with it the urgent question of where to lay her head at night once she's done gathering together all her 'stuffs', as stuff here is called. She's moving in with the new boyfriend, an engineer from Italy on contract for a few more weeks. It's not what she really planned to do, since, I assume, she has to hide from him the fact that she has a hellish temper and how can you do this in too much company of the beloved? She also has to hide that she, now all of mid-thirties, wants to get married, and to whom really doesn't matter. And there remains the sticky question of her being twelve years older than this boy who recently finished university and is still a little damp behind the ears. But love shall be forever blind as he must look at her very good legs and huge boobs. The in-between is where the blindness lies, since Lesley has somewhat gone to pot here in Korea. But she curls those blonde tresses, balances on spiky heels and off she goes.

She has kept herself in check with me partly because I'm officially the English teacher in the sweatshop and therefore the madam of the apartment, bar of course Mister Park, who can apparently burst through the door without knock or announcement. Privacy is a foreign concept.

She's had ample reason to lose it with me. I have departed. I can't get a grasp of things. What I know now, I won't know just now. All I seem to get out of my mouth is a perplexed 'oh'. And I can't get the shoes thing right. You're constantly busy with your feet. Get home, shoes off and into the home slippers, off with them, into the bathroom plastics, off with them again, into the homies. Enter a restaurant, off go the shoes, go to the loo, communal plastic jobs on. They're disgusting. They're definitely not washed and Dettoled. Exit restaurant, shoes on again. And so it goes on the whole day. It's a foot fetish of another kind. Yet the kids freaked when I taught them 'one foot, two feet', which they couldn't get and I then banged my foot in desperation on the nearest desk, saying "One foot." Then I sat down and banged the other foot on the desk: "Two feet."

Never mind *their* disgusting habits. The spitting!

The cons list is growing. What got into me to come to this dump?

Lesley has now taken the last of her stuffs. The boyfriend helped. He's a boy! His parents are going to faint when they meet this sweetest mature woman, who is really a volcano. The taxis won't even bring her up to our block anymore. They dump her three buildings further down. Well, temper or not, I may be a bit lost without her.

But at least Sarah paid attention to the question of the contract, phone and internet. She must have forced herself out of her tunnel vision where she hears and sees nothing but her work. She summoned Park up to her desk from his netherworld, which is way past where the fish in the tanks are. Wife, sitting behind her desk, and the flop husband, standing this side of the desk, had a spitting fight, while the staff pretended not to notice. A fuming Park summoned me to follow him and stormed ahead. I did an undignified walk-run in an effort to keep up and off we went in his blue Mercedes-Benz, the only foreign car I have seen around here.

Talking and talking in the shop, me there as an appendage, just to have a red cell phone thrust in my hands. "Take money when pay you."

"Thank you, Mister Park." I felt like chucking the phone in his face.

I should rejoice. A hurried man appeared at my apartment and installed internet and got my emails up and running without a word said between us. But the internet is in Korean. And Skype won't work. iTunes also not. Thank God for Mae's boyfriend Paul. He says he'll come and help later in the week when he comes from his town to be here with Mae. But I must in the meantime take my computer to a computer shop. How do I find one? There are plenty, he assures me. I must look around. Where must I look? Downtown. All the shops look the same. And I can't read Hangul. And how will I explain my problem to the computer guy? I can try: "Skype no working."

And cross my wrists. "Skype anie." Or is it anieyo?
Oh hell, I'm so exhausted I can hardly walk.

※

Paul was here! I can't believe how much better I felt even though he couldn't get Skype and iTunes to work. He brought along a whole lot of food Leona had bought for me. She must have figured that the money Mae lent me should by now be wiped out. We chatted about South Africa, politics, social issues, and also everything that gets to me.

The woman in the apartment above mine must have a manufacturing factory going on. She bangs, hammers, and rolls iron balls on the floor right through the night. Even the click of her light switch travels through this cardboard place. Cardboard for walls. Everything is plastic. The floor, the couch, the headboard. That damn thing that's a curtain rail keeps pulling out of the cardboard. And I know I should be grateful because at least I have a curtain, one unlined curtain. And this sickening blue/green wallpaper, flowers or waves, it's dirty and busy. The dirty windows. The whole damn country is dirty, the lift, all over, I can't sleep, I'm nauseous, I stay hungry. And I feel bad that Leona is so kind to me. Had it not been for her back in South Africa introducing me to Mae and Paul, I would not have this job. She's invited me to come and sleep over at her place in the university dormitory even though it's apparently small and I'd have to sleep on the floor. This would surely make it uncomfortable for her too.

Paul listened and hugged and said it's culture shock. And then out it came: he wanted to know, he definitely wanted to know, how I write. He wants to write a book and he tries. Heaven knows. But it just doesn't quite want to materialise. Good luck, I think, every second person wants to write a book. Very few get there, because they expect all you need to do is open your newly bought notebook and start at page one line one. And voilà! Your bestseller gets published.

"Paul," I said, "you need a doggedness, like a Rottweiler that gets hold of an object and won't let go. When there's no pleasure in the process, or even in the absence of the meaning it was supposed to bring to your life, you have to persevere.

Morning, noon and night, year in, year out, to the point you become a little touched by your isolation, because you and your book are in a world that doesn't exist for anyone else. And then you don't know whether there will be interest in your great offering or if it even has relevance."

"But there is some magic?"

Paul was grasping at straws. He desperately wanted to believe that the feeling of unease or downright unhappiness he was experiencing would go if he just wrote that book. He's still in the throes of those intense emotions that lose their hold only when you start leaving youth and beauty behind.

"Yes, there's some magic. Like when unrelated and unintended pieces fall together and make a whole – quite outside your control. That's when I trust the unconscious. But, you know, that can take years. And what drives you in the meantime? No magic – that I can tell you."

He got that vague I'm-not-with-you look. So I didn't tell him that all through you're driven mad. An idea or snippet of a sentence comes into your head and you can't go on living until it's written down. You search your bag, but can't get hold of a pencil and take out lipstick instead, but can only find the back of a till slip, or a paper serviette and onto that goes your idea. And then the wonderful relief that it's out. Just to be lost and all you remember is that it was profound. And you're convinced your book won't make it without that. And if you're lucky, or unlucky, as the case may be, you find your till slip, or the by now disintegrating serviette, and decipher what is clearly drivel.

I'm worried now that I may have put him clean off writing. Worse, I have put myself off it. I don't think I have it in me anymore. Perhaps I should give up.

No.

This is not an option. I gave myself three months to settle in. Then, I'll simply have to haul out a steely discipline and not engage with that undermining voice that plants doubt. I have to keep good faith and keep in mind how far this novel has come.

From that lunch hour at the publishers, where I used to work as a publicist, to now, here, in Korea, with many years in between.

That day I was sitting in the scorching sun outside on the patio, which was also the roof. And I had a feeling inside me. I drew a horizontal line midway through a blank A4 piece of paper. Something was going to happen in the top part. In the bottom part, another something was going to happen. Almost at the end of the hour, when I was just about expiring from heat, I thought the top and bottom parts might each have a protagonist who linked somehow. But if so, the top protagonist wouldn't know about the bottom protagonist. And the bottom protagonist? My feeling didn't say. And it would almost be two different stories that made one story. But the problem was, as I walked back down to my office, how was I going to prevent the one story running away from the other so that the reader would not have to page many pages on for the one story and then come back for the other because, somehow, the two stories would have to be read simultaneously to make sense.

The two stories with their paging problem – that obsessed me to sleeplessness.

Paul sighed. I sighed. He turned back to my computer and I to doubting that I'd ever connect with this stuff again. I was so lost in this that when he gave the computer verdict it took me a while to realise the gravity of it: everything must come off the computer and then somehow on again. And where are my discs? Discs? No, hell, somewhere in a box at home.

So I took the thing to a computer shop. The man didn't know the word Skype.

Lesley's engineer will now ask the other engineers.

It's just not easy to get things done here. One smallest drop of snow fell on my camera, which now doesn't work. It's a Sony and they hate the Japanese. Co-teacher Diane didn't know where I could have it fixed. She was most reluctant. She's really an ice queen. But my gentle and persistent insistence got her to ask another teacher. He's a fabulous man. Exuberant on his platform shoes, he's larger than life, a notch louder than the rest, who are just on the audible side of quiet. His blackest hair is spiked to high heaven. He is a rare nonconformist soul, out of place. He smiles and smiles in his English incomprehension. Oh God, he's lovely, I wish he spoke some English.

I had to go to Seon-chang, Paul and Leona's town. At some tucked-away shop. The only option was last Saturday morning, soon after the Friday midnight class and before the next stint at 2 pm on Saturday. I went, but when I came back the world came to a standstill. The bus stopped in the middle of nowhere. I broke Leona's strictest rule that Mae is not to be pestered with our problems. I suppose since she, Leona, doesn't want any proxy of hers burdening her relationship with the woman who is hopefully soon to become a family member. Lest Mae realises she's about to marry into great Western need. And get cold feet. I phoned Mae.

"Mae, I have no idea where I am."

"Where?"

"Here are only many apartments and two shops. And nothing else. I'm not in a town."

"Where?"

"I don't know. I took the Gweng-song bus, but it stopped somewhere. It's not going any further. I have to teach in a while."

"Karin?"

"Wait. Hold on. I'll stop someone. You speak." Red phone now in a stranger's hand. Deep bow. "Gamsamnida." Thank you, whatever, just speak on my phone, please. Perplexed man speaks, then hands phone back.

"Mae?"

"Karin! You are in Gweng-song Eup."

"What's that?"

"It's like satellite. The bus will not go to Gweng-song. You must get taxi. You must hurry. It is not so near."

The misery of the franticness. I don't call the shots in my life anymore.

But at the same time, hey, the sweetest blessing. I had accepted that food had lost its pleasure value and only kept me from starving. I was sitting in one of the many restaurants on the floor with my legs neatly folded under the table. A group of girls passed outside and couldn't miss the only Westerner, the sore thumb, in the brightly lit restaurant.

"Teacher!"

Elation soared through me. I formed 'please' and waved them towards me. I remembered to do it with my fingers pointing down.

Jessica, a lovely outgoing kid, bounced in.

"Jessica, please, I am hungry. What to eat?" The menu is in Korean hieroglyphs.

"Gamjatang. Number one Korea food."

And it was number one. I scrubbed those narrow pork bones, first with chopsticks, then with a spoon meant for the rice and very hot soup, in which the pork, half a potato and strange stringy green veg floated. Then with my African hands, which by now have a callus from the square metal chopsticks. I remembered hunger howling around the next hour. It is impractical to be hungry three times a day. How many millennia before hunger has revolutionised and we eat once a day?

This is not to say, though, that all is looking up. My red cell still won't phone as far as South Africa, which here exists for no one. They simply don't know where it is, or, actually, what it is. All they hear is Africa.

"Where you from?"

"South Africa."

"Aprica?" Why 'p' instead of 'f'? There's no answer.

"Anie, anie," with crossed wrists. "No. *South* Africa. *Nam* Aprica."

No go.

"Mandela!" I make a comeback, with pride. And the face lights up, love in the eyes. "I'm from Mandela."

I am from Nam Aprika Mandela.

Truth is I am not 'from' anymore.

But not to worry, I'm going to Nagan Folk Village. There's a long weekend coming up, meaning I have all of Saturday and Sunday off. In my *Lonely Planet* Nagan looks like Africa – dry, sun-baked earth, open space – no hills around, a wide expanse of sky, and few people around. And somewhere there, Nagan spa, not on the photo, apparently unprepossessing.

I'm going home!

NAGAN. WHAT HAPPENED there? Nothing. I'm undone.
I went on a trip too soon. I've only been here three weeks, says veteran Leona who's been here five years. I am still in culture shock. Culture shock is like a prolonged psychotic episode. I think a shock is a shock. What does it matter which word you bang in front of it?

What has been undone? Me? It's no use thinking, there's language left only for daily physical living. Instinct, too, has disappeared, leaving a void where once there was certainty.

Perhaps it was due to the void that I felt a little bit of dread as I sat in the front row in the bus, next to the obligatory mop in buses. Actually, mops are all over. I repeatedly said "Nagan" to the bus driver and stabbed my index finger into my breastbone, meaning 'I', and then to the bus door, and down, meaning I want to get the hell off this bus at Nagan, please, gamsamnida. After a long while of curving around hills he flipped open the bus door and waved me off.

And there was an African village in all it splendour with a makeshift café, dust, yellowish grasses swaying a little and thatch-roof huts surrounded by a wide stone wall. I walked around on the wall, looking across the flat veld and surveying Nagan. There were no hotels, but there was a hut outside the wall from which a soft light shone. The owner had almost first class English, which has become a status symbol, a symbol of learnedness and refinement. She said there were homes inside the wall that offered accommodation, but they were probably full by now. As foreigners do – and all of Korea, it seems – I had made no booking in advance. Off I went into a wonderful maze of traditional houses built around a courtyard with chained dogs and washing. The rooms were all bare.

So, back to the woman, who was making traditional paper called hanji. 'Han' for traditional and 'ji' for paper. The only option, she said, was to go to the next town. She wrote something on a piece of her beautiful hanji and off I went to wait for a bus.

I showed the driver my piece of hanji with, hopefully, my destination on it. We curved around houses and shops without sidewalks. I watched civilisation fade away as we drove into the night. Eventually we stopped against a long, deserted building. The forsaken place was the bus depot. It felt as if it were on the edge of the world and if I took one wrong step I'd find myself in another universe. But, thankfully, there was a motel. The only place with lights.

Inside was a lone woman in a cubicle, lower down so that she could only see my knees. She handed me a key and I checked in to what felt like an airtight capsule with floor bedding and no heating.

Down again. "The heating system is not working. The heating not working. Heat, no, no work." But there is only incomprehension and disinterest. And out comes my only Korean word: "Gamsamnida". Thank you.

Back in my room I bang earplugs in and swallow the last of my dad's five sleeping tablets. The good Lord's morning brings a craving for coffee and a croissant. Why am I not in France? Why do I make my life like this? But the good thing is that I'm right at the bus depot. And the ticket sales lady seems to understand that I want to get off at the spa, although she looks worried. She writes a note I can show the bus driver.

What does *Lonely Planet* mean by unprepossessing? I throw the word to the wind and see Roman baths and philosophers in extra thick white Glodina towels, sweating and pursuing the realms of the higher mind. We drive way outside any town. The bus suddenly stops and I'm waved off. There's nothing but the road and a gorge, and across from that, high up a mountainous hill, a building. It takes an hour to get through undisturbed nature, with suitcase in hand.

The entrance to the spa sports a mop and bucket. I pay and am given a key to one of the many tiny lockers. I'm also handed a minute towel, far smaller than our hand towels. Inside the locker is a dirty plastic holder. For one's soaps and things, I suppose. I undress and try to hide my pubes with the towel and follow the chatter. Women and children are washing hair, scrubbing bodies and brushing teeth, each with a shower hose in hand and perched on the lowest of plastic stools, in front of a long mirror with a shelf for personal items. Their soap trays are different from mine.

By now I stare openly. There are all shapes and sizes. It's a fallacy that Eastern women are perfect. Their legs are short in proportion to their bodies and many are bow-legged without much in the line of calves. I try to make myself invisible and go to three not-so-much-like Roman baths or pools. From lukewarm to very hot. In front of the hottest pool is a concrete slab, for resting, I suppose. I'm exhausted and flop down on the slab, soap tray under my head, boobs and whatnot down with gravity. If only I could go home! And it dawns on me that I mean Jugong ee cha, Apart 603, Gweng-song. But how am I going to catch a bus where there's no bus stop with unprepossessing Nagan Spa a deep gorge away from the road? I get up and into a pool, determined to relax. But instead am surrounded by astonishment.

One of the women wades up. She has the fingers of both hands spread, her palms hollow. Those hands extend above her shoulders and come closer to me, withdraw, and come closer again. This is a sign for: can she feel those things protruding from my chest? And she's at it. Oh well, at least I have physical contact in this land of no contact. I come to and it's thumbs up from the beaming woman, now miming the shape of something enormous and round. I manage a silly smile, which freezes in mid-air.

A queue the length of the pool has formed. The spa is in silence as they wait their turn patiently, and file by one after another, looking in disbelief at the imprint in their hands of what they have just felt. My God, I'm a hit!

I followed the last one back to the lockers, where I realised my soap tray was meant for shoes. With lots of miming and looks of bewilderment I got a lift with the groping women. They took me to Leona at the university, a town away from theirs, where I slept on the floor in her dormitory room. These unfathomable people shared their heart of gold.

For the uninitiated, counting working, eating, showering and sleeping hours, subtracting them from 24 hours to get the sum thus for writing hours, doesn't seem such a bad idea. But what's not possible to put into this simple mathematical equation is the problem of sleeplessness, hunger, clinging nausea, exhaustion, the general fucked-out-of-your-mindness. All this takes double hours.

I'm in hell, hell. Even though Leona took me to two temples. Out of the goodness of her heart. Hell, hell. At least Mae phoned Brian back in Cape Town and explained all – that I don't know my email address and the password he got me. She told him that I'm fine and that I hope to God he is finer than I am. One wouldn't wish my kind of fineness on a murderer. I can't remember, what can't I remember? No words. Just all nothing, inside and out.

I think, therefore I am. I feel, I don't feel, therefore. There *have* to be feelings, but thinking and feeling can only happen within language. Which has vanished. Therefore I am not. Besides, here is nothing to confirm I am I. Not the café owner, the beggar at the red light, Marko's beautiful all-over-the-showness, my Jasper dog's smell, Table Mountain so close. I miss no one, although they are an abnormal vividness. I can hear their voices. The rhythm, the timbre. Some of them.

But this is undeniable: relentless migraines. No need to think inside language. Migraines are a language unto themselves.

Perhaps it'll help to write a group email. But what will I write? Shock, shocker, shockest. Best is to go on sitting on the veranda with the washing hanging from the ceiling, behind the very unwashable windows, in some former foreigner's blue camping chair and stare out onto the hills while I continue my activity: unravelling the trimmings of my brown shawl, strand by twisted, looped strand. And read Karin Cronje's biography.

How did she hurry through her days? Was she a forceful person, or perhaps shy? The biographer doesn't say. How did she make love? Did she take, without shame? Or not like this at all? The reader will never know. Who wrote this biography full of no answers? Must be long gone dead. Such a bad biographer, only the main events, and those just jotted down.

She was born in Korea, aged forty-eight. The past has evaporated. There are only flat-line snippets, a vague outline with a trail. Look, there goes the trail, it goes and goes, it is lost in the moon. And the moon dissolves, no moon on Planet Korea.

She has become a reciter of the present. It's not a bad way of living – so, without oneself, with the present as oneself. She forgets to wonder: when shall we three meet again? You – mind, body and heart? She is almost sure she believed in something before, which could help her now. Something to do with energies. Like send out into the universe your best energies and you will be provided with more good energies. It is a farce. Is this really what she believed in?

It may help if she starts fixing her novel. It has become a gangrenous appendage. But how will she involve herself with her disintegrating character, whom she hates? Professor Hilette Barend. And Pearl, her professor's case study who simply disappeared off the face of the earth. They do not lie in her anymore. There is just nothing. But. There is fear.

Marko. *Yes*, Marko *is* my son, it's *written*. But he is neither shape nor feeling. He is just a swirl of blondness. It is good. If he takes form their severance will break into a primal-pitched scream and the screamer will be frozen in this contortion. And when she has her midday sleep, or sometimes when she just stands and stares, she goes somewhere warm and soft, somewhere to the left. But then she slides back into her body, which is here, on this bed on this spot in this Korea. The sliding is like plunging headfirst into water. She feels the horror of it, literally a horizontal slide, right back into this bodiless body. The sliding back from the warm left is worse than not feeling the warm at all. She should stop herself, but the warm sucks her in involuntarily.

She decides to touch herself. Those explosions happen *inside* her body and she will then know that she is she. But it's a useless effort. Terrifying, really. There's a slight feeling, but not in her body. Like an earthquake very far from where one is. The Richter scale says it happened, but for all intents and purposes it didn't happen on the earth one is on.

She walks down to the hagwon, past the garbage man, and bows; into the little street where the piano hagwon is with the narrow door, past the café with its unrecognisable goods, past building rubble, left at the hagwon, three stairs up and into the door. She teaches all, from tiny kids to listless, polite teenagers. She is like a mother, says her owner. The parents like this. Yes, she still has a heart. It breaks all the time. The children have no youth. They are booked into this after-school school till bedtime. They sleep little. They learn by heart. The heart is for learning, not for playing and laughing. They break the children in. These young ones, they are ponies that will become horses, obliging.

She, too, is learning to be obliging. That's why the owner trusts that the owned will not do a midnight run. The owned's visa is connected to her owner. So is her apartment and her cell phone, her internet and her money and her life. She has one day a week free and four days a year, and public holidays. She would love to go back to Africa. But she has no idea how she would then feed herself and her ever-munching son. She is stuck and sunk in Korea.

Yes, she may be learning to be obliging, but one thing that can't be trained out of a person is stubbornness. She's from Afrikaner stock.

I am going to address the question of Ryan. That lively little boy should not be in a class. He's stupid, or he is just very slow in English, but he has no clue. He should have private classes, not get lost in a group where he picks up only sounds. It is immoral to keep on milking his parents, who clearly, by the looks of Ryan, have it tight.

I'll have to approach this carefully. Sarah can't lose face so I can't let her know that it's a bloody shame what she's doing with Ryan.

"Ryan. I wonder, perhaps, what do you think?"

"Yes?"

"He's slow. Don't you think?"

"Yes."

"Perhaps he should be in a different class? Or have private classes?"

"His schedule can*not* be changed."

"But he has no benefit."

My last sentence goes unheard. I am merely a deliverer of instructions in this land where each plays his and her role as stipulated by gender, age and position. I'll just have to swallow my indignation and overwhelming rage. As a person in my position must, as all of Korea, actually, seem to swallow. I must remember I'm not a participant, I'm an onlooker. And I can't go back home.

Says Leona, whose cell number, together with Paul's and Mae's, are what I have on my red cell. It takes three months to adapt. Or six. Often longer. Or never, I think. I looked at those foreigners in the dormitory at the university where Leona teaches when I slept over in her tiny room after Nagan. Some of them have been here five years. They seem fine, but they still have a dazed look about them. An incomprehension that moves like clouds through their eyes.

I tell myself: not to worry. You have no past and you have no future. You have only to fill this hell-hole moment, and not with fear. You should fill it with your defunct brain. Begin at the origin of Korea. But the internet is stuck in hieroglyphs, *Lonely Planet* doesn't say, and there are no English books or newspapers. And CNN and Arirang, a Korean actuality programme in English, have vanished. It's useless asking the kids. They get stuck on a bear. Did some tribe follow a bear and settle here? Or they say, "Gaecheonjeol, day sky open Korea start."

Never give up, said Churchill. So with defunct brain I shall try to understand, in the lame, agonising hour with Ferdinand, son of owner Sarah and the flop husband, the beginning of this country. Never mind that all he's interested in is cars. And never mind that he has no interest in medicine, he who *has* to become a doctor and so fulfil his filial duty, the duty of the first-born son. Tonight he will talk history and myth. And able he should be. They do Greek mythology, Roman mythology and no doubt other mythologies Western brains are taught not to take notice of.

The hour with this poor boy breaks both Ferdinand and his private English teacher. He duly tries his best, and it is a damn sight better than the best of the rest. There's a good warmth between reluctant teacher and reluctant student. He knows, she knows, that neither of them particularly wants to be there. But what he probably knew about, and his teacher didn't, was the fact of the spying camera up in the furthest classroom, the room reserved exclusively for the owner's teaching where teacher and Ferdinand have their class.

And so it came that his teacher's broken heart broke some more, now for him, since his parents are only interested in pushing him to breaking point and not at all in anything else, and that anything else at that point meant his performance at the school concert where he was to show off a dance. So his teacher took it upon herself to make him and his dance feel special and also to blow some life into the misery of the hour. She took him by the hand and together they swirled across the room in some concoction of a Western dance, throughout which he had to teach her – in English – the dance for the concert he couldn't quite get right. And both of them laughed and talked a lot, ending with the teacher undertaking to come to his special occasion and clap loudly for him. Not too loudly, he advised her, and she didn't understand, but saw his worry and assured him she'd make her clapping as soft as possible. But when they both came down the stairs and into reception with the orange couch many teachers were still in front of the TV monitor, now relaying an empty room where just minutes ago the unthinkable was happening.

"Karin," said Sarah, "all the teacher saw you dance!"

And because this comment had more life in it than anything that had come before, the teacher didn't know what to make of it. And because she comes from a country with a lot of sexual abuse – never mind that she's female and Ferdinand male – she started worrying, eventually dragging her exhausted self to Goldfinger to ask Korean Mae whether the dancing and laughing would have affronted the sensibilities of the onlookers. At which darling Mae laughed and couldn't quite understand the worry about sexual abuse, which either doesn't happen here, or is just not an issue.

But now teacher's dancing mood is stifled, and the worry is still alive. Tonight there will be proper sitting down with Ferdinand and a good long conversation. About the origin of Korea.

"But first a prince from sky, ask god father may he to go to land. So prince land in earth. He brought also ministers Wind,

Rain and Cloud."

"Are they those huge wooden statues at the entrance to the temples? The ones that look so angry?"

"Maybe. And bear and tiger are in cave, by special tree. They want be people."

"They want to be human?"

"Yes. So they must stay in cave one hundred day than prince will make them into people. But tiger so boring in cave. He goes."

"Okay. Remember those two words? Boring and ...?"

"Yes. He is bored. Tiger is bored. But bear stay. And bear become person. Beautiful woman. Now she wants child. But first she is queen. Than comes Dan-gun. He is boy of queen. He is first people king."

"Oh, he is the first human king of Korea!"

"Maybe. And he takes later everyone to make the main city in Mount Guwol. And now there is shrine. The shrine name is Samsong."

"Good heavens, like Samsong, the computers and so on?"

"Maybe."

We may speak English better, but what do we have in the line of myth?

As I struggle back up the hill in the dead of night with Ferdinand's teaching done, I realise how distant one can be from what's brewing under the surface. I must be so sad.

This morning I was doing 'What's the matter?'

I mime a backache, half of them shout "What's the matter?" and the other half "She has a backache!"

We'd been through all the possible aches. But how instinctive were their 'What's the matters?' So I burst into a mimed sob. And before the third sob was out they were out of their chairs and hugging me with a lot of 'What's the matters?' And then the sobs turned real. "She's crying." Which brought an immediate halt to the tears: they did the present continuous tense! There was a lot of jubilation on account of the present continuous tense.

And now I must be jubilant because CNN is back and a programme on South Africa is just about to start. Viva! I am from Nam Aprika. A luta.

Dire. There is no other word. Endless queues, beggars,

hospitals desperately dire, vandalised schools, rust-ridden cars, and permeating all, dust. How many Koreans watch CNN? How many American programmes are dubbed into Korean? I might have thought I'd left my country behind, but my shame at what we are tells a different story. The programme is merciless. It's now become an in-depth piece on South Africa's disintegrating health system.

Still, the last thing I want to be is a patient in a Korean hospital. The hospital in downtown main road looks all too suspect, with patients strolling up and down in the street, hooked to their drips. Some things should not integrate. Patients should stay indoors with their unmistakable smell of hospital.

Everyone seems to go on drips. Leona says it's because they can't be ill and stay home. They go to hospital for flu and exhaustion and are declared mortally ill by having a drip stuck into them. The average yearly vacation is only a couple of days. Sick leave is unheard of. Attendance is everything. It really doesn't matter how productive you are with your dire virus or exploding appendix.

She, the giant, had better not get ill. There is no sick leave for her. She had better stick to her miserable migraines and get through the teaching, throbbing away. Or she should wear the paper mouth-and-nose masks everyone here wears when they have a sniffle so as not to spread their germs. The giant should don one so as not to catch one.

And she should definitely understand that Nam Aprika is a swear word of a place. And since she, a foreigner, is already regarded with suspicion, she should just say that she is from Mandela.

SUMMER.

It's a loaded word. The crickets are as big as monkeys. The insect brothers and sisters are a busy family, a loyal Korean group. They multiply and thrive in the bath house in the sky. The first question a foreigner asks you is: do you have aircon?

I do not have aircon.

So I hit on the not so bright idea to go and linger, with my all too casual short pants, in an airconned shop. I found my way downtown to a heavenly cool clothing store for men – the biggest women's sizes are too small – I bowed and uttered my polite hello. "Anyong haseyo." I selected a shirt, but the shop assistant, blocking the entrance to the empty fitting room, wouldn't let me try it on. She crossed those wrists vehemently. I didn't understand, but soon realised I wasn't welcome. So I bought the shirt. It was the most reluctant money that had ever been taken from me. I felt repulsive and uneducated, what with the perfect lingua franca not pouring from me, just a lot of gestures instead.

Outside I gave a quick sniff into my armpits. Perhaps I smelled, or perhaps my casual clothes weren't acceptable, with them always smartly dressed. This is what it must have been like for black people before the land turned into Nam Aprika Mandela. How did people keep a good sense of self?

I was too shaken to brave a restaurant, so had a chilled coffee on a pavement under a low umbrella. From this level I could see only legs. An avalanche of fat approached. The width of an entire Korean could fit into one thigh. It could only belong to a Westerner. Without looking up I said: "Are you an English teacher?" And so entered Audrey, braver of this country for five full years. She's loathed more than the rest of us, on account of her size.

Koreans are the biggest of all Easterners, Audrey says, hopeful that she doesn't stick out too much. They have a lot of Mongol left with the broad span from temple to temple and the high cheekbones.

Audrey also had no idea how to fix my Skype and iTunes.

Yes, Skype and iTunes. Had it not been for gone-with-the-wind Skype and iTunes, I would not have had lunch with Lesley's two useless engineers on whom a long, unhealthy life had left its mark. They knew nothing about computers and Skype. All they wanted was to see if I was a candidate for a quick fuck.

Had it not been, I would not have eaten the smallest piece of raw fish on a half-moon of rice and have had a horrendous ordeal, which I later, much after the fact, was told was severe food poisoning. The morning after the half-moon of rice Audrey phoned. I told her I was feeling bad – that is, worse than usual. Off we went to her doctor, a soft-spoken man with the earth's Chinese medicines. He was in a big, beautiful room sitting behind a real sturdy desk. Beside him was some machine thing, the likes of which I'd never seen. Against the opposite wall was an old-fashioned turntable playing Mahler, and next to that three curtained cubicles with real examination beds, though shorter than usual. But everything here is shorter than usual.

With my no Korean and his no English he managed to understand that I was feeling terribly nauseous and corpse-like exhausted. Machine thing employed, readings given, blood pressure taken and acupuncture needles stuck into body, he ushered me out to his receptionist, who mixed and produced medicine. Audrey fumbled around in my bag for the magical medical card, which turns any medical need into the most affordable care. I swallowed a dreadful-tasting concoction, turned to exit and promptly heaved the concoction up.

Just to get home to an email from Hazel, which I thought was going to tell me how well my Jasper dog was doing. But it wasn't that. Her Ernst had died. I started shaking, due to either beloved Ernst's death or the ever-increasing nausea. Or the worst of all horrors: death on this foreign soil. Now I don't mind dying so much, but not here. Not into this foreign and smelly soil do I want my flesh oozing. Death is a very intimate endeavour and it's mortally important to feel at home in the setting.

I placated the death-worry by firmly suppressing it through the single-minded kicking off of the homies and getting into the practical Clarks, and somehow going down the hill and up the school stairs. By now my head was feeling ten feet long, reaching way into the sky. I tottered into the staffroom, straight into Sarah and smoothly informed her that my friend of twenty years had died. At which a fresh wave of nausea hit, now mingled with a torrent of tears. A show of emotion, unless it is an outburst of anger, is not done. Out of compassion or a dire need not to have her English teacher seen in this state she called Park and off we went for a drip in the hospital.

Now, the question of Park, the flop of a husband. Mortally bored is that flop. When his classroom door is open you can see him take his cell phone out of his pocket, flick it open, check the time, sigh. In reception his boredom has a franticness to it. He has his hands in his pockets, paces a few steps and plants his feet, distinctly first the heel then the toe of one foot, then the other, slightly outwards, while throwing his head to the side of the foot in action. It's a deliberate, conscious action to take up time. But impatience grabs hold of him and he starts pacing again. Up and down in reception. All the while smoking and coughing. It's not a phlegmy effort, as you would expect. It's a throat cough, high in pitch, dry, like there's a splinter in his throat he can't get out.

Then he's off to his office and from there shouts into the intercom system so that his voice fills the classrooms at any odd time. There he must sit and contemplate the fact that he was a flop as a lecturer, which is unforgivable, for he has brought shame on his family. He must admit that he was a mathematician, who wanted to do a PhD, but that he's a hagwon teacher; that he's the husband of the owner of this outfit; that he and his wife are close to hating each other; that his wife is not subservient and that he has a softer heart than she has. Also, that his costly blue Merc can't save him from this place he hates, this place which is his livelihood. Also, that he doesn't have it so bad, since he gets his own money. Ferdinand told me. Men earn, then give the money to the wives, who give them pocket money. This gives the impression that women are empowered. Oh no, money is dirty business and therefore women handle it. But Park and his wife have broken with custom and he must realise that it's a disempowering custom and that he has landed himself in the pound seats.

His anger is mostly not like a man's, which is clear and travels in a straight line like an arrow. He has a woman's anger, which is unrecognisable as such and floods into everything, tainting the world with a punitive moroseness.

And now his wife has instructed him to involve himself with the dying foreigner.

He barked something at reception, which I couldn't figure out until a kid whispered from behind that my medical card was needed. And then off we went and straight into a quiet hospital reception room. Before two minutes had passed I was lying in the far corner of a very orderly and clean emergency room with a yellowish drip in my arm. My head had lost its cone-like shape and was now growing into a thundering ball, while the tiniest baby diagonally opposite was being held down by two nurses with a third nurse pricking for a vein, for the ever-necessary drip. The three of them stayed inscrutable, unrelenting in their Korean perseverance, while the baby screamed in torture. Which called forth something primordially traumatic, which in turn turned the fear of before – not knowing what's happening, no one speaking to me – into a state of terrifying anxiety. My eyes must have jumped from side to side, because it felt as if there was a sudden burst of activity, and my entire skin was wet. Just as my feet started pulling towards my shins a lovely doctor passed by, and stopped.

"What's the matter?"

I started telling him everything, but he clearly didn't understand too much although he probably remembered 'What's the matter?' from his hagwon days.

"You are scared? What you want?"

"I want my son! I want to go home."

Bless that man, who injected me with a tranquilliser and stayed around for longer than necessary. And then disappeared into the 50 million people on a spot of the earth not even the size of South Africa's Western Province.

After a second drip of another colour I got myself back to the apartment via taxi. I got worse and worse, but of course turned up at the hagwon the next afternoon. I managed, with many breaks to the loo.

"Sarah, I'm not well."

"Yes, you have finish teaching. My husband will take you. Diane will go also."

Another horrendous fight between husband and wife ensued and off I went again, close to midnight, with a very resigned Park and a long-suffering Diane – the Ice Queen.

"Where are we going?" I managed in the car.

"It is very late." Yes, Park, I know this. "You must go big hospital. Not Gweng-song."

An hour later we were in a much bigger hospital with few patients. There was lots of talking between Park and a doctor while I was shoved into a curtained bed and told by the Queen to take off my top. There she sat on the bed, erect, with her triple-A, twenty-something, uptight boobs, and mercilessly watched me undo the bodice around the Western, forty-something full-on breasts. Her shock registered, but I prayed for Park not to rip the curtains apart. The doctor did the ripping, but Park was really not too far behind.

I'm pushed down, with boobs now sagging sideways, to have another drip, of another colour, banged in. If only I knew what was going on. I know I'm dying, but what of? And how much longer?

The Queen has departed and I hear her and Park talking on the other side of the curtain.

"It take long time," comes Park's voice, in English, meant for my ears. That man there, he is beside himself with rage and boredom.

Indeed, a long time. In come the Queen and the doctor. The doctor knocks around on my stomach and confers with her. "You must have an X-ray," says Queen. "If you want."

"But what's wrong?"

"The doctor doesn't know. It is very late."

And off I shuffle with drip and partially covered boobs. X-rays done, with no diagnosis to be had, even with the help of Park and Queen both inspecting the foreigner's innards on her X-rays. A second drip done and off we go. It is 4 am.

"Tteokkuk."

"What is that, Mister Park?"

"Rice soup," says Park, much kinder.

"Where will I get this?"

"We buy. You must come to hagwon Saturday. Eat rice soup, sleep, two day. You are too sick."

"What's the matter?" But no one is going to answer.

Let me not put Park in too bad a light. Saturday came, so too Saturday evening, with hardly a kid in the 10 pm class. I finished early and got myself down the stairs. There was Park, it was all quiet, and I pointed to my watch, saying, "Early".

He smiled! "You go apartment. Sleep."

"Thank you, Mister Park."

Yes, there must have been a communal heart beating for me, because Sarah with the see-through eyes and Diane, Ice Queen, had been turning a blind eye to the two weeks I skipped telephone teaching. Once a week you have to phone every primary school kid and ask some questions. There are millions of these schools around so this is not done for educational purposes, but for good PR. Parents need to hear their kid say an English sentence, which, when rehearsed in class, the teacher discovered, saves time.

No use not getting hold of the kid. There has to be a tick next to the name with some inane comment and an arbitrary point for the rehearsed effort. The teacher dare not fabricate a tick or the mommies will phone to complain. That's what they do here. They live through their children and so continue their lives, which are cut short by losing their first name and becoming mother-of-so-and-so. Like Sylvia oei omoni, mother of Sylvia. Yet women keep their maiden name. I smell a rat.

How long can a communal heart beat goodwill? So I buckled down and said my sentences I learnt by heart. But one man kept banging down the phone. I shall write down the next conversation and have it as proof, you rude arsehole.

"Diane, here is the proof that I am not successful in reaching Sylvia. I have written this conversation down verbatim."

She read. She translated. An A4 paper appeared on my desk.

"Anyong haseyo. Little Lamb hakyo indaeyo. Sylviarang malhae jusikesoyo." (Hello. This is Little Lamb School. Can I speak to Sylvia, please?)

"Omnindae." (No. She is not here.)

"Gamsamnida." (Thank you.)

"Anyonghi kyeseyo sonsaengnim." (Goodbye, Teacher.)
"Gamsamnida." (Thank you.)
"Sonsaengnim, kenyeoneun obsoyo." (She is not here, Teacher.)
"Gamsamnida." (Thank you.)
"Anyonghi kyeseyo sonsaengnim." (Goodbye, Teacher.)
"Gamsamnida." (Thank you.)
"Michin waegukin!" (Crazy foreigner!)
"Gamsamnida." (Thank you.)

But my Ice Queen, she couldn't see the absurdity of this. Rather she was, and is now forever concerned: the English teacher didn't come across well reciting her telephone lines. How many more undetected blunders does she make?

In order not to expire from the food poisoning which has been lingering for a month, I walk around the Liberace bed, my cone-like head in my hands, and say: I'm walking, I'm walking.

It's better than going mad.

STILL SWELTERING SUMMER.

I do not have aircon, but I have a fan. It is ancient, and it is held together by tape of various varieties, as each new, shocked English teacher added a futile layer and left a footprint: I was here.

To the date – three months after my arrival – as I had planned, I walked to the study without realising the date, sat behind my desk, fan blowing at maximum, and started editing. "There is no editor on earth who can edit this manuscript," Hettie, the editor of my first novel, had said. "Only you can."

It is a daunting task. Is this thing even fixable? All the info is here right to the end. All the symbols, metaphors, motifs and that stuff have been developed – those that can be. There's a strong storyline and the characters are well rounded. I was convinced I had a finished manuscript. But, began Hettie, by first pointing out good aspects, she couldn't always follow. This means the reader gets confused. And this again means that I, Karin, have to go and identify those places. Those places that make complete sense to me. I have to go and see what I don't see. Perhaps everything is all over and not in the right place, yet some is in the right place, but are those the right places? And how can I judge? I can't always see the trees for the woods amongst all these words. Maybe the whole thing doesn't make sense and all those elaborate images and so on, which are so damn important, are too obscure. Perhaps just give up. Besides, I can't quite remember what it's all about.

Nonsense. I'll die writing this book, but give up I'll never do. There's a story here, and it needs to see the light. A story is sacrosanct. Its importance is above all else. I will pull it through even if it means sacrificing myself in the process. Besides, as someone said: life becomes meaningful when it takes a narrative form. And another besides is that though I was writing about someone who had lost control, the writing overall needed to be strong and controlled even if my woman at the centre of my story might seem to be anything but. *I* couldn't lose control. And I haven't.

There was the A4 paper with the horizontal line through the middle and with possible multiple protagonists. As it turns out there's only one. In the top part is Hilette Barend, ad hominem professor of Anthropology (she's ever so aware of this), with her lover and her mother, with whom she still lives and whose needs she has to take care of.

Hilette finds in a dustbin three exercise books filled with the wild writings – in uneducated English – of Pearl Poplin ("... did not know if I was coming or going recived the holy spirt but not baptise I had no where to go no home my sister broters mother did not want me if I get well where will I go to no home no base nothing I said to mrs levin lofes & fises no not fo me must be mad what am I going to in lofes").

Hilette becomes obsessed with her and searches for her in Cape Town, the Karoo and Valkenberg, Cape Town's mental insitution, but never finds her. According to Pearl's writings she was/is? in and out of this mental institution. It becomes clear to the reader, but not to Hilette, that her obsession with Pearl has everything to do with the mental issues Pearl struggles with, which Hilette senses in herself, but supresses. Pearl is the embodiment of the other half of Hilette. Like Pearl, Hilette's own mental state is not all too stable, what with Klaus Hufnagl, the German lover, who she has nothing in common with, but with whom she discovers sex for the first time in her middle-aged life. He is a master at this. This lowers her defences and contributes to her undoing.

Hilette lives with a dreadful pressure. It's a force that squeezes her insides together so that she needs to escape from her body. She is driven by the need to uncover some mystery, yet she is not conscious of this need. This manifests as that pressure and a frenzy, which she experiences as her cells spinning wildly. She slowly loses her grip on the world. Even the sleep therapy she has yearly doesn't seem to restore her. She goes to a clinic where she's given chemicals that keep her asleep for two weeks or longer. Then she comes out refreshed. Like a benign coma.

There's also the issue of Hilette's scalp. A scalp is such an intimate part of a person. There was a dullness there under her hair, yet threatening. And then her scalp started radiating an invisible energy, but I can't find out what is hidden there under her hair. Oh well, not everything can be clear.

At some point she starts seeing white banners that are strung across the road flash up in front of her. On these are red cryptic notes, or reminders of what she is busy doing. It helps orientate reader and, I must say, writer alike. And then she starts seeing a pulverised dog in the road. Its belly and hind legs crushed, red intestines flattened on the tar. Why she sees the dog is not known. It's just part of her mental state.

Now Pearl, she is a lost case, mostly homeless, and belongs to a class that the system ignores. She hurtles from one disaster to another, into Valkenberg, out, and back in again, and never finds a calm spot for her feet. In the end she walks out of a small house with a tin roof in the Karoo. She walks into the scorching veld and is never seen again. She was perhaps better off in the mental institution.

For the longest of time the bottom part of the A4 was a blank. But Pearl had slowly been filling it and by focusing on Pearl's inner and outer life – her psychology – Hilette found a way to get closer to her own tragedies and subsequent contorted psychology, without having to acknowledge that that was what she was doing. Slowly, Hilette's world below the line was taking shape, though her past was still hidden, which I didn't know needed to be known. I was as unconscious of Hilette's story as she was.

And then one day I bent down without having decided to do so – as if in a trance – and opened a suitcase of my dad's that he'd had as a student, and from it brought out pages and pages of notes I had been writing over the years about the hardship of a little girl who incessantly heard a piet-my-vrou calling. All this playing out in exactly the same house and garden as Hilette's. And the little girl standing in the same passage as Hilette would stand. And while writing about Hilette I had forgotten that just like the little girl she also heard the bird. The indescribable excitement and joy. Here were Hilette's formative years, even though it wasn't clear what kind of hardship the little girl had. It was just the girl in the same house as Hilette's. But now I knew why Hilette lived so cut off from herself and I could understand why she was the way she was.

Good Lord, the moment the one lot of writing fell in seamlessly with the other lot of writing! It was my eureka moment.

I do sometimes wonder what kind of hardship Hilette suffered as a little girl. I've written the end without knowing so it's obviously not important. Still, it feels as if more needs to be revealed. To whom? To Hilette? She's all that's left. She hasn't gone yet where she needs to? Nothing to be done about this now. Also nothing to be done about the dog and the scalp and the little girl; they haven't all shown their meaning. It's a pity, but the end's written. The die has been cast.

Besides, our professor is a fully developed character as it is. Unaware as she may be. She doesn't realise people find her weird and pretentious. To top it, she speaks an insufferable formal and modulated Afrikaans. All of this gives me, Karin, a hell of a pain.

At least her English, which she needs for dealings in the world and for Klaus the lover, is everyday English. Our German Klaus, on the other hand, speaks a very ridiculous, ungrammatical English. Like, "If anti pasta is badly disturbing, I am not to having it." Or "You getting dressing now." Or, after he has given her a kind of massage which is supposed to work on her 'energies': "There is some vibration ... your cells, your cells of your body's cells ... around-around some ..."

Klaus senses the vibrations in Hilette's cells. And these vibrations led to centrifugal force. Every second sentence I wrote – there was centrifugal force. And all through there was a fast-spinning earth: a small round object – a globe, way up in the sky seen from up close. Being spun by something. I eventually had to phone a scientist neighbour to explain centrifugal force. I was ecstatic when it all became clear. Deep down I must have known what it is, because the unnaturally wildly spinning earth – that globe – threatens to break apart from the pressure. But it won't break because it is held together by centrifugal force. As it turns out I discovered that this spinning globe represents Hilette's body, her being. She feels every individual cell of hers spinning wildly. This creates such a pressure she may very well break apart and disintegrate. But she's held together by centrifugal force.

It was only much later – years, in fact – that I understood that her childhood traumas, as well as the force with which she keeps these traumas out of consciousness, cause this disconcerting business of her cells. And it is a child's hand that spins the earth. Quite what this means I don't know, but it says: "Hilette sees: a little hand spins the globe around and around. The plump little palm is worn. It is bone, only. The little bone palm. Birdy!"

Birdy also never really revealed herself. And she is so real. She came in the softest way, in a noisy coffee shop, where I sat with two friends at a high table, feet not touching the ground, an ear infection throbbing away. I liked the company so I tried to engage, but a woman I couldn't stand inserted herself in the conversation. And now things changed. With the noise, the groundlessness, the pain in my brain and the need to withdraw from this woman, I felt panicky. I realised the only way not to be overcome by panic was to draw very deep into myself. Beyond where any of this could touch me. And that's when I heard: Birdy. Birdy. And a tenderness I had seldom felt in my life settled in me. Birdy, I said. You've come to me. I have been waiting for you my life long without knowing it. And I just sat there feeling over and over again the presence of this disembodied energy. She still has no shape. She's neither a person, nor an object. But she's an entity that is as real as your dearest person on earth. All the love and protectiveness and tenderness I am capable of – all of this is Birdy.

Birdy, you that break my heart, who are you?

WHEN I CAN hardly walk, I walk down to the taxis and am dropped off right in front of my doctor with his strange concoctions and other-worldly machines.

I am now not much different from the average Korean who works long hours, lives in perpetual exhaustion, foregoes pleasure and embraces duty fully. But I am on my own, which they find hard to understand. Family is everything.

And I have lost an important member of mine. Jasper died. My beloved, my friend. Sir Jasper the schnauzer, old Mister Plod. He couldn't wait anymore. Where did his Karin go? I dreamt Orpheus wanders all over. He is playing his lyre, playing. But Jasper is in the underworld. He cannot come back.

Hazel phoned to say he was peaceful. He was lying in his bed. His breathing became shallow and rapid. She lay on the floor, next to him, with her arms around him. My red shawl was in his bed and he sniffed and sniffed it, his big black nose right up into the folds, and he died.

I said to him: Jassie, you must go gentle into this good night. Don't rage against the dying of the light. You and I, we can't go through euthanasia. You must have mercy on both of us and die gently, of your own free will.

Adel, who is looking after my boxes, was still asleep when I got the news, but I phoned her nevertheless, and she cried for my loss, and I cried, and we cried for the harsh thing I had done in abandoning my dog so close to his end. And for abandoning myself. I sat there crying until the sun, not too long after rising, had me sweating.

A not-so-great idea got me up, homies off and Clarks on. I walked down to the school and into airconned air and promptly lay on the orange couch in reception. I was greeted with looks of horror. The African had clearly lost it: in *this* position, *and* with her bare feet visible. It was a bad idea. So I got up and lumbered up the stairs and did what I regularly have to do: fill plastic bottles with water from the machine, then arrange them in two neat rows of four bottles each, two litres per bottle, 32 kg of weight, perhaps 52 kg, in a large plastic carrier I got from one of the 'pancy' shops that seem to be dedicated to plastic alone. Why 'pancy'? There is no answer. And so, with bag and water, I, the only foreigner people will see in months, proceeded up the hill in the practical Clarks. With each step higher the morale went lower. Sixteen litres of water drag a body heavily sideways. A dripping body in horrible shoes; misery on the face; blackest of Korean-dyed hair plastered to scalp; aching fingers and elbows from water-slogging; crestfallen: a pitiful figure. A sore thumb.

There goes English Teacher.

I stopped. Seeing this foreign figure – as the people in the apartments must see me – brought me to a dead halt and with it a burst of laughter.

There goes English Teacher.

It was a laugh, a spectacle. It was freedom! This, seeing myself through others' eyes, through farce; not wholly being the farce, but observing it, yes. Great wracking laughter. There goes English Teacher. Indeed.

So focused was I on my laughter I almost walked into the caretaker of Garbage Collection Spot. I always check if he's there, for fear of the same scolding Lesley got when she dropped her neat bag into one of his crater-deep collection bins. Why the scolding? She never knew. I always make sure he doesn't see me in the act.

With my sixteen litres of water, he gave me a brilliant smile, which is a rare thing, since no one smiles. Perhaps he smiled on account of my laughter. He had come upright from where he was bent down by the tap beside the garbage, brushing his teeth. He shook his head benevolently.

It's holiday. This means the hagwons brim with activity. The kids book in in the mornings, they stumble out in the late afternoons. They have holiday in the evenings after they have done their homework. I wonder what it does to a society if there is no time for reflection.

With my working in the day I've discovered dusk again. It's magical. The softest colours permeate everything. In these six weeks of holiday dusk I walk up, away from Jugong ee cha, the school, the shops, the neon lights, the bustling of people living their lives to where there are still more hills than new blocks of apartments under construction. Up, and at a specific corner I turn right into an area with no apartments, just a nursery school. Then further still, because there, at the very end of this town, is a real house with a pointed roof and this house has a lawn. It is a lawn that I miss terribly. There are two dogs here and they run around freely, no short chain restricting them. They plonk down on their lawn and look through the real fence of greenery. They don't bark any more at English Teacher on the other side of the fence with her nose tight up in the tiny piece of lawn that has grown past the fence, imagining the smell of freshly mown grass and remembering nonsense, like when her boy was tiny and he and his friends converted the passage into a cricket pitch, bowling out through the front door to the batsman ready under the oak tree.

These nonsense things she thinks make her happy, even though she can't feel the emotion. They are just images that flash up – unconnected to anything else – and then die down. They come one after another, like how she raised her boy; how she combed his blond curls; how she bathed him – that little body! Her hands almost touch him, but he disappears and she can't remember what there is to remember. And I slide back, that horrible horizontal slide from left, where all was real, to right, into my body, where all is too awfully real.

Even the smell of grass.

"Chingu, chingu," says the garbage man and he squeezes a piece of paper between my hand and the ever-present sixteen litres of water.

"Gamsamnida," I say and hope 'chingu' is something you would give thanks for. I do my third-way down bow and slog up to the lift.

"I want to be your friend," reads the note. "I'm Candy and I'm in 503."

So there are more of us here. I go down the short passage and past the dirty windows and there's the hunk of a neighbour in the passage. He has his baby tied to his back in a sling kind of thing the women here use. He has dyed his hair red, like many here do, but it has faded to that miserable orange you see around. He's taller than the average man and I have fallen into semi, forced lust with him, which is hopefully a sign of health. He has a strikingly alive bum. With each step the weight-carrying hip flicks up. It gives him a lightness, as if it mocks his own seriousness. And always the smile that comes with no effort.

His wife is dear too, and I'm happy that I belong. They, of course, have no inkling that they have an extra member in their family who fantasises about the warmth in their apartment where there is no furniture. And it's very nice to have someone to chat with. Worlds can be said with the word 'baby' as an intro to a longer, more fulfilling interaction. A lot of smiling and you can keep your shoulders dropped in their permanent position and drop them an inch further to indicate mortal, constant exhaustion; you can wipe your forehead with an exaggerated gesture and make some kind of sound to indicate God Almighty heat cum humidity. These gestures have to be huge, blown out of proportion to the meaning so as to make sure all is understood. You can convey just about anything as long as the energy behind it is strong as hell, thus using up all the available energy. This, of course, leaves everyone drained, so that everyone tries to avoid everyone.

I plonk down my litres of water and start manoeuvring into the steaming safety of Apart 603. But there's a disturbing pleading sound coming from the third and last apartment, my side of the lift. That's where the horrible man with the limp lives. His wife and teenage daughter and younger son float around in the dread and agony of his presence, never making a sound. He's often drunk and must have been boarded since he's mostly around. He really is a pest and I always avoid eye contact. His wife seems to do her motherly duty during the day and go out to formal work in the evenings, after which she can hardly walk back into that lion's den.

I was hanging out of the passage windows the other night in the hope that the back of the block was cooler than the front. The boy had just come back from some hagwon. He had a normal walk, but it changed to a snail's pace the closer he got to that dreaded front door. His school bag hung from his right shoulder and as he was at the point of opening the door his hand and arm fell, and with that his bag. He laid his forehead against the door and rested there. Then he took a deep breath, got the courage, and opened the door.

The drunk often shouts. With the girl it starts with drunken, goodwill chatter, but soon digresses into shouting. Or his goodwill voice, and then some pleading noises from the girl and pleasing noises from him. Then she is silent.

Please, not what I think! That girl ...

Now the pleading has stopped, but the pleasing continues. Some people should be shot.

The left side of the lift is for the old people. There are quite a number of them in my block. Many are bent ninety degrees. They went through the war with its hard work in the fields, terrible undernourishment and subsequent osteoporosis. They seem strong in spirit and happy, although I can't imagine why. But they would not have been alive had they resented their lot. They put people like me to shame. When people like me can't sleep on account of the noisy woman above and the misery of the hell-hole moment. They are in their vegetable patches in the hills at four in the morning. There they carry water to their plants, with straight legs drop their torsos almost to the ground to weed, plant, make compost and burn stuff, for there are often little fires with lots of smoke. The field work is not the end of the early start to their day. They sit on the pavement, which stretches between the complex and the school, and sort and sell their greens, which are really all kinds of weeds, by the look of them. There they sit chatting, not realising that they should really, by any good standard, feel hell of a sorry for themselves. I have a great thing going with them: they find the word 'hello' very funny and greet me with abandon when I pass.

One of these bent-down women couldn't believe her eyes when she came up close to me in the lift, head tilted sideways in an effort to see my boobs. She promptly set off on the journey to feel them. First one shaky arm went up with a hand waving around until it found its mark, then another came. All along saying something with many vowels.

At some point it was chilli-drying time. Two of the women had spread their mounds of red chillies out in the passage on a blue tarpaulin, their side of the lift, and squatted there, examining them. The short passage seems to be their communal gathering place. It's lovely – they and their chatter full of vowels. I asked them if I could take a photo and amidst laughing protestations they disappeared into their apartments to come out better dressed. I have fallen in love with these laughing women. They feel fully human. Not just another look-alike, do-alike. I wonder if the government looks after these people on whose war efforts the new affluent society is built. Or have they just been relocated to the trash heap of the past?

The limp man's pleasing sounds have come to an end.

I open the door further, shuffle the gallons of water in and close it decidedly in the hope of shutting out the world. But there's a knock. It can only be the Bible ladies. There are many of them and they always come in twos with Bibles in hand. They are very smartly dressed with court shoes, pantyhose and two-piece suits and blouses. I'm told Christianity, and at that the evangelical variety, has taken over fifty per cent of people. After the war the world turned its back on South Korea, and the church – I suppose the Catholic Church, because there are many neon crosses all over – offered help. The influence of missionaries from way back must also play a part.

Instead of interfering with what I believe, the Bible ladies should rather involve themselves with the misery of that girl, for instance. I now just say "English, English", at which they turn around. But now there's another knock. Without opening the door I say my "English, English".

"I'm Candy," comes the voice. "Can we be friends?"

I open the door and see a mop of healthy, bouncing hair. She must be a new arrival. That hair's soon going to go limp in this here Korea.

"I heard there was an English teacher. I'm from Australia. I teach at the school behind us."

"So there are more of us around. Your hair is healthy. You must please ask me if you need anything."

"Where can I get chicken stock? I'm going to make broccoli soup."

"I don't know. I mean, it's been nice meeting you. I can go for weeks without seeing a foreigner."

And with that I have Candy out the door. I am a miserable old thing. I see need, I don't respond. I am being consumed by exhaustion. I'm lost in the language-less quagmire of myself.

But really, all is not misery. I'm making progress. I seem to have carved out a little bit of the known. In the bus, en route back from visiting Leona at the university, I was surprised at how comfortable I felt. The buses are always on time and there are many of them. And they are clean, as the solitary mop attests. I sat there knowing the route there and back. From the school we go up the hill in the broad street with few buildings, then down and through the dip where the highway crosses and we are in country area. We then hit some settlement without name, which is surrounded by farmland – rice, I presume. Then comes a bit of highway, but soon we turn right and into farmland again. This stretch the bus takes at full speed until it brakes hard and stops to pick up people who are assembled around a bus stop made with bricks and with nothing around. Then – oh, how I'll now recognise this place! – comes Gwengsong Eup, where the bus once dumped me.

Then lots of driving and when we go left, up the hill and down, I know we are going to enter a part of Seon-chang no one seems to know of. It's at the nursery with its plastic flowers on the pavement. At this point many people get off and on, mostly older women with boxes of vegetables and bundles tied in the traditional way. The four ends of a piece of cloth are tied together, leaving a good distance between this knot and the knot against the bundle, so providing a handle. We then start winding and you have to hold on. Here the mop sways back and forth, but never tilts over. When we pass the fire station the shops become denser and we're almost opposite the uni.

No, all is not misery. Paul has my Skype and iTunes back on. And there are interludes of happiness. On the last day of the six-week summer holiday Leona and I had ourselves a real Sunday lunch. We had been craving roast chicken, so I went out and bought the fattest I could find of the scrawny chickens they sell here. The shop was nothing more than a cubicle, and chickens were strung up all over the show, even from the ceiling, heads, feet and all.

I had an overwhelming longing for Hazel who is a cook par excellence. She lives on the West Coast where the connection is dismal, which means we don't get to talk as often as we want. Which means I miss her so terribly, terribly much.

Nevertheless, Leona and I laid into that chicken and talked our tongues to a standstill. The kind of talking when your saliva changes consistency. It becomes denser as the pleasure rises. Your tongue, your whole mouth, go supple and sensual. Perhaps it has to do with endorphins. Because the two of us South Africans filled Apart 603 with intense pleasure. While the baby next door complained relentlessly and his mother played the same tune for hours. And outside was a removal van with a noisy hydraulic platform on which furniture went up and down.

I launched into telling Leona what I'd done for so many authors until I came to a standstill. There must be some point in telling all this. And out came the by now defeated anger: I used up my energy to promote others and their books and look where I am today. There lies my manuscript. Where is *my* fairy godmother?

And then I got onto the diversity thing. At first it was a relief to be out of South Africa and the complexity there, I said. Leona understood so well. In Korea there is one culture, one language, one set of social rules. They can barely tolerate otherness and even though it's devoid of complexity it makes for unambiguous living.

I told her about another CNN programme about SA I saw. A panel was perched on a stage in a church. It was all about the miracle, while ignoring the real issues. It nauseated me. Especially when a woman in the audience spoke about her family's return to South Africa, and how they are working toward the new country. Her bristling righteousness, her teary show of goodwill and her 'sacrifice' for the country she so dearly loves made me want to scream. We have a layer of contrived unity with underneath the same animosity as before. And this is not discussed.

But – and this is a horrid realisation, I said – SA is where my heart lies. I could see that I had touched something in Leona, especially when I said that here, or anywhere that is not South Africa for that matter, I am a ghost of myself. Modified. A half person barely skimming the surface of the earth. She started shifting around. She told me before that she's going to settle here, make Korea her home, she at last decided, but I know she is still conflicted about this, even though she has an enviable job teaching English to under and postgrad students.

I told her about an email I had received from my friend Dorrian who works with diversity and that it brought back a realness in me, but that it also brought back the whole boiling cauldron: my collective culpability. And the shame to be associated with those who have not changed a drop. To be looked upon, to know what is seen: you were part of it and many of you – therefore, all of you – are still the same. She nodded. I think reminding her of the negatives of living in our country reinforced and justified again her decision to stay. But she looked quite blank when I said that now there are no longer delineated goodies and baddies. We, the baddies and they, the goodies, are all screwing up. Will *this* twain ever meet?

Perhaps it's better to live as a ghost of myself, I said. Here I am free, I don't drag a history along with me. All she said was: now I am uncomfortable in two countries.

But luckily, as the hydrolic ladder produced its noise and the baby competed with his song, Leona and I knitted our little world tight around ourselves, ate the whole chicken, drank bottles of wine and felt solidly back in our skins, and didn't even dread going back to night-time teaching the next day.

The late teaching has its ups. No matter at what late hour I finish I can walk across the street and a few shops down and enter the bright restaurant where I first saw the kids who introduced me to 'number one Korea food'. I stick one finger up in the air and say, "Gamjatang" and quickly the broad, shallow-ish iron pot appears with the indescribably hot chilli sauce/soup, the various weedy greens, the soft-soft pork on the long narrow bones, and the half potato cut in half. And the bowl of rice. How sensual it is to take a spoonful of rice, dip it into the soup and put the heaped thing in my mouth. Jesus, it's lovely. Then I love this Korea, in which I'm still nauseous.

Candy's at my apartment door again. The shock has hit home. Her bouncy hair is now limp and thin. She's still on about the broccoli soup. Obsession plays a necessary role:

it keeps us focused and thus from sliding off the far side of the world.

"Come in, Candy. Come sit here on the bed. Take off your stockings. Why *do* you wear them? And the court shoes?"

"We can't have open feet. And we have to cover our shoulders and upper arms."

"Public schools don't sound so great. My owner fancies herself modern. My arms can be bare, although I don't think spaghetti straps would do. I had to send them a photo of myself when I was still in SA. They used this for my card. You know that foreigner's card thing? It was vaguely me, a much younger me, with longer hair, and black. And a frilly blouse, covering my neck, up to my chin. How are things for you?"

"I can't sleep. I can't eat this food. No one really talks to me at the school. I sit in a room alone."

"You look frightened."

"I never thought it would be like this. I can hear my own voice. I feel strange."

Do I tell her that culture shock doesn't come to an end? That one dislocated state replaces another?

"And sleeping with earplugs makes me feel weird. The worms here are nasty. When they creep into your ears you lose your hearing. And my hair keeps on falling out. I think I have cancer."

"No, man. Cancer comes after trauma. We can expect it later."

"And the man at the garbage bins is rude to me."

"He's our Cerberus, guarding the entrance to the underworld."

This goes way over her head, for the young Candy is long past that hellish entrance, and has entered the netherworld where social formalities are obsolete, for she's suddenly on her feet, gone back to her apartment and her earplugs and her disintegration.

Skype rings. It's Dorrian. I expect more talk about diversity, but no. What is the atmosphere here with North Korea's nuclear threat? No, I know of no threat.

"That's not possible! North Korea is threatening to unleash its considerable nuclear power."

"Where would I get info from? Who would I talk to?"

"Karin, you're so close. Surely you must ... What do you feel about this?"

"Nothing. I mean, I have four extra classes looming. I was told yesterday. That's what I feel."

"Karin?" Dorrian is hell worried.

"I can almost not breathe any more from exhaustion. Just how will I manage more classes? Perhaps I have a fungus growing in my lungs. They say fungi jump from the mould in the bathroom right into your lungs."

"Okay, look, you go and sleep. Look after yourself, properly."

A nuclear threat? What useless information.

CALLED IN? MS Conscientious-Holier-Than-Thou. Called in!

"Sit down, Karin, please," says See-through Eyes, here in this special little glass room with its plastic plant and pink flowers, all too visible, right next to reception. This is where teachers are berated and parents are seen and hopefully impressed. Here we sit on another orange plastic couch. Does this country make only one kind of couch?

Fucking hell, I am so shocked my mouth is dry. She dare not see this. It's fine to know all about my innards and bra size, but here I draw the line. Some form of mask has to stay. But I'm afraid the colour has drained from my face. Ms-Need-To-Be-Perfect-Worker called in. Ms-Pain-In-The-Arse-Who-Can't-Have-Her-Work-Criticised-For-Fear-Of-Total-Personality-Collapse.

"You did *not* use the book on Saturday with Canada. You can*not* do this."

Canada, together with America and more obscure countries the kids haven't heard of, are the names given to the different primary school classes.

"It was the most successful class! I managed to get them to use, *in conversation*, all the grammar they learnt so far."

"The parent will *not* like this."

"It's what they're here to do. What's the use of filling in one exercise after another? They do that with Diane and at their schools. I must get them to *use* all these things. That's much more difficult than filling in answers." *Not* to underestimate the mounds of energy this requires from English Teacher.

"Yes," says Sarah, and her eyes are soft and far away, "they learn English for many years, but they can*not* speak." Silence, then: "Diane says you don't mark the books?"

"How do you mean mark? They don't get written homework from me."

She draws a little circle. Circles here are like ticks for us. A cross is still a cross and means damn well wrong and now I have one next to my name.

"You can*not* send books home without mark. The parents do *not* like it."

"Let me understand: you want me to mark, in their textbooks, the words we discussed and practised in class?"

"That is better for the parents."

"I'll mark. Have you had any complaints from the parents or students?"

"No, the parents are happy. You are like a mother. They like that. The children understand you. You are patient."

"I don't understand. Why did Diane not tell me directly?"

"Perhaps because you are her senior ..."

It's a really screwed up business, this thing of age, and it must throw Diane. I'm older than she is and therefore I need special respect and so on, but I'm also a foreigner and therefore lower than snake shit. At least I'm an older woman: that makes one high (age) with two lows (wrong gender, anything not Korean). What is higher? Young male or older female? Surely young male. But: young male vs older woman in higher position? Do age and position outweigh gender?

"It's difficult. I am sorry. You cannot read our eyes. We cannot read your eyes."

I am stunned by her poignant metaphor. I look into her eyes. And I see she knows my struggle.

"Diane says you are good colleagues? You go out together. You tell her when you need something."

"Did she? Oh ... yes. You must *not* worry." Good colleagues my arse! What other trash does the Ice Queen spread around? I should tell Sarah she is like ice towards me. But I can't fight dirty. I suspect it's not due to goodness. I'm all too human. But why would Diane want to make things difficult for me? Or is it just the way of the world? Fight dirty, survive or die. Attack, not retreat.

It's a treacherous existence. Between East and West instinct gets lost. We can*not* read each other's eyes. We have words only, which under the best of circumstances are but a small percentage of interaction.

I look Sarah straight in the eye there in the glass cage,

smile and thank her. Quite what I thank her for is not clear to either of us. But as I walk back to my apartment I keep that smile on in an effort to block any misery that may prevent me from what I have to go and do – edit. I've been editing, mercilessly. This paragraph goes there where that one's deleted. This sentence doesn't make sense. Here Hilette is unnecessarily mean, she could be endearing. That character is disingenuous, here the timeline is out, this whole thing is insufferable and this is so obscure even I don't know what I intended. Cut out half of everything. Move p3 to p203 and 203 to 61, or perhaps 120, which should go to 300 or 280 or even 1. This part is English, that part Afrikaans.

Just what is my fascination with English? My first book, too, had English in. An English neighbour offers an antidote to the character's patriarchal world. My flirtation started with my grandfather, school inspector of English, who told us stories from Shakespeare and wonderful mythological stories. I associated these with English. English is perhaps the language of escape, of other worlds. It is a majestically wide, calm-flowing river. And Afrikaans? That expressive language? Afrikaans is the forceful rapids that explode with emotion.

English is more than a fascination. Birdy is also English.

Whether Afrikaans or English I keep on banging my head against the unsavoury tone which simply won't change by tinkering with syntax or toning down Hilette's ridiculous clothes (two-piece suits, pantyhose, patent leather shoes – the whole ensemble in the same colour, such as orange or green). She's also no longer so obnoxious with her students. She even greets them on her way to class. And I have brought in her mother more, who sucks the life from her. Hopefully this evokes sympathy. I've noticed, as soon as Hilette does something remotely endearing, I make her do or think something that slaps the reader through the face.

She now no longer shows her judgement so readily of people she considers the Other. This is anyone not of her social standing or intellectual capacity. Anyone, in fact, who doesn't think, believe and act as she does. In this she's not alone. This is how the world goes around. She finds it difficult, too, not to judge black people. Although she hides this even from herself by being overly friendly to them. But she does sense that there's a divide the size of a canyon between black and white and it's only civility that suggests otherwise.

Another Other is Christians. She's an atheist who can't reconcile herself with magical thinking. And like Descartes, she believes she *is* because she *thinks* – *cogito, ergo sum*. She spouts the Latin. To show her learnedness, I suppose. But she does eventually realise that the Other and the Self are two components of the same entity. In her inaugural lecture, where she starts thinking she's lecturing a class or talking to her mother, she grapples with anthropology, which under apartheid was quite a racist study.

She says: "Anthropology has *no* offensive past. We simply erased our past and attached ourselves to a discipline accepted by the current train of thought. Yes, a new train of thought, as has become the custom of our country. And moreover, far from being a discredited science, anthropology offers a wealth of insight. Into the Other, but also into the Self. Two components of the same entity. An exploration of the Other, thus undertaken, becomes an exploration of the Self. Because we are wont to accuse another person, race, country, another religion of exhibiting those qualities that we deny and do not like in ourselves or the people we come from."

For Hilette's redemption she needs to come to this insight, but I think it may be too insightful for her to say, "There's not a racist left in the country. We all just reinvented ourselves. No one has now ever supported apartheid".

These changes, notwithstanding, are window-dressing. The real problem around the tone simply won't show its face. I have a feeling it's something to do with me, but what I don't know. Perhaps if I stop hating her so much, as she hurtles unconsciously from one disaster to another, to disintegration, the tone will be more palatable. But why do I find her so insufferable? And she's my only real companion. I share more with her than with any other person.

And there's still a nagging niggle of a worry that I don't know the full truth of her childhood. It's not necessary, though. The end still works out well. She gets back home after her inaugural lecture where she lost touch with the world and entered a world free from the world. In this state she acknowledges to herself who she is. And now she can at last say: *Nec spe nec metu*, which is the motto of the book. Neither with hope nor with fear. What freedom there is to neither need hope, because you are strong enough and content enough to bear whatever is, nor at the same time have fear at losing what is clung to, because nothing is clung to. This is a true liberation. And a strong, positive end. I can let go of my unease about the end, which I can't, I'm consumed by my characters, I hardly go out, chat, relax, and what if writing is an illusion? My life wasted on a no-money-spinner illusion. Never mind, these doubts are pointless, writing is what I know to do. And life is more tolerable with it than without it. If every moment is to be lived for its own sake; if the moment can't be mulled over, examined and made into something useful or meaningful, there's just catatonia left. Besides, it seems writing is a compulsion. I make endless notes. Once a feeling or experience is out on paper it becomes concrete and I and the world become a subject I can investigate and understand. When you write you take the forgettable and make it into the meaningful. And with that you rescue potential for understanding and order from the quicksand of daily confusion.

With the tentative umbilical cord to the school with all its horrors gone after the berating business, writing, at least, is something vaguely nourishing.

But still I float away, even though every moment in this strange land is one of extreme awareness. I now realise what the vacant look in foreigners' eyes is. First there is the incomprehension, and in those who stay, a cut-offness; a withdrawal from this society and eventually from yourself. Someone I spoke to at Goldfinger said you come here with all the lights in your house on, but you start switching them off one by one until there's only one light left in the house that once was you.

The plight of the kids is an issue that gets me switching off lights in an effort not to be so affected. There's the question of nine-year-old Mike with his unruly hair that stands straight up. He is bigger than the rest and beautifully uncoordinated. His limbs are all over the show, because he is meant to be outside, to kick his ball, to shout, run himself stupid, to flop down on his bed and sleep a good eight hours long. Mike is not meant to sit in a hagwon. He just can't, can't sit in that chair.

And suddenly Mike was there no more. And because I'm never informed of anything I let him slip from my life. Until one day, instead of at the hagwon, there co-ordinated Mike was on the sports field behind my block, running, kicking, being Mike wholeheartedly.

It gave me such a lift: Mike rescued from the system. Until his temporary reprieve ended and he was back in class.

And little Sonya, with her two pigtails bobbing wildly on the highest and widest two points of her head. Her parents had the good grace to enrol her for English alone and no other subjects. She brimmed and tried her best. But lately she is crestfallen. Her pigtails are limp on her head and her arms are folded across her chest as she shivers under her jersey in this heat. Sonya is in shock. I asked the Queen whether she was ill. No, she said, she's doing very well. She's attending all the subjects in the hagwon. She will now get high marks at school. Sonya is being broken in. It is a horrifying process.

But I won't be broken in. I'm not going to switch off all the lights in my house. An idea has been brewing. From the cupboard in my apartment came a basketball with just enough air to make it through a game. And next to my block is a dusty field with two goalposts. It's here that the Saturday afternoon class is going to have an English basketball game. All I have to do is convince my owner of the educational value.

And my owner says ... yes! And off we go.

Bugger all English as we walk up the hill on this Saturday afternoon. "Boys, remember, English! It's an English class, please."

Tony, with very good English, and God alone knows how he got to this point in this system, breaks the ice and starts talking to Ferdinand. The rest shut up. They fall a pace behind. I fall in with them. Do they like basketball and other such nonsense. Hello! Of course they like basketball. And we've reached the field.

Seven of them must become two teams, and I insist this happens in English. There's a bit of a fight – a semi-wordless disagreement, really. So-and-so is stronger than the rest, so he has to count for two, but the other team wants him and no one is budging.

"Well, boys, that leaves me."

Horror.

"Teacher, you?"

But what I know and they haven't yet realised is that I'm ten feet higher than the tallest of them and that I was a netball boffin in my day.

Now it's desperate negotiation with the objective of not having me in their team. Half of this happens in English, but negotiation gives way to heated argument in Korean and I step in.

"Okay, I'll close my eyes and spin around and when I stop I'll point and wherever my finger lands is where I'm going to be a team member."

Two of them don't understand and Ferdinand translates. Agreement. Spin, point, and I'm in a team.

Netball rules aren't quite the same as basketball and I'm faulted, which I ignore and carry on. But since I have not a word of Korean and they now have to make sure I understand, chunks of English, encrusted in the nether regions of the brain, break loose and are missiled at me.

"Teacher, Teacher, you are wrong."

"Not wrong. New rule for baseball."

"You play baseball?"

"No, I mean basketball. New rule. Africa."

Tony steps in. "Does Africa have different rules?"

But tempers are now hot and my team tells me that I am in the wrong. I'm astonished, once again, at how fair they play. They beg me to play properly: what with all the faults they can see they're going to lose. So I step into my 5'7 and a half inches and the game begins again. They are ants compared to the giant and all their fancy footwork is in vain. Our team scores and scores, in Korean, because English has become obsolete. "Hey, guys," as I score another point, "English, English!" And we start again, now in absolute silence, but for the odd "Here! Here!" And just as I'm getting hell tired, Korean, mixed with an English word or two, breaks out: it's not fair. I must go to the other team. My team can't have me all the time.

"So here's a new word for you: asset. I'm an asset. Tony, what's this in Hangul?" But Tony doesn't know and I'm too exhausted to explain. "Who will check this out and tell us next week?" No one. "I'll join that one's team." Seven boys now undertake to do this piece of homework.

As we walk down the hill, past the vegetable sellers, my face beetroot red, seven sweat-free boys make uncomfortable and self-conscious conversation in English.

Back in reception and Diane, Ice Queen, who hasn't got one slack muscle in her back – she's erect as a kumho pole – is sitting on the couch in reception. She's taken to slouching down between classes. I, on the other hand, stand erect in waiting, my lifeless muscles taut. But I'm learning. The more minutes we miss, the more energy I save. And so today I, too, flop down, with kids all over us. It's quite a jolly little ensemble, there on the orange couch. I'm prodded and dissected from my head to my toes. My name comes up frequently. They point at me and then back again, talking in Korean, Miss Queen heartily too. I can either storm off, leaving in my wake a puff of indignation, or I can clear my throat to make sure they understand that I am very much here and discussing me is not such a kind thing to do. Or I can make light of it with some silly self-deprecating comment. But I merely sit there, defenceless, like a clothes rack that has no say in what's thrown on it.

I must remember the Queen has her own plight too. She's doing more and more classes with probably no extra pay. Hagwon teachers don't have a teacher's qualification and are exploitable. Real teachers are revered, they're almost up there with doctors, although nothing can be as high as a doctor.

I think I should decide that I was wrong about my Ice Queen. It's easier to live in good trust than like a scout on the lookout for a dagger from behind. But what if I'm not wrong? I have to be more cunning. How to learn this at forty-eight?

And suddenly there's a hell of a commotion here in reception. A pair of glasses flies through the air. Mister Park has a dearest ten-year-old boy, Oreon, by the neck and is marching him out of the thick of the throng of kids to where he stands alone. It's as if he is on a stage but there is just one actor shouting his head off. Oreon has no dialogue, and the audience is silent. On and on and then suddenly it's over and I forget that I have to be more cunning and definitely not go against the group and I've swept the by now shaking Oreon out of reception and we sit down on the stairs outside. I talk nonsense, we look at the birds, we laugh at how big my feet are compared to his. My arm is around his shoulder, the shaking is getting fainter. We sit until his cheeks have some colour in them and then off he goes.

Just how will this endear me? I have to wake up, I'm forty-eight in Korea, and I'm going to be stabbed. I must stop stuff like basketball and just plod on like my dead dog, old Mister Plod.

There I plod on up the hill. I stop at the café thing, which is really just a serving hatch in a wall. Should I buy the sticky rice cakes that swim in chilli sauce? Tteokbokki. But my eye is caught by a busy woman whose bum is on the pavement and her feet in the road.

My God, she's shelling oysters! They plop out and fall smartly into the blue plastic bag there on the road. One or two propel themselves that side of the bag, but in a blink they're off the road and back in the bag.

"Anyong haseyo. Nae." Hello. Yes. Bow.

My hands go out and the blue jelly-like thing is on them. I pay, so little, for a whole bag of oysters.

I've got my shoes off, the homies on, I'm on the Liberace bed with the wobbly bag in hand, but think: no, better decant this stuff onto a plate. Like my Hilette and her lover eating oysters and Hilette's arm is stretched out on the restaurant table, her torso on top, looking up at her lover, feeling how he'll later slip into her, like the oysters they're dropping down their throats, all the while moving her buttocks and whatnot, rolling her lusty regions on the restaurant chair.

English Teacher is back from Hilette's chair and she looks at the mounds of oysters. They are so much more enticing in their shells. She slips one down her throat and looks at the mound still to go down that gullet, she remembers that tiniest piece of raw fish that got her almost to die here, die like a foreign dog.

I can't eat this slimy mush.

In Africa there's a lot of hunger, but in Korea, here, one chucks stuff in the bin.

Old Ms Plod, she's pulling out all the stops. She's pulled herself away from the slimy mush in the bin staring her in the face. She's not going to let it drag her down. She's *going* to stay alive. She's going to go to Goldfinger, which is the last place she wants to be.

Good thing she's forced herself along, there, she's gone up Goldfinger's narrow staircase, a skywards birth canal kind of thing. She's touched the walls, which may be terribly dirty in the daylight. She's really trying to adapt. She's even gone to the loo, the squatting-on-the-floor job, and now she's flopped down on a barstool. She has a grimace on her face. She drinks Mae's special concoction and worries that the last time she had sex has already come and gone. Surely there will be a fateful day in some year from where you'll look back and realise that that uninspired occasion was indeed the grand finale. She's gone old in the blink of an eye, because here, once you're just over very young, you're a rag against the skirting. Yes, a gullet, not even good for plopping down the oyster.

There's a youngish engineer sitting beside her. Not one gone to pot like most of them. And yes, he's flirting with her. Surprise has trimmed the grimace on her face, she's got a genuine kind of smile. She remembers Hilette rolling her behind and stuff on the chair. My God, she might take the plunge!

Paul's been watching. He likes what he sees not one bit. He hangs around, but it's to no avail. She knows if she's going to talk herself into a bitch on heat she'll do exactly as she wants. But does she want to? This last chance to be a woman in all the ageing years to come? Although this kind of blind fucking's not her thing. Paul has turned his back to pick up another drink and she's out the door, engineer in train.

"I want to kiss. I want to know if I still have hormones."

The deal is struck and the two proceed, there against the wall, halfway down the stairs in the smell of urinal disinfectant. And the verdict is? He's a good kisser, it'll be a merciless fuck, it'll stuff her up completely, and there are some hormones left.

"Thank you," and I'm up the stairs, back on the barstool. Paul is beside himself. "Where have you been?"

"Just kissing."

He has become a bear with a sore tooth. He's got to get me out and keep the engineer inside. The kisser's drinks are now on the house. Mae mixes triples of all the tots she tots into his glass. And Paul invents an early night for taxis. He orders one and walks me down Goldfinger's stairs. He tells the taxi something more than my address and he bangs the door shut.

I'm so touched, so very touched, at this show of friendship. Such a sweet man, Paul.

TO MY DEAR Friends

(It's just dawned on me that I am now going to swamp you with pages and pages of myself. And it's possible that these pages are more for me than for you. But I'm nevertheless going to send this letter the way I wrote it because these pages rescue me from the quagmire of myself and help me understand this strange new me in this new country. And they most definitely help me feel connected to you and to healthy life. And it's just possible that you will find them interesting.)

Shockest. In a nutshell. Four months in.

It's called culture shock. I call it mind-eraser. People said I was going to explore and have an adventure and a great experience. Just listen how 'adventure' bursts with energy as it rises a few octaves with the immediacy and excitement of it. And the second syllable is stretched with wondrous possibility. Ad ven ture. But say 'experience', that which I'm actually having, and your voice drops, implying dark worlds where meaning comes only after the whole thing is over. And to explore for survival is quite different than to explore for pleasure.

I wonder if it's possible to pinpoint why foreignness has such an effect? After all, it's just something different. They have an expression here: same-same. Well, nothing is same-same. It's a mind-eraser.

Usually the question you ask is what did you experience and what are the consequences? But I now ask who is this experiencer? Is there even a 'who'? Until recently I was in a pre-verbal state. I simply had no way of describing what I was experiencing, or even knew that it was me experiencing. I now understand what is meant by 'I exist because of others'. People in your life are reference points. I am me because of or in relation to this person and that person. But with everything gone, what I thought was me couldn't be confirmed. And I was forced to accept that I could be nothing other than what I was, including not knowing what that was.

This kind of living does offer unimaginable possibilities of being. We make up identities for ourselves and believe these are fixed and permanent and that we are successful because of our strong sense of who we are. Never mind that mostly these identities keep us in bondage. But I have always been sceptical, because our identities are constructed by the theories and beliefs of the Zeitgeist, and these are transitory. Now it's this theory, then that. Where then is the enduring truth you cling to so ferociously?

I see I wrote in my book after the first day of teaching: whatwhat, wherewhere.

Yet an unknown, innate quality kept me going. Or was it just time that dragged this specific shape of energy along with it? Still, I felt relieved, because at home my reference points had become meat hooks in carcasses. The known had become so known that life became lifeless. Here it's the foreignness that dulls and the known is what energises. So I try to develop a pattern: I eat and work at these times; buy at this store; get the taxi there.

But it is fascinating to experience aspects of myself I didn't know were there. Of course I have no projections and am totally resolved and don't see the world in terms of 'us' and 'them'. But others! How they do just this and how I judge them for being so pathetically unaware. It's now backfired on the sanctimonious lady: I am now an Other who somehow offends. And far from being free of projection, my world is the centre of the universe by which all is judged right or wrong, appropriate, cultured, evolved: they spit, they smell, they eat strange food, they have no sense of aesthetics. By whose bloody standards do I measure? Mine? The West's? Really, it's fear, incomprehension and a fragility of being.

Oh hell, listen to this. I have two piles of money, dollars and Korean won. I've just counted the won and put the won next to the dollars under my jerseys, but then I ripped those wons out, because they should not be in such close contact with my clothes. The dollars can stay. I see I have also emptied my treasured purse. The wons now dangle about in anything at hand. Stuff is going on.

Listen, as you know, I'm a drama queen, so water the next bit down a bit. But I have been thinking: if successful Faulkner and Hemingway didn't make it to their natural end, what chance do I have? The more I understand writing the more I know it's a dangerous, treacherous business. You keep alive fearful aspects of yourself you don't understand, have no control over and have little support for by entering an electrical vortex where you shut your eyes and merrily grope around electric wires. But then again there are those highs. But also the lows. Perhaps it's wiser never to write that first word and learn to live with the frustration. But still, writing does to some extent act as a kind of meditative support. While my mind is busy making sense of the current writing, the essence of me is free to be.

More on the death topic: how much stress can strong, healthy genes take before they split open and become proton dust? (I have borrowed *A Short History of Nearly Everything* – hence the protons.) Mine is not a boring life, but I pay the price. Those genes are about to explode. Anyhow, these are just thoughts of a dry brain in a dry season, as Eliot said.

The food's been quite an issue. It's part of the shock, they say. Chunks of livery something in soup. And what look like pieces of artery. And, of course, rice. I'm either going to starve or explode from it. In a nutshell, it tastes like nothing we've ever had. A lot of fermented cabbage called kimchi. Apparently they chuck raw anchovies or something fishy into cabbage together with red stuff and chillies and then pack the whole lot in enormous earthern pots (beautiful) and bury them to prevent everything from freezing and also to ripen.

Korea is an assault on your senses. Smell is the most affected. People have a different smell, I'm convinced of this. If you consider that they sell garlic in 25 kg bags it's understandable. Yet it's more than garlic. It must be the specific spices. Or the fermented kimchi. Perhaps it's that fermented bean paste stuff. Or none of these. I definitely breathe shallower than I do at home.

It's not just the smell. There are chained dogs in the hills behind me in haphazard kennels. They are most definitely not there as domestic animals. I stumbled upon the misery when I braved the hills, really just to hear my shoes crunch on hard earth like at home. I took a turn and there were the kennels left and right of me, with dogs so frantic it was ominous. They say dog meat gives sexual stamina. It's most effective when there's a lot of adrenalin in the meat. Dogs are therefore killed in the most gruesome ways. But I have met only one person so far who says he eats dog. It makes you a man, he says.

I'm still on the assault of my sensibilities. The men spit in the streets. Or in the mornings out of the windows. Surface spitting is okay, but it's when the spitter assembles his contribution from the nether passages. You hear this phlegmy ruckle, but don't know whether it's above or below you, you just have to wait, and then a few seconds later the thud hits the ground. I wish I had no imagination. In the lift my modus operandi is this: avoid the right-hand corner. This is where the lift-spitters ply their trade. So, lean forward, don't lose balance – the lift wall is suspect – make a knuckle to keep a fingertip clean and press the number.

But I must be adapting. Coming to think of it, I now breathe in, let the smells pass right through me. And the spitters – oh well ... And I've adapted to the communal eating. Those chopsticks all go in and out the same bowl. What the hell, we all breed the same germs. And some of the food is fabulous. Still indescribable.

How can I pronounce on Korea? I met an engineer who worked in SA – in one-horse town Ogies. His view of SA was not great. I wonder if my view of Korea is not an Ogies kind of thing. Gweng-song has 130 000 people, or fewer, depending on who you ask. It's a bit like Gatsrand. Maybe bigger towns are different, with a sense of history. Korea has an ancient history, yet it feels as if all was dumped here yesterday. Just the nouveau riche in their crappy apartment complexes opening shops and restaurants and at the same time demolishing the traditional houses in the name of the new. Temples have survived the demolition and they are really beautiful. In the mountains. There is much beauty outside the towns. It's hilled almost all over. (When does a hill become a mountain?) And covered in trees, but without our variety. Our grandiose, spectacular land.

I went to a bamboo festival. In the museum was a photo of two people bent double with bamboo baskets on poles on their backs. It was scorched earth. I thought the photo was taken 200 years ago, by the looks of the people and place. When I saw it dated 1969 I felt ashamed. They come from such abject poverty that you should be astonished at what they have achieved.

I'll try to be Pollyanna and see only the upbeat things. The good thing about these apartment complexes is that I have a sense of community. The buildings are placed in such a way that there is a lot of communal space. I see people walking, children playing and so on. Priceless things. The comings and goings of a shop where most of the veg-selling happens outside. Here I saw a woman pulp red chillies with the communal grinder, which is stored in the shop. Litres, kilos of the stuff. I was curious and went there. I came away with a bowl full and they wouldn't accept money. I did a lot of bowing and said many gamsamnidas.

Sometimes on a Sunday afternoon on the corner, beneath a tree, which is next to the stop sign, there are men sitting on a knee-high table (linoleum coated) drinking and talking. Or women cleaning squid or shelly stuff.

You see food-delivery guys on their scooters all the time. I wish I knew how to order. Imagine I phone. I say: "Anyong haseyo." They: "Nae." (They say 'yes' when they answer, damn unnerving.) Then I say – what? "What's on your menu? Please send me recognisable stuff and without the smell?" But I have discovered a place that sells red sticky chicken pieces. Hot as hell.

Yes, a rich view from Apart 603. There's a lorry that passes regularly and from which a looped voice blares. It drives around collecting old clothes. No money passes hands. It's a beautiful outreach programme. What fascinates me endlessly is another truck that sells veg. The signage is on the roof so that the apartments above can read it. Why this is so fascinating I don't know.

Cabin fever is a problem. And it's no use going out. It's pretty much cabin all over. But yesterday! I went in search of the community centre on the outskirts. I walked forever and was leaving the town and suddenly there was a field of yellow flowering something. A strange, but also known feeling came up in me. It was the expanse. And I heard birds. And I trekked on, because I could vaguely see water. Down some dongas I went and then I was in something of a forest and I went further, down a kind of river bank and onto rocks. On the other side I hit a path, which took me to what must be rice paddies, in which was a man in his yellow gumboots, fertilising. Opposite the field were traditional houses dotted about.

Oh, the colours! Light green, yellow and the shimmer of the water.

I've been trying to understand my deep unsettledness. It's not about surviving among people and so on. I think it's being cut off from the earth. The earth is in our South African DNA and there's no denying it. I sometimes recall far-off coastal areas, or the Karoo, that vast, seemingly arid, prehistoric landscape. I'm on my own, I've come to write, and I discover the veld around me. I'm utterly happy. I can hear my footsteps crunch on the stones. And there's the smell of dust and sun and wideness. And the endlessness of the discovery.

But again in SA there is always a subliminal awareness, or sometimes overt, of danger. It's like a noxious gas. What freedom to walk about late at night in alleys and feel safe. Or the pleasure to sit in a taxi and expand into the outside. No beggar is going to force you to close up, wrestle with yourself, with your position in the country, the whole horrid misery of 'some have and some don't'.

Although this is somewhat tempered by the disgust with which many men look at you. They see Western movies with our brazen sexuality and women doing stuff a Korean girl wouldn't dream of (men and women don't even touch in public) and they think it's the Western norm. A taxi man with his three words of English managed to ask me my age, and when he heard forty-eight, he said: "No thank you, no thank you."

The Pollyanna thing can't help. It is just heart-breaking how I miss people, all woven into me. I try to keep everyone alive, but I lose the sense of people and then feel terribly isolated. Sometimes it's as if the skin on my tummy caves in, just above my navel. And the terrible missing is compressed into it and only a gut cry de-concaves me. But I know, too, there are times it's easier to live in longing than in reality ...

The language is quite something. I hear myself doing what you do when speaking to someone who can't understand you:

first I repeat what I just said. Then leave out frilly words like 'the' and 'is' and 'are'. Then slower, ten decibels louder, with longer pauses between words. Louder still, now with over-exaggerated facial expression. And finally, "Ag fokit, I can't any more," comes out, loudly, with my hands thrown into the air.

Korean has a plaintive quality. The vowels are closer to Afrikaans: 'ê', 'ô' – those kinds of sounds. Many words end on a vowel, which they stretch, then drop an octave, and then say a bit louder. It's in the drop that they achieve that specific wailing effect. You're never sure whether they're in distress or not. Though what must they think of me? A simpleton. When I understand something I hear myself making a high-pitched 'ah', although I know I have a vacant look in the eyes.

How did I manage to be where I am? Like being in the middle of the Karoo. A lifetime's travelling is behind, but hell, the road ahead still stretches far. You must be a something. A doctor, lawyer, civil engineer. A writer doesn't count. It's as nebulous as an office worker or a salesman.

Of course I stare out of the dirty windows and have the distance to see all too clearly. The stages of my life. Mostly I feel sad that stages are over and done with; and did I use all they had to offer? I see how the contents of one stage logically shaped another. But I can't see what this current stage will lead to. Is it even a stage? Perhaps it is forever. Paul Auster quotes Châteaubriand: "Man has not one and the same life. He has many lives, placed end to end, and that is the cause of his misery."

I'd hate to be a doctor – flu and warts all day long, more transfers for the lawyer and whatever engineers do. The grass is just never greener, best to water the spot around you.

I see a fish: now in salt water, surrounded by so many others. He's swimming, his little tail's going fast (brave little thing), he's panting, the salt's stinging his eyes, he's keeping up, where is the finishing line? He's on automatic now, and he thinks back to his fresh-water life. The currents there too were fierce, poor little thing. Is there ever a finishing line? A lake, just a gentle, fresh-water lake.

Anyhow, it helps me to think fish-like, I seem to have more acceptance of myself and I do hit the occasional lake en route. Here life doesn't feel so deadly serious. It's a suspended life in a way, because every thought I have and thing I do is just part of more to come and to go to help me survive. And not shape my life into permanency.

The thing is to keep your heart open. It's easy to shut down and float along on one passing hour after another. But in my heart. Oh, there lies such sadness. And for what?

Okay, I must end this writing. I see now the tone will change from day to day. Today I'm in the hour of my discontent, the dark night of the soul and that stuff. It's getting so bad and what the hell is going on with me? In defiance of the gender-based spitting, or perhaps in true disintegration, I have now spat three times – secretly, but into that street. It is the most subversive thing I've done.

I'm caught in the present continuous tense. No respite, it goes on and on. The worst aspects of myself have been resurrected. I'm in full onslaught. I rationalise all: it's only through acute stress that we really change. And I think to be less resistant and more flexible will come in handy – if this is the pay-off.

And now it's yet another day. I think personality disintegration has come and gone. I dreamt a woman and I looked at Table Mountain and she said: do you know that that mountain is hollow? It has been scooped out. I was about to agree with her, but said: it is impossible to scoop out a mountain like that. It can never be hollow. It is comforting to know that inside I am still me.

Whatever gave rise to the new rise, I'm on the up. I'm not so hypersensitive to smells and sights and I don't know where all the dirt is I saw. Why I was so focused on filth I don't know.

And perhaps they live a more integrated life. Working, constructing, selling, garbage collection, recycling, cleaning, recreation all happen in the same area. We have designated areas for this part of our life and that. Besides, it's more honest that all of what we are is visible. As the all-over mops attest to. We stick them in a cupboard, out of consciousness, but here they are a reminder of the more unsavoury part of us. I have a bloody cheek, really, to criticise Korea. I have not seen one beggar and no squatter camps. At times I even feel a lovingness towards the place.

My herbalist cum doctor has turned out to be a blessing. With his fifty English words we get along.

"Vital energy low," he says. "Symptom not same." He indicates backwards – yesterday.

"Ah." My high-pitched comprehension.

I plonk my arm on the desk, indicating he must take my blood pressure.

"No today."

"Ah. Acupuncture?"

Lots of gesticulation.

Acupuncture down. Herbal medicine high. I understand I'll have to start taking his medicine, get over the taste.

"Why vital energy low?"

But he's lost for words, I'm lost for words. Yet I'll keep on coming to him, with his calmness and Mahler playing on his turntable.

Someone asked me what happens when the door opens. You take more courage than you have; step through; you realise that you left everything behind and it has slipped from your grasp. Back, into the soft light, is nothing. Ahead, you are blinded by the light, you see not at all. You wonder: who is here? It must be me. But you stand in awe as new births are born while you cannot see. And you know: all was; is; and all awaits.

This then the musings from a far-off land where I'm learning to water the spot around me.

Hyundai (as friend Jeff says)
Karin

My telephone number is: 09 82 1048531044 (got it figured after 3 months)

Get Skype! It's not so difficult. You just have a couple of anxiety attacks and then you have it. You have no idea how happy the Skype ringing tone makes me. To talk to you – what a blessing. And thanks for all the emails. They are nuggets of gold. And send a photo of you. And photos with orange in. I crave orange.

Oh yes, Hyundai is pronounced with an 'h' first, then a 'y'. The 'u' is like the 'a' in 'another'. But also not. It's a sound I can't hear, so can't make. But close to this. The end is like in 'day'. Hyundai. Most cars are Hyundais.

Bye now.

But in case you are interested, here's the history of the country. It's quite extraordinary. Perhaps there's a richness here.

Imagine: it's the Korean War in the fifties. People hiding in the mountains from troops, humid, overgrown foliage, trees, soldiers searching, knowing there are people crouched amongst the bamboo, smoking, dropping cigarette butts, moving on. And later: the hills bare, everything eaten, trees stripped of bark to make soup. Empty devastation, and still people crouching, hiding.

- Before this Korea was going along just fine. All of 1 300 years. They made it through the three kingdoms, then through the Joseon dynasty, which was a monarchy. They got through with a little tension now and then between the east of the country and the west. The eastern part absorbed a little from their Japanese neighbours and the west from China. But all in all just fine.
- By 1910 Japan felt indestructible enough to take Korea for itself. Not without strife, though. The Koreans gallantly resisted, but of course lost. Up until 1945 the Japanese were indescribably awful: they abducted the potters, made whores of girls for their soldiers – the comfort women – dumped the lepers on an island and did horrible experiments on them, took half of the rice harvests and generally enslaved everybody. Koreans still hate the Japanese.
- 1945. The war ends and Japan and Germany are in the hot seat, and lots of thought goes into how they'll be punished. All set and done, but damn hell, there's still this thumb-like-looking piece on the map, which no one knows anything about, which Japan had quietly taken care of. It's a hot hub of a thumb from where great power can be yielded. Who will win, the Russians or the Americans? The Americans know they have to win, because if Russia gets the whole place it'll be all too easy for them to take Japan and they will then definitely have trumped the Americans. The thumb will have to be shared.
- Washington hurries and slaps a line through the thumb, cutting off tip from bottom. It's more or less an

equal division, with the line at the 38th parallel. They don't say why it's a horizontal line instead of a vertical line, which would have made more sense given the neighbourly situation for the 1 300 years prior. No, they don't say why, but they secretly know it is so that they can keep Seoul, the capital, which is now safely in the south. And so are created North Korea and South Korea. And because the Americans were the first to do some map work, they gave the shitty, northern part of the map to Russia, where the rice doesn't grow so nicely and all that.

- In all this business everyone forgets that the thumb had nothing to do with the war; that they were all along staggering under the weight of Japanese brutality.
- Now: this division thing is meant to be temporary. Soon Korea will be Korea again. Sure, some Koreans think communism is better, others not, but most are apolitical. Basically they just want their country back. They want the superpowers to get the hell out.
- But America and Russia dilly-dally and refuse point-blank to give Korea back to Koreans. They whisper sweet stuff in the ears of their puppet leaders. By 1948 the South's leader can't contain himself anymore, what with all the sweet nonsense from Washington, and declares the Republic of Korea. Old Kim Il-sung, the grandfather of today's Kim Jong-un, promptly shouts from his northern mountain, with his ear equally filled with Russian nonsense, that his country is called the Democratic People's Republic of Korea.
- And voilà! How can war not follow? Kim Jong-il, who was not first with the naming, patiently waits for two years while stocking up nicely on Russian arms. In 1950 he blesses his men, sends them off south and retires with good quality rice wine. There's a hell of a lot of fighting and people die, die. Kim's blessing helps: his men take Seoul and right down to the bottom. They take the whole lot, but for a small south-eastern part at the coast. Good Lord, what's going on there in our part of the thumb? Washington wakes up, phones the UN,

which in a jiffy gets fifteen countries together and off goes a lot of cannon fodder. They destroy so effectively that the south bit of the thumb gets to be the West's again, and right up into the north they go. But, hey, the Chinese can't contain themselves on the sidelines anymore and, what's more, they smell an armistice coming, so in they step to help push the line further south.

- Everything is upside down. People flee war attacks, they go north, or south, back or not back again, but when the armistice is signed in 1953 they become citizens of whichever half of the country they find themselves in, prisoners of war included. Carved in stone, that's where they remain. To this day. Bar, of course, the three million dead.

MARKO'S COMING TO visit!

To have him close to me, oh! It will be normal and real. Although I suspect he will bring with him that which I left behind. The full catastrophe. It's apprehension and excitement in Jugon ee cha.

Everyone knows, from garbage man to vegetable sellers, oyster woman, red sticky chicken seller, café owner with chilli grinder, gamjatang restaurant, neighbours, doctor: the entire small community knows that English Teacher's boy is coming. "Baby," I say. No comprehension. I cradle my arms and rock. "My," and stab my finger through my breastbone, "Korea, Gweng-song!" It's English Teacher's elation that brings home the message: her baby? is coming. "Anieyo, baby." Not baby. Hand goes up, above head: "Jiggeum." Now. Baby is now tall. "Nae, nae." Head goes up-down, yes, they understand: my tall, grown baby is coming.

And the kids at school! The girls are already infatuated. He's tall, blond, he has blue eyes: he is their knight in shining armour. As for the boys – I don't know why, but they are just as eager. Sarah the hagwon owner, too, has spotted a good thing: a young person, a man, and by Mae's description a great looker. That'll draw more kids.

And she? The woman soon to be a mother again? She works frantically on her book. Before her son comes she must have solved the problem of Klaus's history. She has no clue what it is and she's realised it doesn't work that Hilette's lover is just plonked into the manuscript without a past. In between the Klaus worry she tackles the dirty windows. Those in the passage have been done. The old ladies to the left just shook their heads at the madness – washing the *passage* windows? Those on the veranda these six floors above the earth have patches of circular brightness as an arm, clearly stretched to its limit, washed, while one hand clutched on. There, you can see the finger imprints. The floors are washed, way in advance, on them is not a single Western hair, but there's the problem of no mattress for the boy. It's not as if this is the land of many mattresses. Bedding to go on the floor I can get a lot of: a thinly padded bottom piece, a tightly quilted thing to serve as a bottom sheet, another such for on top. He won't need more. It'll be winter and the ondol will be on.

But how to get him here in Gatsrand, from north to far south? He'll find his way, he says. Absolutely not! One can't find one's way in Korea.

This is all wonderful and so on, but the thing is – the optimistic missive home (I must have sketched Korea in such a bleak way that no one wants to come and visit) – this missive, well, reality is not as neat as a piece of writing. The spot of grass stays brown. Here I sit on the Liberace bed, again, thinking: it's impossible to keep two distinctly different realities alive at the same time. Home worries and Korean survival. The house in SA is instant anxiety. And to think of Marko, motherless. The last thing I need is this horrible horizontal gliding, this time from inside me, out, to the right, right into the misery of the house, and the worry about Marko. All I do is glide: left-glide, right-glide, right-through-me-glide.

The wonderful tenants are awful tenants.

They wanted a shower in the bath, which cost three-quarters of the monthly rent. It's not a fancy thing, pipes run on the walls and ceiling. From them hangs a plastic shower curtain. They wanted a new bin for the kitchen, although there's a fancy one in the kitchen already. But too old, not quite white anymore.

They wanted a new house, all crisp and white. The house had just been painted, with Plascon Double Velvet, nogal. But not white enough.

They didn't want Marko there. He is noisy.

"Mams, I had friends over. Once. And I offered to make them pizza in my oven. He's a baddy. We had to whisper."

Marko is such a generous soul, but they wanted his pizza oven gone. It's unsightly. The child designed and built it himself. It cost thousands as one failed attempt was transformed into a new one.

"Marko, have you been flirting with their teenage daughter? Have you kissed her? Other stuff with her?"

"No. You told me not to go near her. But she is very sexy. Mams, he's a menace. He had bad flu all along and his job didn't work out. And she was full of herself, with her important job. She walked around as if she owned the place. They liked nothing in our house!"

Liked? Walked? Past tense.

"Yes, they have left."

"They gave no notice!"

"They were awful."

"Marko, I'll transfer money for Victoria. She has now lost a job."

"Mams, I can get a very good deal. A double bed plus coffee table."

"Where will you put a double bed in that small place?"

"It looks great."

"Oh, it's already in."

"It was a good deal, Mams, but now I don't have bedding. Size is a problem."

"Okay, you couldn't let a good deal pass and your bed wasn't so great in any case. I'm not convinced you kept that girl off that bed. How far is the new bathroom?"

"It never started."

"My God, I thought the building was happening. I get almost no rental. Last month they paid the builder a fortune. For what?"

"To draw up the plans."

"But his draftsman was going to do it, for little."

"Mams, yes, I took the plans in and they have now been approved, and I paid."

"Why don't you tell me this stuff? You've now been without money! And you just disappear. I can't get hold of you. Cell phones can't phone South Africa, I told you that and you don't answer emails."

"They cancelled our internet."

"Never mind all this now. Have you got enough food? And get fruit. And go and get that fancy jacket. I'd feel better if I knew you were warm. And find out about internet." That boy! He's been keeping everything going. "And go to Dorrian. She'll give you good food." And she'll mother you a bit.

Absolutely impossible to keep two realities alive. I phone Hazel, but her phone once again gives a strange engaged signal. I miss her!

Frantic. Well then, make a list of all that's baffling. One can work through a list and tick off as one finds out, and feel better.

- Korean age (man years) vs Western age. Don't ask Ferdinand again. I just can't understand him.
- What happens when babies are a 100 days old? It's a big thing. They count the nine months in vitro as well. 9 x 30 = more than 100 days. Perhaps when babies are a 1000 days old?
- Chuseok, other than being a public holiday. Is it thanksgiving? There's bowing in front of graves?
- Seollal, to do with the moon? Planting? Seasons? Also public holiday?
- Ancestors, they seem to be alive and well. Will fall under 'Beliefs'. Also whole thing about Confucius. Everything is based on his principles. What are they? How do we see that in society? It's too big for now. I'm wasting my time. As soon as I get up from this Liberace affair I'll have forgotten about the list. Well, how else? Must I just conk in and accept I'm a moron?
- Commemoration of parents' death? When Park and Ferdinand went to Park's father's grave. It was a big thing, they were gone a day or two.
- Those giant wooden statues at the entrance of the temples. Are they the three kings?
- The lights festival. Has it to do with Seollal? Is Seollal also a public holiday? It's already on the list. Never mind, find out if it's a public holiday. Ask Ice Queen. No, rather ask Leona.
- Leona says they abort female foetuses and now there aren't enough women to marry. The men have to marry Russians and so on. Is this true?
- Ask Queen to ask her boyfriend where he has his hair cut. Ask her to write down the address in Hangul and in English. Ask her to ask her boyfriend to make an appointment. Or do they not make appointments at hairdressers like they don't make appointments anywhere?

Then ask her boyfriend to write down, in Hangul, how his hair is cut so that the hairdresser will know to cut mine in the same style. He must write that she mustn't use a razor. Razors and Western hair don't go together.

- Ask why I sometimes get half a potato in my gamjatang and other times not. Potatoes are rare, but still. No, don't ask this. There are too many other things already.
- Ask that she must write down the name for sleeplessness and that I need a tablet or something. Where? I haven't seen a chemist anywhere.
- Ask where I can get proper tampons. No hell, don't ask this. Leona says their vaginas are horizontal. This is bullshit. How did the veterans get to have their knowledge? It's nonsense 'truths' passed down from one to another. And that flabby one at the uni, she says the men have a lot of staying power. But that they don't kiss. How the hell would *she* know?
- Get the word for 'excuse me'.
- Ask Leona what are my chances of teaching at the university. She's mentioned the possibility before. I don't need to teach postgrad and professors like she does. Any old grad will do.
- Why do ninety per cent of people wear glasses or contact lenses?
- Why are there only white and black cars?
- Ask Mae to ask my doctor why vital energy is low.
- Why is there an invisible band around me so that I see, but can't see, and feel, but can't, and hear? There's an echo almost. As if there's a relay between me and the world. And what do I mean when I say Pearl is in and out of Valkenberg? Was this a lifelong pattern or only at a certain stage in her life? I can make this clear when Hilette goes to Valkenberg to look for her. A psychiatrist can look in her file, for instance, and give Hilette this info. Also, is it necessary that Hilette's thighs are out of proportion to her rather small upper body? Doesn't she have too many peculiarities?
- Ask Audrey, she of the heavy thighs, she's been here five years and she should know, ask her what those places are where there's a rubber kind of curtain, cut in strips, in front of an enclosed parking space. So that one has to bend

down to see the cars. Is it perhaps that the cars are meant to be hidden? And a woman who sits in a cubicle in what looks like a small reception area, but she sits down from floor level, so that she speaks to your knees.

- Never mind all this, it's worse asking than not knowing.
- Rather ask the Lord in heaven why I came to this place. And now can't escape.
- Remember to remember that the end of the book's been written and that the doubt about it that recently set in is unnecessary. Also, remember to remember this: Ice Queen Diane is worked off her feet.
- The thing with Diane: you'll never know what's brewing there. You can't ask, you can only assume. You, alone, without the ear of another, simply have to soldier on with your anxiety.
- Ask what I believe in. Oh yes, the energies we all send up to float in the air. Make sure yours are positive, keep good contact with them and the universe will send good ones your way. The universe, which is same-same as God.
- No, much better idea. Get Sarah and Mae and me to have lunch together.

THE LUNCH WITH Sarah and Mae was something of a forced affair, even though Paul was also there. It was a very fancy place. Sarah went out of her way to treat me in the way she thinks I'm accustomed to, because Mae told her my house back in crumbling Africa is one to dream of, which, for someone from here in one of the endless apartments, is not far from the truth. She did everything possible to show her good standing in society. But the effort backfired and caused her the greatest embarrassment.

At the table behind us was a group of smartly dressed women. At first muffled, soon their voices started climbing heavenwards. I made a slight backward double-take and went on cursing myself for suggesting this lunch. Sarah stiffened. She clearly knew what was to come. Mae talked more, in a hushed tone, and Paul made a gallant effort to wake up. And then all hell broke loose. The women had jumped up, abandoned their table and were now smack in eyesight. They had each other by the permed hair, fistfuls of the stuff, and they shouted.

We went on in our hushed way. Sarah asked, hopefully, whether the same thing happened in South Africa. I could honestly not say yes. I later realised how bad it must have been for her and Mae, because the group is yourself and they had disgraced themselves. And that in front of a foreigner, who in that situation was not only a hagwon teacher, but also a witness. An English-speaking witness.

But I also saw that honesty of theirs. Sarah could have brushed it off, but instead she owned up to these public outbursts. There was such pain on her face. She was so vulnerable in her honesty.

Although no sooner had I had this glimpse than things became tighter at the hagwon. Ice Queen was now downright unfriendly and dismissive towards me. And Sarah – how can you read her? Perhaps I was being paranoid, since I couldn't trust my instincts anymore, but I felt distrust from her. So I made an appointment with her and she suggested we go to a coffee shop. A coffee shop in Gweng-song?! I couldn't help asking.

I had prepared properly. I used a sample of five of the levels I taught and showed her exactly what I did in class. The syllabus book, which was so neat with the Queen's three colours of ink, was proof of my doings. There were my notes to myself in my horrible handwriting and every child's different struggles and accomplishments, from one day to the next, recorded as reminders to myself. And look here – I showed her: this is how I bring in previous learning, and integrate it with the current learning.

"You can do this already?!" She was bowled over. "It is for very experience teacher."

But.

See things from their point of view.

Who *are* these English teachers? We are an endless sea of indistinguishable whiteness: the tide comes in, the tide goes out. One Western face after another. They hate that they are dependent on an outside force, which has the one thing they lack and want: English.

And we are loud. We are rogues and rebels back home. We've come to the frontier. We've left behind our comfort and ourselves. We skulk around in faded jeans, washed-out shirts and incomprehension. We are dazed, un-ironed, we sweat, we stink, our hair hangs limp. They dress themselves as neatly and formally as money can buy. They have high heels and stockings, frills and two-piece suits; they have pressed pants and they have blazers. They put their best foot out the door.

We hang onto each other; men and women kiss and hug in public. We have no decency as we flaunt our only strength, our English tongue. Of course we should be watched. Yes, you come to our land. You intrude, you stick out, you disturb our group, we'll break you down.

With us come our problems. A tide of them. No sooner have you got your teacher through her food poisoning than she's looking for a mattress for her son.

"Please write this in Hangul, Diane, on this here A4 sheet of paper: 'The English teacher wants to borrow a mattress for seven weeks.' Thank you."

Diane shook her head, but wrote.

I stuck the sheet of paper on the staffroom door.

"Karin," said Sarah. "You don't trust? We already have mattress. Ask math teacher. He has."

"Sarah, thank you."

But why did you not tell me and spare me the worry?

Because in this here country we are a group, and we can trust ourselves. Because we *will* look after each other.

"Karin," says Mae, "Marko is coming! We wait for him. He must welcome. We are so excite."

That darling woman, Mae. And bless Audrey, who will drive and drive into the deep night until we are right there, there where Marko will be.

Yes, these foreigners, they are just one problem after another. For instance, there she goes, the English Teacher, dressed to the nines – in a long skirt no less – through the university entrance, up the path with the very neatly dressed students. There she goes, the last vestiges of youth desperately clinging to that heavily made-up face in this land obsessed with youth and beauty. She moves resolutely. She's trying to change her lot. She's going for an interview with Professor Gang. She hopes she'll get the university post next year teaching English to undergrad students. Which aspects of English is not clear. Just English. Leona, who has recently been selected as the organiser of the foreigners, suggested her. And voilà, she has an interview.

She keeps the fingers of her left hand curled. She's stuck a diamond ring, meant for her bigger middle finger, onto her ring finger. This land is obsessed with marriage. The ring will hopefully signify that there is a man and a marriage in the picture. Or was. This means divorce. No, not good in this land.

She's reached the professor's office. The professor is a

woman slightly younger than her, but still, she's middle-aged and her hopes are up: two souls of a kindred age; surely this must count for something.

Yes, she's making a good impression, although only the band shows, the diamond now hangs downwards. The professor in her navy court shoes, stockings, pleated skirt and matching jacket says she's not going to interview any more candidates, she's happy with what's in front of her. The only hindrance is this: will her contract at the hagwon have come to an end by the time she's due to start her important work here at the university? And, as instructed by Leona, she lies about the contract, which will not have come to an end at the hagwon. She discovers that need is the best teacher: she can lie without even blinking, although she feels her pupils dilate at her reckless daring. Yes – and she smiles earnestly – she'll be free as a fiddle. She has the presence of mind not to add the fiddle bit.

She's got the job. What a good thing she lied. She's learning the ways of the world.

Back she goes, down the same route, she must hurry, there's a whole hour's bus trip and she can't check in late at the hagwon. She's sorry now that she wore this full-length skirt. It's too narrow to allow long strides. Oh well, it served its purpose, she's got the job. The only horror now is to get Sarah, her owner, to release her.

Her whole life depends on a piece of signed paper, handed in at some registry office. Plus a letter explaining the release thing. Don't even think of taking a chance. This country is perfectly computerised – it is not Africa – with programs that will undoubtedly show if you are still owned elsewhere. Besides, what will the fall-out be for Leona if everything goes wrong? No, it simply can't go wrong. She'll thank her tonight once she's done her stint. Hell, Leona's stuck her neck out for her. Perhaps it's because she makes Leona feel normal, not so disconnected, as she said. She knows it's because she with her South Africanness brings back something from home. But how can she be sure? She knows nothing anymore; understands less and less about life. Perhaps that's not a bad thing.

Anyhow.

The days come and go. They come, and they go.

The light is different now. It's the silent winter light. It's an intimate cloak around all the same-same fish in this shivering pond.

My boy is coming!

It's the hour break before Ferdinand. It's cold and dark and I walk down to the paved park with its one tree where few people go. Everything is quiet and I think, but for the occasional outburst, this is really a muted country. It's the women who laugh softly, giggle like girls with their hands in front of their mouths; it's the men who keep the women, and themselves, in check. Perhaps it's the low, low sky that lies lightly just above our heads. Perhaps it's the water in the air in summer, and the colourless air in winter.

There's a wailing saxophone and I follow the sound, out of the park, down, further than I've been before. It's the man in the moon calling, it's getting closer, down this street, across that one.

Here he is, this man with his saxophone, in a large and empty room. He wails, he sends his sounds up into the sky, down into the earth, through my feet, my body, my mouth says aahh, I am born here today, I am sound, I am a man in an empty room. I am a saxophone who wails through the cloak in the sky, a continent far, into another soil, the hard earth of my beginnings, where he calls my boy, this man with the arch of his back and his saxophone high. My boy is coming.

HE IS TALL. His cheekbones are high. His cheeks are red. His eyes are blue. They are smiling and laughing in the night light, his arms are around me, he has grown, this boy of mine, in the eight months and a lifetime apart.

We're huddled in the car, which is not much warmer than the minus outside. Our breaths make little clouds as we speak, Marko in the back and me turned around, holding hands, talking, talking, so many puffs of clouds, and how visible my boy remains. Every moment is crystallised into forever. And we are almost there. Audrey has a sensitive heart and leaves after she's dropped us off.

In sparkling Apart 603 he makes a beeline for bed. I tuck him in, this boy/man. There he lies, cocooned on the math teacher's mattress, with the ondol boiling from below. I tip-toe out and feel a wave of excitement that I have to do the tip-toe silent walk.

Out on the cold veranda the stars shine their light right through the semi-clean windows. I've been brought back from somewhere I didn't know to somewhere I used to know. The sharp-light band around me, through which I see, but can't see, and touch, but can't feel, has gone, and with that the mayhem of the whatwhat wherewhere. Something slower has taken root.

I stand there for a long time, waiting and not waiting. And then, suddenly, my heart goes throb-throb, bang!

Marko is here. I am.

From his suitcase came a book on love from Dorrian and a note on the positive philosophical choice. It seems you choose a belief, or a set of guidelines, and you live by them wilfully. She also sent a photo of the two of us in the Bain's Kloof river, hanging onto the small island and drinking champagne. The suitcase also offered my red shawl, the one

I draped over Jasper when I left him with Hazel, and a letter full of Hazel loveliness. There's a link to a site of a marvellous place in Zanzibar she wants us to go to. From the suitcase also came *New Yorker*s from Helena and the most gorgeous sheepskin slippers from Adel; utility bills from my friend Janet, who has taken over my admin (bless her); a CD named 'Karin's House' from Brian, who must have gone there to take the photos; sleeping tablets from my dad with a fine letter, in total, reading: "Karin, sleeping tablets are addictive. Take only half, half an hour before sleep." Also half a suitcase full of oddly squeezed Western tampons. I am ready for Korea. And ready to cry for the effort Marko must have gone through to collect all these things.

And to make everything more lovely is the success – temporarily? – of Marko himself. There is much lighting up of teenage faces at the sight of him. Sarah also seems enthralled. She's paying him to do Ferdinand three times a week, with my Wednesday evenings falling away. Rejoice, the saviour has landed!

Even the gamjatang restaurant is now a different place. Marko gets invited to sit with whatever table of men. He's plied with soju, the clear alcohol they drink by the gallon and that you buy at a café. And he is stuffed with gamjatang. He gets more than half a potato.

The lone woman remains at her spot on the floor. But the mother is happy for her boy. Besides, now I live like I'm used to. Everything is more valuable when the child experiences it too. What a waste to experience for yourself only.

And he's doing those classes. Even though he's started complaining. The novelty has worn off. I can see it's just a matter of time before I have the teenagers back. But I insist. I'm good at motherly sacrifice, but need has killed that spot in my heart. Marko drags himself down to the hagwon, and I sleep. He takes the middle and high school up there on the first floor and afterwards he's nicely warmed up for Goldfinger, where Mae has him working her bar. He loves every smoke-filled, loud, hyper moment. Right up and beyond 3 am when Mae, Paul, Marko and Soo-mi have washed up and locked the door and taken themselves off to a restaurant, where they eat the giantest of crabs and consume more bottles of soju.

"Mae, you don't need to feel obliged to employ Marko," I told her.

"Karin, no! Marko is doing so good for business. He is selling all very expensive drinks. And now, also, many Koreans coming. Marko talks and he laughs."

Blessed be that boy's heart.

He has been pushing me to go to Goldfinger to join all the jolly people in their drinking festivities. And Mae is going to make her special food and pack a few guests into the private cubicle behind the bar. Saturday after Marko's late class with the teenagers. But – "Please, Mams, please" – he can't do those teenage girls anymore. He can't get them talking and they are not interested in his philosophical topics.

And so I duly arrive at the bar, after not being able to discuss with teenage girls the pain and confusion a young heart goes through when a projection onto a male falls to pieces and you are left with the un-wondrous reality of yourself. Or perhaps I'm reading them wrong. It could be their usual exhaustion that I see as disappointment. These kids are too polite and reserved to let their feelings show.

Feeling way too old and sensible to have infatuated projections ever again, I climb up the narrow stairs, each stair with its candle, past the squatter toilet and into the warmth of Mae's heart.

Sam, the foreigners' unofficial GP, is here from Seon-chang. He is an enigma. He's a doctor, which is the highest god here, but he seems to have only foreign friends. Class consciousness is something I am unable to pick up, but I do wonder why he mixes with us, the losers back home, as Leona calls us English teachers. Although it's a strain to follow his English, it's much easier than most. He learnt English from singing at karaoke evenings. He is forty and, it seems to me in my state of old decrepitude, young. But, he says, for the next ten years he's damned. (The word for forty is the same as the word for death.) Tonight probably doesn't count, because he's relaxed and almost at the point of being unreserved. And he has time, since his very blonde Russian wife and child are in Russia.

Candy is also here. She looks terrible. Her hair is now pitch black, courtesy of a Korean hairdresser, and thin. She has a new affliction: she's going home for the holiday for two months but when she comes back the taxi *will* take off with her luggage. Between her getting out of the taxi and walking to the boot. I'm astonished. They are such honest people. No, she's been told it happens and can I meet her when the taxi stops? Although she may perhaps not go. They may want her to sit in an empty classroom for some of the time. Her co-teacher can't really speak English and he's not able to tell her what the headmaster says. He just bows. And her recruitment agency has also long since banked her money and is not interested. Then, out of the blue: "The garbage man doesn't shout at me anymore. We have been dumping our trash in the recycle bins."

Mae appears and gathers us in her private cubicle where huge plates of various delicacies await. There are thin pieces of crab, Korean sprouty things and God alone knows what else. All to be deposited with dextrous chopstick movements onto paper-thin, crackly seaweed wraps, then neatly folded into a parcel. And consumed by the many.

It's a solitary affair. Once you're done eating you simply get up and join the rest in the bar. Sam the GP and Marko have hit it off. As with all the friendships here, this one, too, is instant. Whether Marko's drinking on Mae – Marko being behind the counter, serving – or whether Sam is buying is not clear. But between them the bottle of Johnnie Walker Blue is going down fast.

Mae and Soo-mi are slicing fruit into complicated mini works of art. It's on the house for any of the Goldfinger clients. Fruit is their highest offering, and it's not just any old banana and apple, but extra juicy pears the size of small melons, and fruit I've never seen.

Sarah has materialised and somehow she and Marko are now drinking in a cubicle. My God, I think she's flirting with him! She's rapidly losing that tight control over herself. I stay out of her sight. When she wakes up tomorrow and realises she let her guard down in front of her English teacher, English Teacher will bear the brunt. But now Mae, with one grand swoop of her soft, fat-free, muscle-free arm, has Sam and Paul and me and some other loner or two seated in Sarah and Marko's cubicle.

Sarah is on the topic of her mother-in-law. She has to do her filial duty tomorrow, visit what is here the original meddlesome mother-in-law from hell. She controls that son of hers, Mister Park, the flop husband, his wife and child.

"It is for me very difficult," says this proud, independent woman. To top it all, Park is the eldest son, and as such his wife is the mother-in-law's slave, says Leona. The worst thing you can be is the wife of the eldest son. Often first son and wife have to move in with first son's parents. Wife is then in servitude. Women think twice before marrying a first born. But Sarah is in too strong a position to be beaten into submission. She prides herself on her progressiveness, hence she – a woman – is here in a bar, drinking up a storm. But tomorrow she'll be at that mother-in-law, cooking, cleaning.

"Tomorrow I want quit Gweng-song."

"Quit?"

"Go to outside, my home town. I always want quit Gweng-song."

Gweng-song is the place where Park grew up and therefore the place his wife had to settle in. She had to leave behind her way of being and adopt that of her mother-in-law. Centuries of Confucius doctrine is not going to be undermined by the aspirations of an individual woman. This goes for Mae and her quandary with her Western boyfriend too. With my Western mind I would say Mae may be okay breaking free from the rules, but when it comes to her parents she's not going to step out of line. Paul's not going to be introduced to them and I would think they probably don't know of his existence. We all watch Paul and Mae like hawks: the only thing standing in the way of a wedding is the introduction to her parents.

Suddenly a Korean jumps up, gives a slight bow, and he's off.

"Mae, what happened?"

"He is so angry. Sam says not nice things about Korea. We don't say that to foreigners. Also, that man knows the brother of Sam. And Sam says he is not married."

"Yes?"

"It is like shame. The brother. He is not married. And he is also not so young now. He will not get a wife."

I can't for the life of me see what's shameful about not being married. But it seems the longer I'm here, the more there is of this culture to understand. But I don't understand the first thing about this culture.

Anyhow, Mae has lost a client.
And Sarah is definitely flirting with Marko.

How these days etch themselves into me. We laugh, eat at more restaurants than just the gamjatang place and laugh some more.

Sam, who is still without Russian wife and son, has invited us to go to a bullfight. We leave Gweng-song and arrive in a farming area. There are rows and rows of identical blue trucks, where there is a dispute in progress. One truck has dented another and the younger man is the guilty party. The two men use the honorific, though it's not so in tone, but, says Sam, the younger one will soon address his senior in the informal way. This will distract from the actual dispute and it will then be about the younger one's rudeness. Luckily the older man's wife is not present. Because his pride, too, will have been dented.

People are picnicking under the pavilion. The bullfight is in full swing. It's nothing like bullfights in Spain with matadors and cloaks. There are just two men with their bulls in a dusty arena. The winner is determined by the horns of one bull being below those of the other bull. As soon as one fight's over another follows. It's like those porn movies where one loops into another.

Out of the blue Sam tells us, in a whisper, that his brother isn't married. He seems really worried by the shame his brother has brought upon the family.

At last the bullfights are over and Sam, the dear person that he is, wants to treat us. We're going to have dinner at one of his up-market places that foreigners don't know exist. Class sticks to class. How would we, the losers back home and losers here in this country, get to go to these places?

We park outside a building, unpainted like all the others around it. Downstairs we are greeted by someone in uniform and taken upstairs. We step into a different world. Everything is understated quality. On either side of a short passage are private, raised rooms behind rice-paper sliding doors.

We're formally handed over to our hostess. She's in traditional costume and bows deeply. She leads us to the biggest room at the end of the passage. I hide my happiness when I see that the floor under the table is dropped and there are backrests.

We are handed thick, moist handtowels. Sam says something and the feast begins. Plates and plates full of raw fish arrive. The fish is indescribable: every crawling, swimming and dead thing so fresh the sea is still in them. Our hostess must be hovering outside our door, because no sooner has a plate been half consumed than another arrives. Marko eats every morsel and I enjoy many of the morsels.

Still, I have a thought I try to suppress which I can't: how long still? My throat won't stay open anymore and that sliding door is relentless. Sushi, with tiny pieces of fish stuck between mounds of rice, is one thing. But kilos of undiluted raw fish is quite another. Here comes a mountain of octopus arms. They are crawling about. Sam says they can get stuck in your throat and throttle you. There's a special way of eating them. And right there I have my excuse: one should be more experienced in these culinary matters before one risks one's life.

My smile, which shows my faked delight and which has become a permanent fixture, breaks out in genuine delight, because Sam announces it's the end. And just there I feel deeply thankful that I had this experience, because a new world did open to me. But still, I am more thankful that that world is now behind me and that soon I can let my smile drop, flush the thing down the loo.

But, oh no. Sam has decided that now is the time for steak. Our hostess brings a low braai contraption that sits on the table. She produces the costliest piece of steak ever, which Sam proceeds to braai to cinders. He is on a roll and has broken out of his constraint. He tells us with an animated face that his brother gambled away on the stock exchange most of his parents' money, which they got from selling their farmland to the government. I break through my laboured smile and stop him in mid-sentence: why didn't he stop his brother? No, he couldn't. His brother is the first-born son, there was nothing to be done. My God, man, pension comes before culture. I'm about to launch into Korean culture, but am saved by the ball of chewed meat obstructing my tongue.

And now he's into a short history of the financial

transformation of Korea. Like everyone else in Korea, he grew up poor. In the 60s or 70s (I can't quite follow) he was eight when they got their first telephone; ten when they got a TV; twelve when they got their 'refrigeration'. Forget South Africa with the miracle transformation. Here was a true one. Sam is now an affluent doctor. His son will go to the best schools. He will have the worst of the gruelling hagwon system. And one day he'll be able to take a guilt-ridden foreigner for a costly raw fish meal.

Marko has gone with Sam to Seon-chang. They are painting that town red. He shows up days later, with a Korean girl in tow. She's from Seoul and she's no innocent thing. He is in heaven. He absolutely loves Korean girls. Of course he does. She fetches and carries, she's a step ahead of every need of his. They disappear for the night. Thank God.

Dorrian, ever the researcher, sends information on Korean teens. The article says their social skills are dismal when it comes to getting along with others. A survey done ranked the country 35th out of the 36 nations that took part. It's due to the educational emphasis on knowledge, not interaction. It says the system should pay attention "to the fact that Korean children scored well only in areas with a strong emphasis on written assessments and performed very poorly in areas related to internal and external activities. There is a need for measures to change the policy on developing knowledge toward nurturing independence."

They scored down to zero for "relationship promotion and social cooperation". Social interaction skills are linked to the ability to live harmoniously with culturally or socio-economically different counterparts. But their score for conflict management is second only to Denmark, thanks to their rich knowledge of "possible democratic solutions to conflicts".

I see these 'democratic solutions' daily. Whenever there's a dispute their hands automatically go behind their backs and away they go playing 'rock scissors paper'. It's touching to see the kids abide by the outcome. And I love what they call it: kawi bawi bo.

Marko, without girl, is hardly back before the ants in his

pants drive him wild. In a mad moment I had told him we could go to Vietnam.

"Oh come on, Mams! You said you wanted to go. We don't need to make bookings, we'll stay in youth hostels."

"I'm not staying in youth hostels."

"Hell, great!"

And with this feeble resistance he's persuaded me to go to Vietnam and Cambodia. Things progress quickly. I have three days' holiday, plus Christmas and New Year's Day. The rest – to get to ten days – will be taught by Audrey, whom I'll pay. Tickets have been bought through Leona's travel agent, who can read English. We have no reservations anywhere, we're going blind. We are packed and almost out of the front door when the red cell rings.

It's my niece. Her father was shot and he's most likely going to be paralysed. Three robbers came onto their property, which borders a nature reserve, and held up the eight people drinking coffee on the patio. A scuffle broke out between one of the guests and the men, at which point my six-foot-tall brother-in-law, the marathon runner, the deep-sea fisherman, the part-time farmer, the law man ran to help his friend. Eight shots were fired, one of which was stopped by a credit card in a handbag, and one by a spine.

Marko and I pick up our suitcases, lock the front door, which here you really have no need to do, and set off. We talk too much; we are silent; we decide that in spite of this news we have to enjoy our trip. On the night plane I can't keep it up anymore and move to a seat away from him, and sob. When my shoulders don't shudder anymore I look up. Marko, too, is sobbing. His shoulders contort in their violent abandonment to grief.

When we retrieve our luggage we fight because my borrowed rucksack is too heavy. I'm slowing us down. We simply *have* to move at a staggering pace: away from South Africa, away from our grief. Marko takes over my rucksack.

We have come from minus to the tropics of Southeast Asia. It is beautifully hot, it sweeps us off our feet, we're in another world, we are free in this functioning chaos, we laugh as loud as we wish, we shout, jump, run, we wave our arms, we might as well be back in uninhibited Africa.

AH, IT WAS the maddest and most wondrous time!

Everyone is out to do you in. You live by your wits, improvise every moment, you are drenched in sweat and sensual pleasure. We were fully brought back to life. I discovered again how great it is to eat – the food is exotic, yet known. And I managed the terror of crossing a street. You simply walk into many lanes of oncoming scooters and trust them to weave around you. Marko took my hand every time. It was strange to have our roles changed like this.

We soon worked out how to co-habit as a young adult and a has-been. On long bus trips, which take double the time, probably due to the terrible roads, I blended into the bus, leaving Marko free to chat up the young crowd. And when he found no one interesting we talked and talked and kept our eyes on the countryside, which, in its sprawling, unkept way, reminded us of home. Third World is the best world.

We had many massages, one of which left us not saying a word about it. We both went in to what appeared quite decent premises, a double volume, two storey building. We were taken upstairs, where cubicles were divided by not much more than curtains. I was taken to the left, and Marko to the far right. My massage proceeded as expected, but Marko's was no ordinary one, as I realised when I heard a mighty groan from his side. For the next three days he went back twice a day.

In the Cuchi tunnels, in Ho Chi Minh City, the old Saigon, I had my own groan. During the war soldiers had dug kilometres of warrens of tunnels. Those tunnels are so small you can't arch your back from your crawling position. They will be the death of you if you get anxious. It was downright terrifying. No guide accompanies you. You're a crawling line of people, you can't see in front in the dark, you can't turn back, you don't know where they're leading and how long still you will have to go. Marko was way in front. I heard him wonder aloud, at what must have been a fork, which of the three tunnels he should take. God help us, what if he had taken the wrong one that led deeper down and with no exit? He, of course, emerged through the smallest of holes, exhilarated.

In Cambodia we stayed in Siem Reap, the closest town to the Angkor temples, which are just outside the town. Built of heavy stone, they are magnificent and mysterious, with jungle growing around and through them. We ate and drank and sucked up every moment. We bought metres and metres of silk. I also bought a kind of fold-up wooden bird on a frame.

Back in Vietnam we took a hellishly long bus trip to a small seaside town. We were the only people at our hotel. One evening we were eating a hot-pot of Vietnamese food practically on the beach. Not far out was a little fishing boat and everything was imbued with strangeness. Marko, who strives to make my life easier, dreamt up a silk business for me back home. I was going to transform my house into the most exotic place imaginable. And right there we had a fight. About how the profit was going to be divided. I was going to run it, make trips to Cambodia to buy silk – although I couldn't imagine where I'd get the energy – and pay for everything. Obviously I should get the profit. But no, it was Marko's idea and so we should go fifty-fifty. When our voices climbed to the high heavens Marko saw how ridiculous we were. We were sitting in paradise and quibbling about profit. But such was our abandon that even our fantasies were real. It was a heightened time. Discovering the world together in total abandon, how can we not be rich with this?

Back in Korea we realised with relief that it was great to sink into the upholstered seats of a quiet and clean bus, right on time, taking us safely to our destination.

Marko must be grateful for the trip, as he offered to do the Saturday late-night teenagers again.

But he comes back baffled. He can't figure these teenagers out, perhaps I can enlighten him? How can he teach them when they can't "relate to internal and external activities"? How exactly are they supposed to "practise living harmoniously with culturally different people" when there are no different people? I should never have shown him the article on Korean teens' social skills. He is on an argumentative high. He has the just indignation reserved for the young.

"Marko, we have to keep things smooth here at the hagwon. Your blond looks, your maleness and no doubt your flirting with Sarah are still counting in your favour. And therefore mine too. I have more standing now because I am the mother of a son who is here and who needs to stick his temper in his pocket. Sarah hasn't signed me off. I'm still her property and as such not free to take the job at the university. Because I started six weeks later than contracts at formal institutions do there's an overlap that won't disappear. I am forever going to be stuck here unless I can get myself signed off. I won't survive another year in this sweatshop. Korea is now my lot. I won't be able to support us in South Africa. And I'm building a pension. This means I'll have to stay here indefinitely, as I had planned from the beginning, although then I didn't understand what the effect of being here would be. Also, forty-eight years of myself there, together with the country, have vanished into the sea. So learn to buckle down. I know nothing in your young nature enables you to do this yet – but buckle down. And keep smiling. Besides, it's good for you to know how generations of black people in our country had to live their lives."

As Marko throws his hands up in the air I storm off, rid myself of the homies, get into the plastics and start washing the toilet.

Only to have to stop to answer the soft knock on the door. It's Candy. This time with a chicken in hand. "I'm going to make broccoli soup. There's lots of chicken stock around this chicken. What do you think it's stuffed with? I'm just going to chuck out the chicken."

"Candy, this is the most wonderful dish. Mae took me to a restaurant that serves only this. You get a small chicken in a scaldingly hot cast-iron bowl, swimming in soup. But the beauty is it's stuffed with special rice and chestnuts and stuff. It's very delicious."

I turn around, back to the toilet. Candy follows with

chicken in hand. I start cleaning again, feeling uncomfortable to be washing a toilet in the company of another. Much like picking your nose. We all do it, but it is a more private part of maintenance.

"Okay, bye," says Candy, not having registered where she is. Does one ever become normal again?

NOW THAT MY boy is gone. Now that my boy is gone. Whatwhat wherewhere? He is far, beyond knowing. But he was here. He did walk out of the airport. His cheekbones fitted into my palms; I buried my fingers in his hair. Gone was that sharp light band around me. I was flesh, not light masquerading as matter.

But I am in this strange place. The sounds are all high again. The neon lights flicker, high. The people are high in their politeness. Where is the moon, where are the shadows? Where a low earth?

Careful, now! The little fear, it can jump up and throttle. Out with you!

That's better. Only the word remains. One can't feel a word. But I feel the word. It is fear enough.

Not to worry. All this love with Marko and the care and the normalness just wiped out my defences. That's all. Not to worry.

But I'm afraid, afraid. I am afraid.

I hope Marko didn't leave with what I was left with: ringworm.

I did another Sunday trip to the uni, after which four of us, sardined in Leona's little car, went to a fancy restaurant by the sea. We got very lost and found the Koreans' directions useless: a single word spoken with a finger pointed in a direction. We eventually got there, having travelled through mortifying colourless country, only to find that the sea was listless water stagnating in what was an ocean-like pond. But there were many potted flowers in a small landscaped garden and – green lawn!

It was a fancy place with the most spectacular and confusing toilets. So many buttons to choose from, with lots of Korean instructions. I eventually took a finger to a button and all hell broke loose. A strong stream of water was propelled over the cubicle door and onto two women washing their hands. Anyong haseyo, kyeseyo, juseyo, gamsamnida, hello, goodbye, please, thank you, all mixed, and I bowed and got the hell out.

The owner in traditional wear looked splendid. She had seated us in a separate room full of Korean antiques. There were the most beautiful wood and brass pieces. I surreptitiously produced my ankle. The ringworm was easily diagnosed. I was quietly beside myself: do I have worms in a ring under my skin? Not quite, but I'd have to have it treated, otherwise I'd find them spread all over my body.

It was one thing to know what plague I was carrying, but how to find the word for this? One of the women with us promptly phoned what is here a lifeline: a Korean friend who speaks English. She wrote it down in Hangul. I could show this to a pharmacist. We made our deflated way back home. No one really enjoyed the outing, but it was the best highlight we could have and we – who had little in common – were the best friends available.

On one of my scouting trips deep into downtown, which I now know rather well, I poked my nose into a small shop that turned out to be a pharmacy. I confidently went in and showed the pharmacist my precious piece of paper, but he declined to help me. I had to wait a week to ask Ferdinand to go with me in our class time. As we walked away from the hagwon, out into the business of the neon night, Ferdinand's English tongue came alive. I hoped his mother would see the benefit of our little outing. This innocent and dutiful boy, oh, Ferdinand, my heart breaks for you. Even the choice of his name must come from his ambitious mother, who, like Ferdinand, strives to be as Western as possible. It starts with an 'f', which sound they simply can't make, and then has an 'r' close to it, which is a much-dreaded and mispronounced sound. But Ferdinand, to exalt himself and his parents above the struggling masses, can make both in close succession!

Apparently there's a belief that the 'r' can be made if the fleshy thing underneath the tongue, which joins it to the bottom of the mouth, is cut further in. Nonsense! I've got a nice game going with the younger ones: running around while loudly making the Afrikaans 'r'. There's a hell of a commotion between tongue tip and palate. It's a trilling with a great amount of voice thrown into it and they make it with gusto. But now, how to make the demure English 'r'? The tongue has to take a dip in the middle of itself, with the sides slightly curled up and the tip a bit back and hovering in space, which is not a comfortable position. It's fabulously exciting for them, but when they get to the English 'r' the exuberant little faces turn to perplexity: a moment ago life was so good. It's no fun learning English.

I had a good mind to get Ferdinand right there to trill and tremble that tongue tip, but we had arrived and Ferdinand said some words. He told me to produce my piece of paper, which I did, but the pharmacist crossed his wrists.

"Ferdinand, it says here what I have, what I need to be treated for."

"No," said Ferdinand in a quiet way, not used to contradicting an adult.

"Yes, man, it's right here." I shoved the piece of paper under the pharmacist's nose again.

"No. It gives instruction of how to cut your hair. Not use razor, use scissor. The top more longer, not too very short, not straight line when the neck start."

Bloody hell, it was the hairdresser's note. My bag produced no other piece of paper.

Desperation knows no bounds. I plonked my foot on the counter. The pharmacist and Ferdinand recoiled in horror. Not only was there a foot on the counter, but a foreign foot at that. But evidently, this was not the worst transgression. The pharmacist said urgent words, at which Ferdinand turned his back on the offending foot. He was not to see the pest his teacher carried. Then the pharmacist slid a tube of ointment my way, making sure not to touch me, checked that Ferdinand was still facing away, and turned his back on me.

"Thank you, Ferdinand."

Did he now know the teacher he had danced with was an unclean person?

When we got back we were flushed and Ferdinand animated and Sarah in tunnel vision. While all seemed fine I took the horrible plunge and spoke to her about ending my contract six weeks early. And the question of the bonus. She could work it out pro rata. Just deduct six weeks' money.

"Yes, I wonder what you are going to do. I think maybe you go to university."

I must have looked relieved, or perhaps still worried, because she added without my having asked: "I will sign release form."

"Have you got such a form? And where must it be taken?"

"My husband. He will do."

"Thank you, Sarah." Big smile, big bow, big worry as to how to get Park to do this form thing. "And the bonus?"

"I can*not* pay bonus. If you get other teacher, I can pay the bonus. It is very good for you here. Other schools sometimes make a big fight with the teacher and let the teacher go before the contract ends, and then they don't pay a bonus."

"You have been most kind to me, Sarah, thank you."

I got straight onto the job of finding a teacher. The emails now fly to South Africa, ads go in, there's a taker *and* he's youngish, at least he's younger than I am. But his eyes look strange. I present Sarah with the wonderful news, omitting the eyes. There's great relief all around, though his eyes keep worrying me and I take a closer look. There's one small problem: he's blind. He convinces me he'll manage.

"In Korea we can*not*. We can*not* help for this."

What? Do they not accommodate disability?

Not deterred, I am spurred on. Never mind the bonus, it has dawned on me that if Sarah is left high and dry without a teacher she may not sign me off. It is not easy for her to find teachers because of the Saturday teaching. And Park will then most certainly be more unforthcoming. Whenever I ask him where to get the form he mumbles some stuff and disappears into his warren.

But things light up: there's another taker. A young girl, and pretty. Now I want my bonus. Only thing is, Paul has left the university and is going to fill my place. Paul, here?! Why? But no answer comes. And by the looks of it, no bonus. I think I have been cheated, but I'm still not signed off. My bows grow deeper and longer. They've become a compulsion, like laughter you can't stop.

There is dreadful tension. Park and Sarah have shouting matches; Park's angry voice on the intercom system booms more often into the classrooms. The math teacher has disappeared and Sarah can't be disturbed with the question of his mattress, which is still in Jugong ee cha. Diane is definitely working herself to a standstill. Her back is now so rigid it may snap. And I have realised that she is at the mercy of Sarah's and Park's whims almost as much as I am.

There are two weeks left before I have to leave. Preparations can't be delayed. As soon as I've hardly slept in the uni dorm, I'll have to somehow find my way to Japan to get a visa. I've been receiving information from foreigners on how to make the trip. The main problem is how to pay your fare on a Japanese bus. There's a picture of the bus, and there's the pay point, or not the pay point, that is the problem. Leona has also phoned to say that in addition to teaching English to university students – still no one seems to be clear what exactly – I must also give a writing course. For students, adults, and children. Three classes of writing, every day of the week? No, one class, every day of the week. Adults and children writing in one class? Just so.

I may have published my own work, but what do I know about getting others to write? Karen Bruns, our friend in publishing, is in Europe and she's promised to look for this one book the internet says is the alpha and omega. There's no such book in SA. I think – don't get side-tracked, never mind the bloody book, ask Park again about the form. Stand in front of him, turn when he does, cling to his movements.

And deliverance comes unexpectedly. Sarah tells me I must go with her husband to office in downtown. Now? Yes, he is waiting. He cannot wait long. Indeed, waiting, furious, just a grunt to my "Hello, Mr Park". Off we go in his Merc.

I trail behind him into the building like a child. Talk, talk at the counter with the official and he barks a word at me: card. Ah, I must produce my card with that photo that is not quite me. Card produced, lots of talk, please dear God make things work out and help officialdom to start and finish a task in one quick blink of the eye. And oh, merciful joy, it is not Africa, and a completed, filled-out form, with stamp and signature is gruntily shoved into my hands. I am free!

"Gamsamnida, Mr Park." My thankful bow is deep and keeps me down and when I emerge I see Park's back leaving the building.

Back at the apartment there's mail from a friend to congratulate me on my job at the university. "It sounds at least prestigious for purposes of CV etc. Puts a different slant on teaching in South Korea." CV? I've never thought to build one. This is more proof that I don't know the ways of the world. At least I have now lied blatantly, and with potentially good result.

That greener grass on the other side of the fence looks very green to her. In her despair of herself she sees my situation as one of freedom. She wants to travel, she says, on account of the four walls. She feels trapped. But from where I stand in the misery of what I've organised for myself, those four walls of hers will still be her freedom. In a few years she'll have a pension, with a real profession behind her. And when she wants to move she'll simply look up a number and phone a company which will effortlessly move her furniture. She'll talk in full sentences; she will be answered in full sentences and she will not have to rely on absurd gestures.

But here, look what happens when you break the four walls: my big move from Jugong ee cha, Gweng-song, to Beak ship o, number 515, in some building on a campus, has been and is still going to be dreadfully cumbersome. Many bus trips have already been done and many more are to come.

There is by now a rhythm. Gather armfuls: uncomfortable plastic/wooden fold-up chair, rice cooker, shoes for all indoor occasions, now-emptied ceramic pot for beautiful future plant, sponge floor-washer so as not to have to get hands embroiled in sticky dustballs and hair, Lesley's old vacuum cleaner held together by Sellotape, her pan with mismatched pot lid, suitcases, bundles, stuff from Vietnam and Cambodia. Gather all these armfuls and leave, walk to bus, wait, struggle to get on while being pushed aside, bus driver impatient, clutch stuff to body on wild route; disembark while losing footing due to shoving of fellow travellers, proceed to walk up the hill. Arrive. Ascend four storeys. The end of this trip, at least, is nigh.

Leona is there. She says Paul is furious. We had ransacked his room for his desk and almost-comfortable and much sought after lounge chair. Although he doesn't want to see this fake leather thing ever again, he may have wanted to pass it on to a friend. We did it in the dead of night when things here are moved from vacated room to the next-to-be occupied room. We also swopped the mattresses, though this he didn't notice.

I notice nothing but the glaring neon light that shines right into my room and onto my bed. I'll have to get curtains, but this is near impossible. Leona brought hers from SA and another's mom is making her some as we speak. I'll have to ask Sarah if I can take her unlined one, since she's not going to keep the apartment. Paul will live with Mae. She must be very sure that he will stay in her sweatshop for ever. It's no small matter to rent an apartment. You need key money. This is a very big, once-off sum you don't get back when you move. Or do you get it back, but without interest? But, and here is the wonder, you never pay rent. Perhaps I don't have this right. Whichever, key money is a big thing.

Sarah is going to give me half of my bonus. I say thank you and ask whether I could possibly have the curtain. She's so relieved that I didn't quibble about the bonus that she urges me, please, yes, take curtain. I can*not* read her eyes and between East and West much gets lost. There is more care and goodwill here than I give credit for.

Tomorrow is my last day. I have already said goodbye to the old women on the pavement and those on my floor on the other side of the lift, to the unfriendly café owner and the man who sells the sticky red chicken – the one who once drove me home when he saw my exhaustion. I have also said goodbye to my neighbours. Goodbye went like this: index finger jabbed repeatedly into breastbone, meaning 'I', followed by crossed wrists with a single 'anieyo Gweng-song' for 'no', and all finished with an outstretched arm and index finger pointing behind me, away, with the word 'Seon-chang'. And a bow.

And so it is goodbye-day. Damn hell, I should never have become so attached to the kids. It's very hard to say goodbye. Oreon, who was left shivering by Park's shouting, has quietly snuck his hand into mine. Sonya with her non-bouncing pigtails has pressed herself into me. And Mike, the irrepressible, sits meekly on my lap.

But back up the stairs things are worse than ever. Under the neons the staffroom hums with whispers and repressed animosity. Diane, for one, has been fired. No severance pay or notice. She has to be gone by the end of next week. Her boyfriend is leaving too. Though whether his leaving is voluntary is not clear. And it seems the Korean teacher – in his absence – also has to go.

"Diane, you must have some rights. This can't be legal." But this is Korea and anything can happen. Diane is devastated. She must make lots of money. This is the reason for being alive. By now she is sitting down, her back hunched. I hover on bent knees next to her. It transpires she is a deep-sea diver and that there are quite a number of reasons for her to be alive. If she could break free from the numerous constraints here and, unfortunately, the security they offer, she should have a good life.

I get up and walk to my desk in the foreigners' far corner in the back. I make a neat pile with the books I used, and also those with the notes to myself. I leave them on the desk. They, together with the children's documented progress or lack thereof, will end up in the trash. The children will start anew, to eventually leave school and the misery of the hagwon system, still not able to have a conversation in English.

I have bowed to Sarah and thanked her. I was the slightest bit short of sincere. I did have it good. She paid me on time; I had decent lodgings; she signed me off. I have made a general bow to the teachers in the room and am now walking up to Diane, my Ice Queen. She astonishes both of us. She grabs me and hugs me. "Oh, Karin!" Gone is the barrier of age and culture. I hug back, the giant in her padded jacket, gloves, her shawl and her beanie. "Make a good life for yourself, Diane."

At the door I turn around to make another bow, but the teachers are back hunched over their desks and Sarah is in her tunnel. It's a lone Diane who stands there and looks on. She smiles, sadly, and waves. I smile, and wave back.

I have slept, dressed, done the last bus trip. I have walked up the hill to the dormitory and climbed the four storeys up.

I look around my assorted bundles and odd furniture. Never give up, said Churchill.

Never give up.

SEON-CHANG

WE ARE IN the furthest corner of the university grounds, wedged between buildings to the left and a hill cum mountain behind which stretches to the right. On the right is also the side road I braved up and down with my bundles. From the road you go through a gap in a low wall to get to our building. The wall ends in the mountain, which is thickly covered with bamboo, creepers, trees and undergrowth. There are vegetable patches here and there where the forest has been cleared.

It's blissfully quiet, everyone's on holiday. Brenda, the only person here in the foreigners' dormitory, is a fifty-odd-year-old Australian. She's very helpful and correct. Our conversations are shot through with lots of smiling. She looks a bit like a parrot: her thick dark brown hair, hacked by a Korean razor, stands on end on the top of her head. I get the feeling she can be prim and proper with her short and neat body. Miss Parrot Priss. Her room doesn't have an Eastern thing in it.

What worries me is that she's put me on the highest of pedestals. I'm perfect in all ways. It's probably the perfection she strives for in herself. I see a bad thing coming. I can only fall from that pedestal. She wants to join my writing class. It's going to change her life. No, I want to say. You're going to be as prim and unfulfilled as you are now. She's too ordered and controlled for the messy business of writing.

She has taken me around the campus to scout for discarded furniture. The campus is not big. Leading off the main road is a broad walkway in the middle with buildings left and right of it and buildings at the top. There's a breathtakingly lovely pond, around which are trees neatly cut into spirals and various shapes. Near the pond we find a discarded ball and claw coffee table. Not one I would love to possess, but it's real, with a glass top and wood and the height of a Western coffee table. How did this thing get to Korea? It fits perfectly in my room.

My room is drenched in the softest light. There's not an unlit spot in that room in the corner of the L-shaped building with the men's bathrooms and their morning spitting next to it. At the far end of the room are glass sliding doors almost the width of the not-so-broad room with glass I can wash to my heart's content. The wooden Cambodian bird hangs from the ceiling to the right of the doors next to the head of my bed and plays in the soft light. It perches on the bottom bar of its frame and is supported from the top bar by string. The string is also attached to its head. He – this bird is a he – has a long neck which is a string with wooden beads. There's even a fish that dangles in front of his mouth. If the bird's wings face downwards his long neck and head drop, and he sleeps. But when you have the wings horizontal his head and his fish come up and he's awake. I love him.

But the best of all is the balcony, surely the smallest balcony there could possibly be. It's exactly the width of the length of my legs. Lesley's uncomfortable plastic/wooden chair is small enough to fit. I sit there in the cold and drape myself with blankets. One can't take Africa out of an African. Outside we have to be.

The balcony sitting is most instructive. The café on the far side of the road sports a neon sign above the door and lots of writing on one wall. Brenda's given me a booklet with the Korean alphabet. I sit and spell, like we did in Sub A. That thing must be a 'k' and that an 'a'. Each character represents a sound and they are composed of a combination of lines and circles.

It's vastly different from Chinese writing, which uses logograms where a character depicts a word or a phrase. There are thousands of these characters. It was only the educated Korean elite who could write this; the writing brought about the meaning but not the sound of the Korean language. It was also unsuited to convey the complex Korean grammar. Some or other king was concerned that only a few people could express themselves and so developed Hangul.

In Hangul characters aren't written in a linear way like ours. They write from left to right, but they stack two, three or four characters together in a square, the first one on top of the second and three on top of four. It seems there are sometimes three stacked one on top of the other. It has to do with vowels and consonants. Something like this. Each square is a syllable. Several of these syllables make a word. But where does a single word start or end? By the end of a lot of concentration I've either spelled one very long word or a sentence. They say it's a hellishly difficult language with sounds we simply can't hear. There are three different sounds for 'k', for instance. We also can't hear the different forms of 'd' and 't'. And I suppose they all mean different things. Added to this is the problem of romanisation. It can't reflect these sounds and meanings fully.

Next to the café is a building under construction. Many men scurry back and forth. They don't have wheelbarrows. They stand with their back to a person a bit higher up. A sack is draped over their shoulders on their back and then filled with sand, and off they go. They all wear the same cotton gloves with rubberised palms that everyone else wears here, from the person behind the meat counter to the toilet cleaner. There's a solitary dog barking there. I wonder how long it will live there before it is clubbed to death and eaten.

And I wonder how long before this country's clubbed me to extinction. Back I can't go. Besides, some internal process has started. What it is, I have no clue. I'll have to sit it out.

The sun is setting to the right. The colours are most unimpressive, but their softness echoes the gentleness of what lies under the surface of the harsh striving here. There's a single tree in the vegetable patches. It has lost its leaves in the winter cold. In its top is a bird's nest. The mother or father has come home. Amongst the dense growth on the ground is movement. An old woman shakes the soil from her hands and looks one last time at her vegetables. She squats, lifts her dress and relieves herself.

I am going to be happy here.

❉

The ferry for Japan leaves from Buson, a modern city, more modern than any city I've ever been in. Here I had to get official papers at offices in warrens before I could get onto the ferry. It's full of young foreigners doing the visa run. Next to me is

Ross, early thirties with a sharp brain. It's her second time in Korea. She couldn't make a life back home when she first went back. Hence her coming to Korea again. But she tells herself she's back because she's doing an MA in some social study of foreigners. We laugh at the lie she tells herself. Not a single interview has been done. She's at a dreadful Buddhist university. Every movement, every thought is policed. Her lodgings are dismal too. She has no bathroom, fridge or cooking facilities.

We wonder what would happen in the case of a cholera outbreak, what with all those chopsticks in the communal bowls. We discuss Korean building practices. What if the slightest earthquake were to hit the peninsula? Is anything even reinforced? Buildings go up in a flash. I talk about the built environment and she is astonished. The level of conversation here is so low that 'built environment' is a sure sign of intelligence.

She's also heard of the bus problem in Japan. With this worry we disembark and make our way to a bus. And indeed, paying on a bus is no easy thing, but it's over and done with so quickly I don't have a clue how we did it.

Japan is different from Korea. The design of buildings, artefacts and clothing feels streamlined, somehow. It's quite a beautiful and tranquil place. The millions of Toyota taxis hardly make a noise. There are many bicycle lanes and people use them, as well as coffee shops. The atmosphere is much more Western than in Korea, except for the very low bowing. Their foreheads almost touch the ground.

We have a day and a night to get everything done and dusted before we start a frantic scramble back to be ready for the start of term.

But done and dusted doesn't mean the scramble has left me migraineless. The migraines are relentless. Sleep is a migraine's first casualty. I wish I could have Hilette's sleep therapy. Be knocked out for two weeks. Or more.

It's twelve-thirty here. Dead of sleepless night. In desperation I swallow one of the last remaining migraine tablets and disappear into a fantasy which I hope will bring comfort.

In this fantasy I have a brain tumour. A scan was done

and there the thing was: big, with tentacles lying all over the brain like an octopus. The octopus is of course responsible for everything: fear, exhaustion, migraines, my inability to grasp anything, all the misery. But how does this thing find space between brain and skull? Never mind, I'm whisked off to Seoul by Sam with his okay English. There's an excellent brain surgeon in Seoul.

By now the tablet starts working ever so slightly. Earplugs are in on account of having a room next to the men's bathrooms and also on account of being me. It's as dark as can be with the neon light shining through Sarah's unlined curtain. My fingers lie lightly over the afflicted eye. My head's propped up high in the hope that less blood to the brain will curb the pain. The brain that is about to be operated on.

And the operation is done. The thing was literally plucked from the brain. There it lies in a kidney-shaped stainless steel container, all intact. And the tablet's working even better and sleep may just claim me properly. But my eyes sprint open. I'm lying here in this dormitory – this is real and no fantasy – and it's about to happen. What is about to happen? The fantasy may tell, so I sink down again.

I open my eyes in the hospital and am defencelessly horizontal and know I can't talk to a soul. And then, here in this dormitory, in this single bed not far from the wheezing fridge and the men's bathroom, the pores in my being open. And what they release is terror. Crystal sharp. Because of the tablet and the lateness of the hour and the pain all defences are gone and I realise: this terror is no fantasy. It is what I feel. Every moment. I am petrified.

As the good psyche will have it, the fantasy takes over again and looks for the answer. I'll only regain my senses, I realise, if I'm out of this terrifying place. So Marko must come and bring me back from desolation and the desolation in myself. But how will I get money to him? I'm horizontal with an octopus in a container. At this point a tear starts forming because my heart breaks for Marko. What sorrow and panic he must feel for his mother and her octopus! Here I must skip a bit. I can't cry full on, because the pain will be worse.

Good I skipped, because here comes Marko. He was whisked up to my hospital room. He somehow didn't have to go through the language incomprehension thing at reception. But, for God's sake, the fantasy evaporates and what to do with this terrible fear.

So I wake up, I cry rivulets down my neck and into this miserable bed in the room that the ondol over-heats.

And now it's one o'clock and my heart's shattered by terror, because how can I go back to South Africa? And so I get up to open the sliding doors and the movement brings some relief, but it's temporary. I have no hope. At best I can hope to bear what is.

The thing is, the whole Korea business would have been easier if I could believe in God. Terry Eagleton said standing outside faith allows for a freedom of sorts, but there's a price to be paid. There's very little solace. I came upon a quote on my computer from his *On Evil*. Turning down God's love "… is the final, terrifying consequence of human freedom."

Perhaps faith is the positive philosophical choice you make, and so defy logic and reason.

My sister and brother-in-law's deep faith is astonishing, now more so after he was shot. Although it may very well stand in their way of acceptance. He *will* walk again, God *will* grant him this. I shut my mouth. I know nothing of what they are going through. But this is certain: they have made the positive philosophical choice. As a consequence of their faith they will not hate those who committed the crime. They will not dwell on the incompetence or disinterest of the police; they will not consider what-ifs. They will live their lives the best they can. In their faith.

It's all too overwhelming. The night will soon come to its end and I should try to get a few hours sleep, propped up high with my fingers over the afflicted eye.

※

Indeed, all ages have been dumped into the same writing class. There are ten-, twelve- and sixteen-year-olds, university students and adults. I said on the university's website that this course will help you discover what you want to express and guide you to do so. But the kids just want to swivel on their noisy chairs. They want to discover nothing. The teenagers have some vague wish to free themselves, through writing, from teenage angst and confusion. The adults want to discover something, but they are dismayed by their lack of good English through which to discover. They hide their frustration behind silence. Only a few want to develop a creative voice. There's one woman who's not bad. She's clearly powerful, but tries to hide it. Her hand movements are strong, but she curbs them. Her hands should naturally move away from her into open space, but she keeps them close to her by choppy, short movements as if she's caught herself in a bad act. I can't see her laughing girlishly behind her hands. She must have it difficult here where strength in a woman seems not to be a plus.

I can't pitch myself to these diverse groups at the same time. I'm a jack-in-the-box. I pop up everywhere. The one very good thing is that Miss Priss didn't make it to the writing class.

The university classes are somewhat better. At least there's grammar, which is easy to teach. But there's still the conversation element. I try to do it through literature. But to get them to make a single sentence! They are too prim and proper and overly respectful. I now have to get up at the crack of dawn to prepare for the first silent class at 7 am. Then drag my body through the day – with time off in the middle – to 8 pm when I finish with the kids.

The kids' building is appropriately off campus. It is a new building with good plumbing and the loos don't have bins for semi-used paper. A lot of energy goes into the kids. I'm trying not to get too attached, as I did in Gweng-song, and I'm definitely trying not to undermine myself again by making them naughty, just because I can't stand to toe the line. Although I've proved they learn better in rowdiness than in non-participating obedience.

But on the balcony I'm free of the whole lot. I have wrapped myself in a blanket. From up here everyone's strides seem too short. But truly, we are all caricatures. We, the waegukins – the foreigners – on the campus of the daehakyo. I sigh and wrap the blanket tighter. There goes Miss Priss, early as usual, on her way to class. As the longest-serving member she is now head of the children's section.

There goes spaced-out Fred, the bodybuilder who lives

above me and who dumps his weights on the floor and therefore on my ceiling. He's in his early twenties and has a disconcerting vulnerability. His eyes are always glassed over on account of culture shock and depression. Even from up here I can hear the slouch as his heavy-soled shoes drag on the ground. He has his earphones in again to cut him off from life. He's really not a baddie, but for his spitting. He bends forward while in a circle of people and out it comes. Jesus, Fred, have a heart, I said to him once. Now he turns his back on the group and bends over.

Then there's Andrew from England. He's made it clear this teaching job is a stepping-stone. He's headed for the diplomatic world. Quite how teaching in Korea will land him on the ladder to ambassadorial heights is not clear. Although he seems to be together, he must be on the down. The last couple of days heavy metal's been pumping from his room. I suppose, like Fred and his earphones, it's to block out Korea. And when it's not his heavy metal it's the slow, heart-breaking sound of his guitar.

The young, hard-as-nails creature, John, is thin and completely nondescript. A cartoonist would have a hard time drawing him. I saw a girl go up with him to his room and the next morning, in the café, I heard her on her cell telling a friend that it was ghastly. Everyone knows everyone's business.

Cindy is the youngest woman here, late twenties, and attaches herself to one of the older women and then moulds herself to that one. It's disturbing to see with what fluidity she changes. There she goes, just a few steps behind Fred, who is her bosom buddie. She's off to the café. She's in her jeans. They never leave her body. She's started clicking again. The sound you'd make for a horse. The tenser she is the more clicking comes from that Canadian mouth and the stronger the smell of vomit from her room. It's at its worst after lunch. She must be dabbling in bulimia.

Dennis, in his thirties, from Ireland, who's been here a long time, talks without any inflections. He has a deadpan face. Not a muscle moves in that face. He told someone, who told all the other someones, that he suffers from Asperger's. This intimate detail is now all over the place, as is the following: he thought he got himself a faithful girl in Vietnam, to whom he sent money regularly, but then he came back from his last vacation with gonorrhoea. Now he's not sending money.

It's a bit too early for Jeremy from the States and his snail's pace and limp. Now *he* is a cartoonist's dream: slightly sagged belly, neck thrust forward, head tilted to the side, exposing that long lower part of his face. He was a preacher in some Christian sect who's somehow washed up here. He may be slightly ahead of Leona in pushing 60. He and his wife, Greta, huddle in their small room where, the gossip goes, she prepares her husband's lectures. Usually he's led by the hand by her. When they're not together she's in a hurry. The hurry must be on account of all the myriad things she has to do for her husband to keep him in a job before she sprints down to her churchy hagwon where she's not paid properly. She's a long, wily whirlwind, with her black pumps and white ankle-high socks neatly folded over. The right sock is always slightly higher than the left. Her pants don't quite reach her ankles. But it's no joke. She never used to have epileptic fits, but now she gets them. Her tension levels must be sky high.

Leona's pants too sometimes don't reach her ankles. She's descended the stairs in her white sneakers, and with short strides and stick in hand, she and dog disappear into the mountain. As if I'm one to criticise. I sit on this balcony hour after hour and latch onto a misery. It's as if I'm not alive until I find a misery to occupy myself with. At present my misery is Leona. I don't understand what's going on, but she's become distant and cold.

Leona's greatest foe is Susan from America. Loud, over-weight, unkempt, she's the spitting image of a bullfrog. She's probably early forties; there are vestiges of youth, but she has that look of weariness that middle age brings. There's a terrible chasm between her self-image and her living self. She has a photo of herself in her room taken about fifteen years ago. She was beautiful. When she says age hasn't really changed her I'm gobsmacked. What she sees is clearly not what the world sees.

Leona has warned me against Susan, and Susan, the Frog, has warned me against Miss Priss, and Miss Priss has warned me against Cindy, and Leona again has hinted that I should be warned against everyone. And all of them have warned me against Leona. They seem to think they can only survive if they trample on people and so rise higher on the pile of corpses. Exactly where you're rising to is unclear, since there is no promotion, no higher pay, no real reason to curry favour with Admin.

I wonder how a cartoonist would draw me? A frowning gash so deep it clefts my head. Hunched shoulders. Strides too long so as to get the moment over and done with. A speech bubble would show a stream of sighs.

Here we become the shadow of ourselves. You have a place in the hierarchy and that's it. Or actually, you don't have a place and so you stay an unacknowledged outsider who will be nothing more, who will forever fart against the Korean wind.

The ensemble is not complete without Admin, the gents and ladies who determine our lot. They are possibly a microcosm of the greater society, which is held together by hierarchy. I read somewhere that their society is vertical because of filial piety, age, respect for seniority and the worship of ancestors.

At the very head is some or other professor who is never seen. On the ground floor behind the counter is Mrs Kim, whom we are not to talk to. She's high up or something. She speaks no English; you just bow and say thank you in two octaves higher than your normal speaking voice, and with honey dripping from it. This is the sickening way we foreigners talk to Koreans. Each sentence ends in an upward inflection, like a question. This is to show subservience and that you won't challenge the status quo, and that they can mould you into the perfect indentured labourer.

Anyhow, what you thank Mrs Kim for I don't know, but it's in line with how I am here. Thank you, thank you, that's almost the only thing that comes from my mouth. What's wrong with me? I'm very tired of myself. Someone told me not ever to thank a Korean. That way you admit you are indebted and you are obliged to help that person in future.

The rather anxious Ji-hu, in his early thirties, who is responsible for the teachers, syllabuses and programme, is next down. He got a hundred per cent in the dreaded Test of English for International Communication – TOEIC. This test means he has perfect English. Yet he struggles to string two sentences together. There are so many stops and starts, repeated words and nonsensical words thrown in that it's almost impossible to follow him. It's exhausting standing there with your smile, bent lower to his face level, and hide your impatience.

Ji-hu's a good example of the way things are, according to Leona, done in Korea: spontaneously, last minute. One moment there's nothing, the next there's something. Usually a change of plan. And of course no consultation. The top dog gets a whim and down the line it travels without any challenge or input. This swift decision thing can be seen as a beautiful spontaneity, but when you're left picking up the pieces it loses its beauty. The writing class is an example. It was Ji-hu's brainchild. It just popped into his head and was never thought through. I now sit with what can only be a failure. Ji-hu is also constantly on the brink of a nervous breakdown. If saving face is paramount, there's no respect for him. He's not supposed to show a thing.

Next in line is Mun-hee, although I'm not sure whether he's perhaps above Ji-hu. He's older than Ji-hu, which gives him an advantage, but to my mind his job is less important – though this may mean nothing. Mun-hee minds the computers somewhere in a computer room when he's not downstairs in the office.

The older Mun-hee may very well be below Ji-hu, because Ji-hu is slightly lighter skinned than Mun-hee. In the past uneducated people worked on the lands and were tanned, says Leona. But Mun-hee is also the eldest son. Does family position count for anything in the working environment? Mun-hee as the eldest son works his fingers to the bone every weekend for his parents, and after that has to endlessly bring workmen to the foreigners' dormitory he has to oversee, the dormitory which is about to sink into the mountain according to Leona. She consulted an engineer who is now a teacher. We live in grave danger. Jesus, I care not a hoot. I have my wooden bird, deeply loved he has become, computer and balcony with a view of the café and street and the vegetable patches and the lone tree with its bird.

On the lowest rung is kind Seo-yeon, the secretary, who speaks good English. She comes over in the afternoons to the building where we teach the kids, to spy on us. Although she has her nose in her computer and doesn't mind us. But perhaps she notes every move we make.

Admin simply means that the locus of control is not inside yourself.

But really, I cannot fathom their sorrows that lie below their hard striving; below their anger and their softness. But I feel the sadness. I only need to look into their hills and their valleys and their faces with their vulnerable honesty. Their insularity has preserved them. They don't know what psychic adaptations are necessary to incorporate clashing cultures. Their innocence in not knowing what is out there; that is what breaks my heart.

But what do I know what lies beyond their inscrutability? What does it mean to have your will and wishes, from an early age, subjected to the greater good of the group? They are a closed book forever.

LEONA, THE HEAD girl, or HG, let me know Mun-hee wants to see me urgently. Now more bowing, high voice and sweet smile. En route I hear a lawnmower. I follow the sound deeper into the campus. Walking on the campus is being in a time warp. Songs from *The Sound of Music*, Abba, or German marching music play through loudspeakers. And once, in between, a bizarre English sentence like this one: Will you have tea with me today?

It must be the lawnmower, because up come two, no less, memories, replete with emotion. Marko and I are in the car on the way to school, chatting ourselves dilly. There he sits neat and fresh with his red blazer and his red cheeks. And one where I fetch him from rugby practice. There he comes drenched in mud, his rugby socks are down around his ankles. He turns around, has a last word with a friend. I have plastic down on the seat. The back door opens, in go his bags. The front door opens, down he plonks on the plastic. "How was it?" "They killed us today."

I was a mother once.

I get to Mun-hee hurried and dishevelled. It's proof of the urgency with which I responded to his command. He informs me I "have bad virus on computer". I "must back up computer". He "must have computer".

I try to explain that I'm editing and will need my computer back soon. He doesn't understand 'editing'.

"I write, I write book. I must have computer."

He turns his back on me. He's so bloody rude. I bow.

I go down and ask Seo-yeon to please ask Mun-hee how long he'll have my computer. There's much subdued jubilation behind the counter. Seo-yeon is pregnant. Everyone hopes it's a boy. I catch Mrs Kim's eye. She is smiling. I can't help myself and exclaim: "Mrs Kim, what good news!" I've over-stepped the line. I bow and get out.

There's great pressure on Seo-yeon to produce a son. Someone told me there was a time a man could divorce his wife if she had only daughters. Now she's not divorced, but she has no status. The obsession with sons has something to do with lineage, which is passed from father to son only. And lineage is all important, it is your roots, because it binds you to the ancestral background, which determines the identity of the family and thus the individual's within it. I wonder how many generations back the lineage is celebrated. I think Chuseok has something to do with these ancestors. Anyway, all we in the West know about our genealogy is Adam and Eve.

Now with my computer gone there's a lot of balcony sitting. It's in one of these sessions that I have a heart attack: what if Mun-hee reads my stuff? There's the missive about Korea I sent home. And there are steamy emails with a very distant lover. Perhaps it's still culture shock that made me dig out our emails, print them and start writing to this man again. Or my need to remember my past. Or my hormones that are all over the show and also dead at the same time. I reckon the truth lies in the body and if I can feel his presence I may remember what came before I was born here at forty-eight. God help me, Mun-hee must be reading this, perhaps right now:

Darling woman, I think of you daily; of how your lips feel and how you open to me; your wetness and urgency; of my need to be enveloped by you. We are entwined in ways that I can't fathom nor really wish to. There is between us a strength of desire and purpose that we don't understand and which I am sometimes (and you, too) mightily afraid of. There is something that consumes us both and we spend an awful amount of time trying to pretend it isn't there. But then the moments when we release ourselves into it and into each other are sublime; and for that I would never stop seeking you out. I miss you in all sorts of complicated ways; not only from the sexual energy we nurture but because something inside you remains unknown and elusive. And there are moments when you are completely wrapped about me and our eyes meet that I think I have come close to knowing all there is to know about the world inside you. But then it slips away and we are once again circling each other, waiting for that moment our barriers drop and passion and true understanding emerge from the sweat and delight of our being.

∞∞∞

V, there you were on Skype, your photo, I mean. You're still the rugged sexy thing with the devil's look. I can smell you. The memories have burst in me like the clear and over-bearing sound of a bell. In my new, disinfected life I miss the muddle of our passion, the anger, hurt, the force upon which we acted. The dark blueness of it all. We gave so little of ourselves. But perhaps this enabled us to give so much. I feel sad for what we did not explore, but still, I'm happy for what we did. Have we now stepped into a different age where things are only remembered? Sliding my body on and through the sweat of yours. The perversity of opening your pores to another's fluids. Sinking into our base bestial humanness. And so, did we come to the end of it all? Not having given ourselves to love. Much like my Hilette who can't even say the word 'love'. Perhaps you and I can't really love. Or perhaps we knew that to love would destroy us. Are we so fragile, or was our passion so strong that it excluded much else? But still, with you I showed that which I always hid. But not my love. Not my love. Oh, why were we two stunned animals? What did we have and never have? We must not regret.

Our passion had very little to do with ourselves. Do you see it the same way? Not specific and personal to each other. No, a depersonalised force. A free force which visits the fortunate ones and is complete in itself. And so we should not mourn its passing.

I have just looked: the evening star shines bravely. The sun has left behind beautiful hues. The evening is spread out against the sky like a patient etherised upon a table. In the room, the women come and go, talking of Michelangelo. What did Eliot mean, what did he feel? It is a love song, but a strange one. Perhaps a love song, like ours, without love.

Here, well, here the women come and go, talking of each other with their rattlesnake tongues.

Much love then.

∞∞∞

I've been thinking about what William Ernest Henley said – not that I know a single poem of his: "I am the master of my fate: I am the captain of my soul."

Well, I am master of bugger all.

I've been reading *Moby Dick* since there's nothing else to read. It's got me thinking about free will, because I chastise myself: wasn't it I, me, myself who chose to come here? In *Moby Dick* Ishmael says a soul's a sort of a fifth wheel to a wagon. Gone was a soul choice when I realised it would be next to impossible to get my boy through university and me through life with those cancelled contracts at the publishers. Coming here was necessity. There was little room for choice.

But this aside. Here's the thing: with what's conscious you make destiny. The unconscious stuff, now that is what makes fate. I'm living in fate. How much of my decision to come here wasn't guided by what I had no clue of and no control over? For one: our historical time allows for only certain choices, as does our geography. And what about genes? I come from extreme people. Nature is not always subject to nurture. Ishmael also says:

"Though I cannot tell why it was exactly that those stage managers, the Fates, put me down for this shabby part of a whaling voyage, when others were set down for magnificent parts in big tragedies, and short and easy parts in genteel comedies, and jolly parts in farces – though I cannot tell why this was exactly; yet, now that I recall all the circumstances, I think I can see a little into the springs and motives which being cunningly presented to me under various disguises, induced me to set about performing the part I did, besides cajoling me into the delusion that it was a choice resulting from my own unbiased free will and discriminating judgment."

Free will is pie in the sky.

On the brighter side, I have my wooden bird. In the mornings I push up his wings and his head comes up and he's awake. Then I kiss his pointy beak which moves on his neck and I tell him it's a good, good day. And in the evenings after the teaching I give him another kiss and push down his wings and he goes to sleep. And then I pour a Korean cupful of soju and drink it on the balcony. Soju is distilled mostly from rice, yielding a twenty-five per cent alcoholic kick, or more. One cup makes for a nice light head. Sam told me that Koreans consume 3 billion bottles a year. There are 375 ml in a bottle. That's a lot of soju.

Also brighter: Miss Priss took me with her to her yoga teacher. A Mr Kim, though why she's so formal with him I don't know. Across this terrible divide between East and West we immediately recognised something in each other. He is very humane, and gentle. Dae-ho is his name. Not like in 'day', but rather as in the 'de' of 'delicate' and 'ho' as in 'hop'.

But on the darker side: I'm now certain I've landed in a nest of gossip. I go to Y, she gossips about X. I go to X, she gossips about Y. I go to Z, she gossips about X and Y. But when I see X, Y and Z together butter won't melt in those hot mouths. I'm not going to survive. I won't keep track of who's in and who's out, with who holds the power when. Better stay right out of it, concentrate on my editing and get stuff to keep that writing class occupied. I faithfully consult all possible sites, but everything I find is soul-destroying. So I basically suck stuff from my thumb for them, which means all of me is engaged. It's more work, because there's no book to follow, but it's lovely to see people use freedom. And despite the bad English hampering them there's a deeper value to them writing.

One more darker thing. There's this cute but hyperactive little boy who can't be more than eight. He must be ADD. He's really a menace. I don't know how to control him.

Never mind all of this. Next week is Seollal. I can't figure the difference between this and Chuseok, though last year I must have known. What I do know is that it means three days of holiday. I asked the kids what it's about.

"Down."

"It's about down?"

"Go down."

"Go down where?"

"Teacher, no. Down floor."

"Please, show me." No takers. "Please."

One gets up, is overwhelmed by shyness, but makes a bow.

"Oh, you bow. One calls this bow. Bowing."

"But boys not."

"Boys don't bow? Only girls?"

"Teacher, no. Boys down too. Boys little down."

"Show."

Now two takers. The boy gives a kind of halfway bow. The girl sinks with crossed legs down onto the floor.

"And get money." Many smiling faces. "Many money."

"Oh, a lot of money. You bow and you get a lot of money? Who do you bow to?"

"Ancestors. Grandparents. They give money. We have photo of ancestor."

"And put on hanbok. Eat rice cake."

"So you wear traditional wear?"

"When moon comes. Moon first in year. But also when year comes. First year."

Could it be a lunar celebration, honouring grandparents and ancestors all in one? At New Year? But it's far from the end of the year. Never mind, whatever we're celebrating, we're going to have holidays. And confused as I may be I feel certain that culture shock is wearing off.

Bull Frog, the shabby one from the States with the warped self-image, it transpires, is the expert on culture shock. She sent me info. There are stages of culture shock, like in the shape of a 'U' or 'W': the honeymoon phase, crisis, resolution and stabilisation. They say all the uncountable ways and clues with which you orient yourself and are mostly not aware of – all the familiar signs of interaction – are just gone. Hence disorientation and so on. At its worst it's like schizophrenia, where everything is threatening and you're defenceless. When you're not so immersed in your horror and start looking at everything from the outside – like I'm doing reading about culture shock – you are on the way to full recovery and self-development. But this part of the 'W' thing I can't see happening: the isomorphic attributions which will come. This is that Koreans and foreigners will see the real reason for one another's behaviour and not assume incomprehensible reasons. I doubt it. This twain is not ever going to meet.

But what I don't doubt is that Mun-hee must by now have read every last word on my computer.

THERE WE GO in Leona's little clapped-out car no Korean would be seen dead in. She invited me to go with her, Bull Frog and Miss Priss to a temple. And since I'm bent on stepping out of culture shock, I'm going. She's come out with what's been eating her. She wishes I'd drop in more and become more involved. She clearly wants a closer friendship and is hurt by my withdrawal. But I don't want to get embroiled in the gossiping and jockeying for power. I notice I'm saying less and less. Just watch, really. But I do feel bad. You are loyal to a friend and she's been good to me. But there's something strange in her voice. Like something's there that's not there. Or the opposite.

"Leona, you navigate these roads so well, but you've just smiled and bowed to that man who cut you off."

"Yes, I smile and apologise."

"Why?"

"I'm a foreigner. Plus, I'm a woman."

This country sucks all entitlement from you.

She and Frog chat as if they're not arch enemies. And Miss Priss laughs at the weirdest points in the conversation. The only thing that stands between me and enjoying this outing is the problem of speaking. Everyone sits ready to pounce on everyone. Leona told me that the Frog had made a grammar mistake in a conversation, which is unforgivable. Not that perfect English is uttered here. Fred and Miss Priss had a stand-up fight about 'gonna' and 'wanna'. She assured him that there are no such words, that the words are 'going to' and 'want to'. He insisted and she got her face all red from trying to keep herself in check. And there's Dennis with his Irish. Me mommy is making me some or other thing. Or this priceless one: it takes two to tangle.

I'm now overly cautious. If they cotton on that English is not my first language I'm done for, although nowhere is it stated that it has to be so, and there are many people here whose first language is not English. The consequence of all this is that every verb, clause, adjective – the whole bloody lot, which before was perfect enough – is checked while I speak. I stop midway in a sentence, because my brain has raced ahead and warned me that trouble is coming. Then I drop that sentence and frantically look for another way to say the same thing without the looming obstacle. All this happens in the blink of a second. I must sound very odd, what with half sentences and hand movements to complete a sentence.

In this internally fraught way we're happily speeding along. We're heading for the mountains where the temples always are. Halfway to hell and gone we stop for something to eat at a suspect-looking place surrounded by mud. There's the obligatory chained dog looking miserable. The inside is old linoleum and steam. We sink down onto the floor. Miss Priss and I don't struggle, but the Frog and Leona go down groaning. They try to smother it.

They all tuck in heartily. I'm back at the start of culture shock's 'W'. I'm nauseous in anticipation and I have that barrier between myself and what's presented. The fog from the early days has invaded my brain. I swallow and swallow and we are done and back in the car without shock absorbers, and drive into the mountains to a nameless temple. We've all known for days which temple we're going to so I definitely can't ask and reveal my undesirable foggy state of mind.

We are at our best for the sake of this outing. Bull Frog even smiles broadly at Head Girl and she, HG, is at her best compliance. I participate with my half sentences and feel bad that I see only the absurd in our jolly efforts.

We've parked. Leona doesn't lock the car. These temples are so safe there's no security needed. We start climbing the mountain to get to the temple. Climbing here means walking on a stone path and entering a mythological world with an abundance of trees that cast a mysterious light. En route are the watering spots. These are big hollowed stones into which fresh mountain water runs. Next to these exquisite things are big and deep plastic spoons with long handles to the side for easy drinking.

Suddenly HG speaks to me. In Afrikaans! I answer in English.

We're about to enter the temple gates with those huge, horrible-looking wooden creatures that flank them. They are really snarling monsters, much bigger than life size and painted in muted colours that are vibrant at the same time. They use naturally dyed colours, says HG. Perhaps she knows I can't remember a thing.

Suddenly it comes to me that I do know about these creatures. They are the Four Heavenly Kings. The one hears everything, the other enlarges, one maintains the state and the last one sees all. They protect the world from evil and the temple's dharma. They are also the Heavenly Guardian Kings of the East and West. If I have it right.

Surrounding the temple complex are ancient stone walls topped with roof tiles. The pillars are engraved with Korean words and have turrets on top. Inside, the buildings and rooms are loosely arranged in a square around a big centre with paths, terraces, colourful flowers and bridges of the same ancient stone as the walls. But what's especially catching are the high hip-and-gable roofs with their many layers of eaves. Their overhang is deep enough to cover the raised walkways around the buildings. The first layer is made with round logs and is shorter than the layer that follows on top of it and that again is shorter than the next, so that the roof is tiered. These layers are made of logs of different shapes, like square, oblong or flat, and are painted in various colours with intricate designs. The corners where the logs fan out are the most spectacular. On top of the corners are different tiles that look like dragons or monsters. It's all finished off with the top layer of the roof tiled with blue-black ceramic or stone tiles. From the sides the roof gradually flows downwards towards the middle, forming a curved line. The whole lot together is a dazzling sight of colours, motifs and shapes. Adding to all this is a bigger than life-size bell with ornate patterns. This one hangs in its own open temple in the right front corner of the square.

We're talking in hushed tones, because temples make you small in the presence of something higher. Just to the right of us is a couple walking aimlessly, staring into space. He is Korean and she a blonde Westerner. Her ring finger sports a wedding ring. There is absolutely no connection between the two. Whatever drew them to each other has dissipated into the Korean air and what's left is a defunct marriage and boredom. I wonder how Mae and Paul will work out. These marriages don't work, but men have little choice. It is true that, although illegal, female foetuses are aborted and now there aren't enough Korean women. Sam confirmed this.

Behind the bored couple is a building with a door of rice paper. From this hangs a thing that looks like a calabash with a handle and a stick stuck through it. I want to know what it is. Leona is about to answer, but Bull Frog cuts in, stumbling over her tongue to be first to answer. It's a moktak. It's a hollow percussion instrument – a hand bell – made from wood to call the monks to morning prayer. But, says Leona, it's also used when they chant.

Leona is on a roll. She explains so well and has so much knowledge. I can see why she teaches the most advanced students. Anyhow, the moktak. The elongated opening in the front and the two round holes on both sides of the moktak are like the mouth and eyes of a fish, although this one doesn't quite look like a fish. The story goes that a monk's baby fell out of a boat and was swallowed by a fish and was found alive inside the fish three days later. Much like Jonah and the whale, I say. Perhaps, the two of them agree doubtfully. Miss Priss concurs. She is really like a parrot today; that head bobs up and down as she agrees.

We turn away from the moktak and look at the walls all around. They are covered with paintings in the same muted greens, yellows, reds and blues that the temple gates have. They seem to tell stories like comics turned holy. Yes, says Leona, the top parts depict the worship of ancestors and spirits and the bottom parts depict hell and the suffering there. But the Frog won't be outdone and adds that there are also scenes that depict the most important teachings of the Buddha, or events from his life. There's one of a Bodhisattva on a white horse. Then there's the birth of Buddha, though it doesn't look like a birthing scene. In one scene Buddha leaves his grand palace. In the next he subjugates the demons. Another depicts him under the tree where he became enlightened. There are also pictures of a man looking for an ox and eventually finding it and riding it back to the village. This has something to do with how the mind is tamed from wild thing to oneness. Probably oneness with the disappeared self, I almost add.

Further along is a smaller room. It's a shamanist shrine. Buddhism and shamanism together? Leona explains that Koreans don't have one exclusive faith. Buddhism, Christianity, Confucianism and shamanism all co-exist with ease, although with the coming of the missionaries shamans were persecuted. But they are still entrenched in Korean culture and their rituals use traditional costumes, music and dance. The shaman, or mudang, is a channel for mountain or ancient warrior spirits and helps a person resolve problems by connecting that person to the spirits.

We've left the best for last. The most spectacular is the big shrine hall. It has real wooden floors and high ceilings made with many beams and painted with lotuses and unrecognisable patterns. Inside are golden Buddhas, much bigger than life-size, and all raised off the floor on a platform. We are quiet. It's as if the air compels you to bow inwardly. It brings peace and it's touched all of us. We leave, almost in a spirit of real friendship. I walk behind and turn back. I want a photo to add to the collection of Buddhas and temples I've been gathering for Adel. I wish she could be here with me. The temple would have touched her so. I hope my boxes aren't in her way.

Outside is a man in traditional pants, which are tied at the ankles, and a shirt that hangs freely. He's sitting on the edge of one of those low tables, or pavilions, where they socialise. One knee is pulled up under his arm, the other leg hangs down. He's upright, but his head hangs down. He's sleeping. We walk quietly past him and down the dense mountain. In the parking lot a woman is selling her wares. I buy a dozen ginger peelers. It's a nifty thing that slips over a finger with a cutting edge at the bottom. It's just the kind of thing Hazel would appreciate. I should have left my boxes with her.

On the way home in our silence I think: so what if I'll soon forget everything I learnt. The temple in the mountain with all the beauty will remain with me.

THERE IS NEW life in me.

Miss Priss's Mr Kim, Dae-ho, is definitely my friend. My guru man, healer, yoga man, friend. He is a rare, beautiful being who embodies the best of Buddhism. He spent time abroad and his English isn't bad.

"Karin. Anyong," he'll say hello in his singsong way. He lengthens certain vowels like the 'i' in my name and ends the word in an upward inflection. There are many little laughs in his sentences. They don't go outwards, but in, and down his throat, shaking his whole body. His smile stretches the width of his face and his tongue then slides to the left and peeps between his teeth.

I have been to his house, which is near the uni. It's a real house with a garden behind a wall with a gate. There are two dogs, and they are not chained. His wife has the same gentleness. Theirs was not an arranged marriage. They met when they were young and fell in love. They went down to shinae, or downtown, the old part of Seon-chang, and Dae-ho took her hand, which was, and still is, not allowed, and walked with her through shinae. Thereby announcing their love and commitment.

His little boy is a darling child. I have never seen a father love his son with such gentleness. He is worried about schooling for him. He doesn't want him in the gruelling system.

The first thing he noticed was my exhaustion and laboured breathing. Breathing makes movement, he said. Movement makes habit. Habit makes destiny. And he had me 'attach' my feet – bring them together – and 'vacate' my lungs – breathe out.

Three times a week I go and see him. Down the hill to the main road I go, where the buses come promptly every five minutes. The road is the liveliest place. The shops are open all hours and students mill around. They are soft-spoken, they don't hang onto each other and they are neatly dressed in their frills and stuff. It's an ordered, silent chaos.

We also have here on the main road a post office, the bus depot, pavement shops selling all kinds of food, makeshift shops of tarpaulin, and restaurants by the dozen. I often come to a sun-filled one, Woori Mandoo, to eat bibimbab, which is a steaming hot lot in a cast-iron pot that's just come off the gas flame. Inside is rice, of course, chilli paste to give it a red hue and to burn the hell out of you, strange stringy green veg, bean sprouts and a teaspoon of mince. Into this lot is dropped a raw egg, which quickly cooks in the intense heat.

Here the ajumma makes me feel welcome. These middle-aged women seem to be the only people free of constraint. They have earned the right, after many years of conforming to what femininity here should be, to be exactly as they wish. They're strong and outspoken, they have nothing of that girlishness. I love this woman. We have a beautiful bond formed by not more than two words. She's been teaching me to read by spelling out words from the menu, after which it's my turn.

Just left from Woori is a tarpaulin effort which sells those lovely fishes made in a jaffle iron with sweet bean curd inside. Then there's the Sand and Food shop. Sand is for sandwich, though there are no sandwiches, but they sell the best coffee. Here an ice-cream poster reads: 'Refreshing dessert candidates'. Frank Sinatra sings happily away.

Down you go in the bus to shinae. There was no town planning. It developed organically and is the expression of everyone's involvement, not only architects and town planners. I've come to love every square metre.

I get off where the bustling little streets start. They are so narrow that cars can hardly pass. There's lots of colourful writing in Hangul which seems to the illiterate like an extended abstract painting. Next to a more fancy-looking shop is a place that fixes scooters on the pavement. Opposite is a clump of trees that escaped the clearing of the forest and next to that a meat market with lots of flies in the entrance. It's set deep into a dark building. I have no intention of finding out what goes on inside. Into this mix are traditional houses with their hip-and-gable roofs, which are patched with corrugated-iron, held down by stones and pipes and broken pieces of tiles. Dotted all over are brick chimneys with four little arches at the top. Here and there, elevated to roof level, are small pavilions with the same elaborate roof structure as the houses, but covered with thick bamboo. This is where they socialise. Among all of this are satellite TV dishes, attached to any upright thing.

Along the length of the pavements traders have their wares – colourful fruit and veg and grains – spread out on the ground on tarpaulins of different colours. The fish shop, which mainly happens on the pavement, competes for space. Plastic buckets are filled with strange moving eel-like and crawling things. Fresh water is somehow pumped into containers higher than the buckets. Pieces of hosepipe then carry the water down into the buckets which are filled to overflowing. This goes on the whole day so that the pavement around is a bit of a dam. Next to this, also in buckets, are the biggest orange/brown mushrooms I've ever seen. A single one won't fit in a hand.

Where the pavements disappear altogether is the tiniest fabric shop, almost in the road. The owner has her afternoon nap on her mat between folded pieces of fabric, her head resting on her outstretched arm.

Further on there are no cars, just paved walkways with shops. At lunchtime trolleys stacked with food for delivery are pushed up and down. Each order is neatly wrapped in colourful cloth and tied into a knot at the top. And in winter, in the middle of the main walkway, a 44-gallon drum is placed horizontally on a stand with wheels. In these drums they bake sweet potatoes and chestnuts. At the bottom of the drum is a small opening to make a fire. Around the top edge there are holes where long tube-like things slide in and out. They are cut through in the length. One such tube can take quite a number of sweet potatoes.

Dae-ho is on the second floor above a restaurant in a sunny, most spacious room. Coming here is unadulterated pleasure. I'm never sure what's going to greet me. He may be doing yoga or sitting on the floor treating someone or making tea at his low table. The tea business involves a lot of pouring water from one container into another. Today he is alone. It's

Buddha's birthday, there's no teaching, and we have as much time as we need. I'm lying on the floor in the winter sun with Dae-ho sitting right beside me.

"Do you believe me?"

"Trust? Yes, I believe you."

"Tell me about your home."

"I have a beautiful home in South Africa. An oak tree of about two hundred years is in my garden. Golden light rolls down from the mountain and falls through its leaves. I often sit on the lawn with my back against the oak and feel the grass with my palms. I have very good friends. And my son is there. I don't know what I'm doing here."

"Perhaps to meet me," he says.

He has a needle the size of a crowbar approaching my sternum. And in it goes.

"Now your tears will come."

Crying is for the strong. Not for those holding on for dear life. But I cry for my lost life with the golden light and for the incomprehension of what I am now.

"Yes, perhaps to meet you."

We get up, put on our shoes and go out for lunch. As is my habit, I'm into my long strides, but today my shoulders aren't hunched and my lungs breathe in and vacate that air.

"Karin, slow," singsongs Dae-ho.

We've entered a part of shinae no foreigner will find. There are just too many twists and turns. We go into a fabulously packed restaurant where the food comes in a blink: mounds of unknown salad leaves – the best are the sesame leaves – to wrap around mouthfuls of food, a wide, flat cast-iron bowl with thin pieces of meat in a thickish chilli sauce and, spread across the table, the many side dishes that always accompany the main meal. They are called banchan and together, hanjeongsik, says Dae-ho, and the chilli paste is called gochujang. Some of the dishes have fermented soybean paste, which is called daenjang, but Dae-ho can't say whether it's this that gives Korean food that particular taste I can't name.

The food today is so lovely that I even eat the daenjang and before we know it we've finished the lot. But not yet the afternoon. We're going to the tea shop lady and her tranquil shop, where the floors are covered with thickly woven grass mats edged with fabric with Chinese script. You sit on the floor, facing the lady, at one of two long tables, which form a corner. For privacy a rice paper and wooden lattice screen divides the tables.

Our lady is beautiful again today with her deep purple, long silk skirt, which is slightly gathered at the waist. Her white silk top has subtle cherry blossoms on branches, in lilac. It's styled much like a fitted Chinese top and has the ornately knotted buttons. It's all finished with her lilac scarf, which is neatly tucked into her top. She is really grace incarnate and embodies all the qualities Dae-ho says one finds in a teahouse: respect, peace and purity.

There are many teas to choose from: green tea and chrysanthemum or persimmon leaf, and many more. Some teas are a hundred years old. And there's an array of doll-size cups and teapots on shelves all along the walls.

We've made our bows and sit down while our lady assembles what she needs for the ritual on a tray with a lattice surface through which water can flow onto a solid bottom. She uses a number of cups and teapots since different shapes and colours are used for different teas. There is always an unequal number of cups. Unequal numbers are lucky, of which nine is the luckiest.

With all this in hand she glides to her spot opposite us and sits down cross-legged. Without wobbling. She's erect, but fluid, unaffected. Inner calm emanates from her. Graciousness has to do with economy of movement, I realise, as I observe her. She doesn't make a superfluous movement. When her arm stretches, for instance, it does so from her waist, her shoulder doesn't move. And that arm has the most beautiful curve. Her other hand, palm down, rests lightly on her sternum. All her movements are gentle and light.

The ritual is not stylised, but natural, though everything probably symbolises something. This is a country with a rich heritage of symbols. Although I don't know what goes for what, I do know that I'm in an elevated, spiritual place.

As always, today too, she starts a gentle conversation by asking Dae-ho how he and his family are and then moves that lovely arm in my direction. I then have to tell Dae-ho how I am and he translates. All along she prepares the tea.

First she drapes a folded linen cloth around her arm, which she uses to dab up the odd droplet of water. Next to her on the floor is her kettle. She doesn't pour boiling water directly into the teapot, because it makes the tea bitter. The water first goes into a wide-rimmed jar to cool down to just the right temperature. After this she rinses the cups. The solid bottom of the tray catches the water. The cups are then placed on tiny wooden saucers.

With delicate wooden tongs she picks some tealeaves from a container and drops them into the tiny pot. The water from the jar is now poured from up high into the teapot and then poured into her tray. This is to rinse the leaves. Finally she pours a little bit of tea into all the cups and then comes back to fill the cups in the same order as before. This is so that all the flavour doesn't end up in one cup only. She pours the tea from such a height that it makes little bubbles in the cups. It has something to do with luck, if I understand Dae-ho correctly.

She makes just enough tea to fill the cups once, because the leaves shouldn't sit in water. The tea is then gulped down in one swallow. A cupful is half a gulp. Eventually you want to burst. Dae-ho told me only recently that if you don't want any more you leave a bit of tea in your cup. We go on in this way until all the flavour has been extracted. Then out comes another pot and another kind of tea.

I thought I was being polite by handing her my cup, but Dae-ho gently explained that it's more polite to sit and let her take my cup. How many small misunderstandings are there?

After a while she brings out what I would think are sticky rice cakes of various flavours and something that could be glazed fruit.

And in this lovely way we spend an hour or so.

The tea lady has a sad history. Her husband abused her, but she couldn't go to the police. Perhaps domestic abuse is not seen as a crime. Things got so bad that she attempted to hang herself. There are cuts in her bottom lip from where her teeth bit into it. Her situation was so dire that she eventually divorced the man, the consequence of which is that she has no contact with her child. In divorce children are legally part of the man's lineage and they go to him and his family, while the mother is cut out of the family and society. Some mothers meet their children in secret. Hopefully it's not so severe now that the country is changing.

The tea lady wishes she could be more like me. Laugh and show emotion. But this is 'forbid', said Dae-ho. "We don't make big motion, we don't show big happiness, or big smile or tears. We must hide our emotion. So Western feel good with Korean and don't get big smile. So, our feelings are same, but not express same." This must be why Westerners feel they're greeted by a wall of politeness. "Also we are one blood people. We don't have chance to get together with other people. So we don't know them. Big motion and big express is exaggerate and we can't help we are discomfort." I must be causing shock and resistance wherever I go. If there's unspoken resistance to your basic way of expression, and there's nothing around to confirm you, something has to give. No wonder I've become smaller and smaller.

The puzzle gets worse. Even their concept of friendship is complicated. "Our emotion must not show. Only show to old friend."

'Old friend' is someone you grew up with and who is the same age as you. Anyone else, even if you feel close to that person, is a social friend and is introduced as that. Social friends come and go. Loyalty lies with an old friend. With social friends, Dae-ho says, they are "just friendly in out way, but in inner way, don't share. If you share there is responsibility and now I must help you."

What complicates matters is that you can't be friends with someone younger than you. That person is your junior, but not your friend. "Language is different between young and old. You use honorific for old and stranger. We must respect older. It is the Confucius way."

I wonder how formal Dae-ho and the tea shop lady are. They are close, but custom forbids them to be true friends. And she is such a lovely person. I hope her teahouse brings her joy. And luck, which here seems to be money.

We've come to the end of our tea time. Suddenly I'm exasperated with myself. Korea is also this. Then why do I struggle?

"Dae-ho, why?"

"Just accept. Just accept."

Also accept the end of this lovely time with him. Hop on the bus, back to waegukin's little room at the daehakyo. And straight to the balcony.

It's very quiet here in the corner of the campus on this public holiday. There goes the Chinese teacher with his hands locked behind his back. He carries his loneliness with stoicism. Out the gap in the wall he goes, stands about, and back in he comes. He turns around, looks up into the bamboo. He must be thinking of his family back home. Here comes Miss Priss up the road. She's going to her room where she will while away her loneliness. The Frog has emerged, she's off to the café for food to quench her loneliness. A young couple, not touching, say their goodbyes.

We have a small respite to renew ourselves in order to repeat our labours again. This is how the world goes around. To repeat it the day after, and the day after. To this repetitive world I now belong. I am part of a class that forms the foundation for the strivings of the higher classes. We are the insignificant ones, the replaceable ones. We are ants scurrying around in our designated jobs, making sure the hive stands tall.

Just yesterday it was today. Tomorrow will be today all too soon.

I HAVE MY computer back, which is now in Korean. Never mind, I can still spend my days with Hilette and Pearl and Pearl's trips to Valkenberg. How fascinating a mental institution is. Instead of imagining it I'd love to know what goes on there where the full spectrum of our humanness is given free rein. Perhaps it's a place of freedom from constraint and self-censorship. What unknown aspects of yourself might you discover there? I should have found an excuse to go there before I came to Korea. Now I will never see the inside of such a place.

Do I still hate Hilette so much? Probably, because of reasons I just can't figure. And I suspect Hilette is the repository of these eluding reasons. Perhaps it's something to do with home. But I am not home and I am not confronted with our complexity and our past. Oh, what freedom to be here in Korea away from my world. Here I am just Karin.

Anyway. My fridge packed up and Mun-hee has brought a fridge man to fix it. We've done the greeting bows and I do a quick second one for goodbye, because I have to go and teach. Halfway down the passage I remember I left something behind and go back. And there is Mun-hee, brimming with excitement – mid-air – on the way to drop his bum on my desk chair, his hands ready to strike the keyboard. He's going to read my stuff! All the steamy exchanges with the ex-lover, and that letter home. Through my shock I realise he has to save face, or I'll bear the brunt of his humiliation.

"Oh, Mun-hee, while you're here, won't you please make my computer give commands in English?" And I am out the door. Bloody disaster. I caught him in the act and he did not save face. Instead of doom settling over me I feel 'damn it', I can't square myself into a circle anymore. And the mother of all insubordination rises in me.

I'm ready for those classes with a demonic energy. The first two go relatively peacefully, but come the third one we race through the book. I give them the answers, the way Korean teachers apparently do. Done and dusted and most of the time's still left. No use staring at the clock.

"We're going to have a performance today."

They choose the three best ones to write a script, who duly churn out a half-formed thing. It's hardly written and they're up, acting it out. It's to do with thieves and police and some other characters I can't figure.

"Stop!" shout the police.

No one stops.

"I catch you!" shouts a cop.

"Caught," shouts English Teacher.

"Caught," echoes the cop.

"Good job," pipes English Teacher.

"You don't. You don't catch me," replies the thief.

"Didn't. You didn't catch me." Teacher mindful of her educational role.

Jesus, now there's chaos. They're out the door, down the passage and back. The script's been abandoned. The scriptwriters are part of the mob, or of the cops.

"He catched you. He did."

"He *caught* you! For God's sake, kids, the past tense of catch is caught."

"Teacher, he liar."

"He *is* liar," corrects Teacher.

"He is liar," parrots the cop.

"Oh no, sorry, man, he is *a* liar."

The mob has now joined the cops against the liar. Everything is in Korean. Their voices rise and rise. That's it, kids. Shout to your heart's content. Get it all out. Catch, catched, he liar, what the fuck does it matter, you're never going to speak this dreaded language, because by the rule book we should now be on page two million doing exercise one million, allowing no time for conversation.

"Teacher, Jong-hun was caught. He didn't stop. He is a liar."

"Brilliant!"

English Teacher claps her hands. Tears in her eyes. One person in Korea can say three perfect English sentences.

"Go, kids, go home!"

I run out with them. Halfway down the stairs I come to my senses. I have one more class left. I am the English teacher and I should be demure and happy to be a round peg in a square circle. I haul myself up the stairs with the exhausted teenagers who have come for their last class on this Friday night. Okay, you have the most boring book, I told them. But get through this book we'll have to. So best do it as quickly as possible and then do other stuff.

Other stuff today is as yet unknown.

"Okay, let's go."

We go so effectively that we finish long before our time is up. A silent one pipes up: where am I from? Dear awkward, exhausted teenagers, I come from deepest, darkest Africa, and what do they know about this mythological place in any case?

"We have no cars in South Africa. We ride on lions." Miming with bent legs, open wide enough to fit a lion in between, bum backward and body up and down as the lion runs.

"But they not eat you?"

"No, they only eat Japanese." They like this bit. "And teenagers," I can't help adding. Now a look of empathy. "And we live in trees. Our muscles are specially adapted so we can jump from one tree to many trees away." More miming.

"Liar, teacher liar."

"No liar. True." They themselves are now into miming: a fast horse galloping, a slower lion. "No, lions much, much faster. Horse slow."

"But their tooth. Big, eat." Miming of big teeth sinking into a hand.

"No eating. Lions don't eat the horses. Only Japanese and teenagers."

I check the clock. Still time left.

"We don't have gas stations. We have special places where we take our lions when they are hungry. You park the lion next to this machine thing and out come the Japanese and teenagers and straight into the lion's mouth."

"Teacher!" Incredulous. Confusion, belief, disbelief.

Still more time on the clock. "And we don't have aeroplanes. We have enormous birds. Ten people can sit on one. So we fly everywhere." Miming of flying. I've reached the door and can easily fly off.

"Teacher liar."

So I fly back. "No, check the internet. Type in South Africa + transport."

And with this, time is up and the whole lot fly out the door. At least it was an exercise in listening.

In the staffroom Miss Priss says in the form of a question: "You had an unusual class?" She and bulimic Cindy, who aren't on speaking terms at present, look at each other knowingly. They have found a common enemy. I shrug it off and leave to go back to my bird and my balcony.

The night-time walkers are coming down the hill. There are usually three of them and they vary according to who's the source of power and who's close to it. Leona is mostly top dog. I'm starting to understand my reticence. She gossips with this one, then that, then smooths it over with the first one. Her voice has an undertone or overtone – a two-tone voice, so that what you hear is not what you hear. Plainly said: it's duplicitous. In tone as well as content. And yet, she means well, I suppose.

In answer to my bemoaning this strange lot Marko told me what Nietzsche said about existing beyond good and evil and therefore operating outside the Judeo-Christian moral system. Not seeing the world in these terms and therefore not adhering to the status quo is a threat to the moral code of the group. Ours, by which we have to orientate ourselves, is formed through, and based on, gossip and is young and unstable, because people constantly come and go and everyone is in some form of shock or displacement.

Also, the more secure a moral code, the more willing the group is to accept dissent. But the younger and weaker, the more severe the punishment. I'm going to be ostracised if I don't chuck my morality out the window and join in. I'd be a wangtta, an outcast. Oscar Wilde said if you hear no evil and speak no evil you'll never be invited to a party.

No! I can't do this and lose the last shred of myself. I'd be an amoeba.

Back in my room I go to my desk. In my inbox have landed two disturbing emails, which cause instant anxiety. The one is from the new tenant in my house in SA. She needs this and that and Marko talks to her too much.

Now, how to tell sociable, unsuspecting Marko that he's to become a ghost? When I am universes away in a time capsule?

The second, much more upsetting, email is from Adel. She has neatly repacked all my boxes into new boxes. I know, oh, I just know that some of my boxes have gone missing and this is her way of concealing the fact. In one of those boxes is the lock of my mother's hair I cut from her corpse. There are philosophy books that belonged to my grandfather, with his notes. There is my granny's mixing bowl she used all her life. Her crystal and her linen and her bone china. There is Marko's first tooth. My notes for future books. There are my treasured TS Eliot anthologies. All my photos. Those boxes were a physical link to a life I will have to pick up again in such a distant future that the years are uncountable. They say: yes, you will come back, and yes, you do exist. My life has been stolen.

Adel knew who had access to the room my boxes were in and she knew things had gone missing before when those people were around. Could she simply not care? How is it possible? We've had such happy, heightened times over many years. The lunches! And us full of difficulty. No, we don't like this table, or that one, here the light is too gloomy, there you look into a corner. But at this restaurant the butter is the best and they have linen serviettes, but, and, on and on, hours of happiness.

I get up, kiss my bird and go and sit on the balcony. It will still be spring here for a while. Summer will come and autumn. What is autumn like here? I can't remember from last year.

What is really inside one? Yes, a kind of nothingness, as I suspected.

There are many changes here at Seon-chang National University.

Jeremy and epileptic Greta are moving to a Christian university. They are going to be professors. Professors?! They're half brain dead. This title clearly doesn't have much gravitas.

But necessity dictates. Every university needs X number of A1 visas and only professors boost this count.

Miss Priss is leaving at the end of the academic year, as is Cindy. The Frog and Asperger's Dennis too. Our budding ambassador has realised that teaching in Korea won't get him onto the ambassadorial ladder. He is also going.

A new woman in her fifties, Claire from South Africa, is settling in. This is her second time in Korea. There are many foreigners who come back to this place they couldn't wait to leave. I wonder why. Our Head Girl says she's going to get her in her camp, Bull Frog won't stand a chance of recruiting her. Claire should not trust a word, but perhaps I'm wrong and everyone means everyone well.

There's also a new guy from England. He has a PhD and perfect British pronunciation. What is anyone with a PhD doing here? I smell a rat. But he's bright, so perhaps the level of conversation will go up. He tells me it's a toxic place and I should get out. And our HG never does anything without a reason. What does he mean? I'm not going to ask and set up a gossip spot. Perhaps it's his instinctive distrust. People have to earn his trust. No, man, I told him, I'm the opposite, I just trust. Anyhow, he's into Brahms, which he lets thunder through the dorm. I love it.

The problem with him, though, is that he smells. He wears the same thick jersey his daughter knitted him day in and day out. It's a pungent affront. It's now fallen to HG, as the organiser, to tell him to wash the thing, and himself.

There are many complaints. The professors, whom our PhD guy teaches, complain that he gives formal lectures and they don't get enough opportunity to talk. The parents complain that Fred chews gum in class; Cindy they can't follow what with all the nervous clicking, I presume. The mother of the hyperactive boy has complained about me. Quite what her complaint is I don't know. HG, as the harbinger of bad news from Admin, couldn't elaborate.

A good thing is that a mother of one of the writing boys begged me, through her teenage daughter with her limited English, to keep on teaching her boy in the holidays that are just around the corner. He's become far less withdrawn and has gained confidence and he wants to become a writer. I should let this be known to offset the other complaint, but so entrenched is negation of the self that I won't blow my own horn. Pity, also since I'm going to throttle that hyperactive child. He disrupts the entire class, which has now changed to a writing class for kids and teenagers. The adults kindly fell by the wayside.

One wrote me a touching note to say she was not continuing: "Thank you so much, Karin. I feel to you: thanks, sorry, happy, trust, and so on." I kept on commenting on her writing after she had left, but now we're just back and forth on email. This year, she, as a teacher, should do very well. She gave the principal and vice-principal big gifts and took them to a very special dinner. Now she will get extra points, which will enhance her chances of promotion. And she gave certain staff members gifts: the bigger the gifts, the higher the points they give her. She's applied to another school for a higher position. She gave the principal of the new school a lot of money and the position will now be hers. I'm horrified. What if this principal has a thriving racket and she doesn't get the job? Oh no, she says, the one whose money she accepts first will be advanced. "It is not proper, moral, to take money and not give position."

"This is bribery?"

"No, not bribery. If not sure, don't give money, just gifts. It's how you make advancement in Korea."

She tells of a friend who worked her fingers to the bone in her husband's boss's house, only for her husband not to be promoted. "This is very bad." She is a treasure trove of info.

I'm also learning more through the daughter of a friend of Dae-ho's I'm teaching. She's twenty and the loveliest thing on earth. Hye-mi. We've developed a close bond. She's so innocent, although there's a lifetime of sadness.

It's against the law to teach privately and you can be deported. So I sneak out of the dorm in broad daylight and meet her a block away where we then drive to Dae-ho's studio in her red Mini Cooper, the only red car I've seen here. You should not stand out.

Every aspect of her fascinates me. Her tongue has a firm fleshiness. It's smooth and pale pink. There's a little ridge where the underside, with its darker colour, joins the top.

Hye-mi spent a few months in Australia and can speak some English. She says: "I'm living in ordinary days. To me like you are a very special person. Nowadays, I found relationship is difficult. Because of my work, I met so many people in a day. Always smile and have a chat but I can't feel anything. Most of them talk about something. But that isn't from their inner. They are from their lips. It makes me exhausted. The most afraid thing is I started to don't expect them. Actually I got so many struggles. I could be calculating, I have really no idea. I did hundred per cent thing to someone, and after then, I expect at least fifty per cent. I know it's not good for me. But if I did something to someone, that means I have a interest to someone. How can I give up about that? Especially friendship I weak. Before I told I have two best friends. With them, everything is like normal. But other people, expecting is problem. Now I try to give up. Yes, because of these things I can grow up."

This young girl also carries the burden of her mother, who is depressed a lot of the time. Hye-mi feels it's her responsibility to lift her out of it. Her mother went to a psychologist, but it's a shameful thing to do. She paid in cash so that it wouldn't reflect on any records. Hye-mi really wants to study psychology, but was advised not to. It's best not to be on the outskirts of society. I wonder what the state of mental health is here. How do people cope with the relentless stress and over-work? Hye-mi says Korea has one of the highest suicide rates in the world and not a single school has a mental health professional; and there are only a handful of universities that offer psychology.

"We have to hide. Maybe better go to shaman," she says. "Or talk to you. Really I have no experience left someone close to me. I can't understand your mind, but I can feel. What can I say for you? If you beside me, I just want to hug you. It's very difficult. I want to say many things, but I can't. But please, Karin, feel my heart. Next week is so long. I hope time goes fast. I felt somethings from you. I remember that in my heart. I have many things to talk, you know, you are the one of closest person. Someday, I tell you more stories. You don't forget me. Really, really, you are in my heart."

Our friendship must be difficult for her because of the age difference business. You can't be friends with someone older than yourself. Perhaps this is why she can be inexplicably formal.

She once brought a friend along who tried to hide her unhappiness, but started crying. Her mother was a kind of second wife (although whether she was married to this man is unclear). He died and she married the man who is now her stepfather. They seem to be indebted to him for his kind act, because before they really belonged to no family. She tried to explain what she called hojuje. It seems it is a family registry system. All family members are registered under the hoju, who is the male family head. But stepchildren don't belong to the hoju's family and can't take his surname, which the friend did and now has to hide that she's his stepdaughter. She and her mother have been walking around with this secret for most of their lives.

Leona says things may become easier. The country is being transformed into a pluralist society, although what this actually means on the ground was not clear to her.

I'm in a complicated place. And a place where all is not well. It is now clear why our PhD, with his recently washed jersey, is here. He hits the bottle and misses classes. Well, there you have it. He's not going to last. And, as I feared, the life has been squeezed out of the new Claire from SA. She doesn't understand, but everyone gossips about everyone. Yes, I wanted to say, and I almost blurted out my struggles. But while revealing your weaknessess and insecurities is taking a step into deeper friendship, I now know here they will be used against you. Besides, I've become too silent.

My mistake was to tell them I write. Unpublished, would-be writers are a dangerous lot. And there are a number of them here. Standing on the sideline while someone else does what you feel you, too, can do, but deep down know you won't, because you lack the discipline, courage and tenacity, makes you resent that person.

"You aren't still working on the same book? You spend all your time doing this?"

By the second person who made this comment I knew the tongues had been wagging. People expect the artist to be like they are: sociable, easygoing and somehow able to keep everything effortlessly together. They know nothing of the pressure that builds from keeping a book in your head, of developing motives and symbols in the face of fear. You don't know where these emotions and thoughts come from and where they lead. And this while you are consumed by an unfolding you wrench from yourself. You grind your teeth and you push beyond exhaustion, doubt, loneliness, the cry in your throat.

You stake your life on one piece of writing. You fall flat or you don't. You shut out the world, because writing is not something you do by taking a little time off for your endeavour. No, you take a little time off for life. And you'd better be good at that life lest the whole house of cards comes crashing down.

Still working on the same piece! You shapeless slobs, while you gorge yourself into a stupor I battle it out word after word. Nefarious is not too strong a word to describe them.

Susan signs her emails with a quote from Kurt Cobain: wanting to be someone else is a waste of the person you are. Hopefully none of us are the person we are.

At least I'm becoming a healthier one. Survival has forced me not to internalise their negativity. When there's no positive confirmation you can't turn against yourself like I used to. How quick I was to point out my shortcomings.

Yes, things have indeed progressed. The tone of my novel has changed. It can only mean that I no longer hate Hilette so intensely. I'm now rather fond of her and her brave struggles, misguided as they may be. She could very well break my heart. If my time here could free me of whatever caused my hate for her, it will have been worth it.

To hell with the vipers. Next week I'm sending my manuscript off. I've made contact with two publishers and they seem keen.

Summer has come and with it the humidity, but I don't register it. I'll be home for four weeks' holiday soon! I don't even begrudge the fact that at the last moment, as is custom here, things have changed and we have to teach teachers in the first week of the holiday.

It's a close call who hates being here more: the teachers, who sit like lambs to the slaughter, or the foreigners, who want to bugger off home. But we soldier on and the teachers all brush their teeth after lunch and complain about Miss Priss, and Cindy has the nerves and shakes so much she can't turn a page, and I talk so fast I shock myself, and Ji-hu is a spanner in the works. He changes the programme daily and causes confusion.

And then we are done.

I have all my gifts. The many ginger peelers I got from the temple, and bottles and bottles of the best sesame oil. I pointed to the many oils and said to the shop assistant: "Korea Number One?" A finger went up in the air. All is set. After a year and a half. I'm going home.

IT WAS WONDERFUL to see Marko. There he was at the airport looking like a Christmas tree. He had dressed himself in his best: light blue linen jacket, a shirt somewhere between pink and orange, cream pants that balloon out madly and then tie at the ankles, and formal brown shoes. He could have stepped straight out of my novel. My Hilette also donned all her best garments for her inaugural lecture – where she unravelled.

But home: was I even there?

A few frantic weeks in which I saw everyone for the shortest of times. How can I keep my life in SA alive by jetting in and out once a year, flitting past people?

Everyone seemed downtrodden, anxious for their safety and the future, withdrawn into their individual selves. Like dung beetles, each rolling its own ball of shit. For them nothing had changed. But I have been to the moon and as a result the earth no longer has the same shape. I couldn't quite relate.

At least Helena, one of few people who actually does well in the publishing world, was still tackling life with gusto and she gave me some hope. But Janet's anger at her ex-husband hadn't subsided. She was a stuck record and I could hardly listen to her; and then I felt bad because she has dutifully been collecting my post and seeing to admin. Dorrian had a calamity with her house and was still working with diversity. Brian was still kind, and we kind of kept to our non-lover status.

Courtesy Marko (how he's been keeping everything going at home!), all my remaining boxes had been taken to Brian's, since Adel had to move. And yes, many boxes were stolen. She tried to avoid me, I suppose on account of the stolen boxes. In my time away her face seemed to have dropped to below her jaw, where folds of debris were now gathered in a busy dance. But she was also still the same. She had had yet another fall-out with someone. Strange that I didn't feel her plight the way I used to. But I do love her so.

The best, really, was my niggle of flu, which drove me straight to Hazel and into a bed there with her sitting beside me and chatting till the cows came home. I felt fortified and a little afraid as well. What if something went wrong and Hazel, who is a mother and friend rolled into one, is not there anymore? It's very unlikely, though. She did have cancer, but that was cast out.

The country was in a way worse. A deeper sense of foreboding hung over it. Our country is slipping into the sea. All that will be reported is an insignificant plop as the southern tip of the African continent sinks into oblivion.

But I did walk on hard, red African earth. And I heard and felt the stones under my feet.

While I was there I also saw the two publishers I'd sent my manuscript to and lo and behold: they want to publish! One was an impressive woman. She seemed to me like a strong matriarch who would keep everyone who works for her toeing the line. She has access to funds and good scriptwriters and she'll also get this thing transformed into a play and me onto a stage. I decided to go with her.

I was struck again by my sister and brother-in-law's faith. It was then, being so disconnected from my past and future, that I wished I had but a splattering of their faith. They sounded unreasonably optimistic. It was as if the Lord hadn't decided yet, but the odds were in their favour: my brother-in-law was going to recover. It's optimism raised by denial. His spine is shattered. He is a paraplegic. I took the plunge and hauled out the positive philosophical choice. Surely, the force of all that praying would get the Lord or some such to decide in the patient's favour. Or Dae-ho would come and conjure up his energies and make him walk again. But the positive philosophical choice was useless: trying to mix the rational with the irrational. Besides, my brother-in-law has a much worse condition. He suffers neuropathic pains, which aren't to be confused with phantom pains. No, these hellish pains, a result of haywire impulses from the brain, are ten times worse than the severest pain. It leaves him a whimpering mass. He lives in the only hell we can be sure of: now, constant. As simple and horrible as that.

I thought of him every time I wanted to succumb to despair, because Hilette clung like a burr. Perhaps it was being back in the cauldron that brought her up again. A bit of that hate still lingers. Rather fond of her and her brave struggles? How patronising!

There she walked around with her wounds. One almost feels sympathy for her. God help me, such a wounded old thing. Whatever stuffed you up is long gone. Get on with it, Hilette!

And while you're at it, acknowledge your part, collective as it may be, in the harm we whites caused. Everyone should say mea culpa. At least then I'd be free from flagellating myself to pulp to make up for those who will not admit that terrible wrongs were done. Because as Hilette says: there's not a racist left in the country. Everyone just reinvented themselves. They sleepwalked through apartheid and woke up after the fact, refreshed like Rip van Winkle. A luta!

For God's sake, still harping on mea culpa? We are all racist. It's the original us and them. But there's now so much shit flung around in this country by all and everyone that my anger may very well wipe the slate clean. At last we'll be equal. And free. Yes, but free in bondage to greed.

You can protest all you like. And you can delete that piece from the *New Yorker* from your computer, but you can't delete it from yourself. "... such cleansing self-reproach is merely part of liberalism's dance of survival."

Hilette in a way saved the day. She, the embodiment of our racial problems, managed to trump them all. She stretched herself like a leitmotiv through my comings and goings, and I was almost relieved when I saw an upsetting family interaction that made Hilette's issues seem insignificant.

I was dragged to a small-town bar to watch a rugby Test match, which proceeded in silence. No one made a peep.

To my right was a family on barstools sitting in a row, one behind the other, against the bar. At the back in the best spot furthest from the TV was the father, in front of him the mother, then the son, somewhere in his early twenties, and a daughter a little bit younger, who was closest to the TV. In the inexplicable silence there in the bar, the man leaned forward a bit and put his hand with its wedding ring gently on his wife's upper arm. It suggested something soft and healthy in their relationship. He withdrew it and sat back again with his arms folded on his stomach. A firm, upright tummy. And on went the silent rugby. The wife now turned around to him and whispered something. He shook his head: no. She stretched up to be closer to his face and sought once more what was clearly permission. Again the head from left to right. Not a word said. The wife turned around and went on watching. But she couldn't give up; she turned back to him again. Now with an arched back and breasts slightly thrust up to him. But still that head. What struck me was that when she turned back to face the TV again, she did so without any resignation, frustration, anger or any emotion. She fully accepted his decision.

Mother and son now said something. He then turned back to watch. He was a perfect opposite of his father. A gentle boy whom his mother understood, but most definitely not his father. I could see how the mother might act as go-between between father and son and skilfully twist the truth to protect her boy against the harshness of the father.

The boy now turned around again and stretched over the mother to say something to the father. It was a comment on the rugby that ended in an upward inflection, turning a statement into a question. As you do when you don't have the confidence in yourself and you're not sure how your comment may be judged.

Without taking his eyes off the TV the father said nothing. The boy turned back, then a while later repeated the whole business. And so it went on. He tried hard to win his father's approval: first making an observation to show he knew rugby and when that failed, asking a question. The most the man ever said was "Hm", without looking at his son. Boy, I thought, your father is never going to accept you; his disdain of you, his rejection of you and anger for your not being a manly man like he is, is too absolute. You'll live your life suspecting you're not up to scratch, that you are wrong somehow, not worthy of approval. And you won't know why. At best you may in due time see it for what it is. And perhaps turn your back on the world that bred you. Or live in defiance. However you turn out it will be because of, as a result of.

Hilette didn't grow up with this kind of scarring. There's a lot she and I don't share.

Anyhow. Being back here in Korea my bit of horror is to buckle down. I figure if I do a lot of balcony sitting I may accept my lot again. At least I no longer latch on to a misery every night to remind me of myself. Perhaps it's because of this that the strangest awareness sprang from the blue. With the past wiped out and the future too ghastly to contemplate, and not escaping into fantasy, because the coming back is too horrible, I'm aware that there is just this entity, sitting on a balcony, trying to read a sign above a café. There is nothing more and nothing less than a being spelling out a word.

Whatever is inside has changed so often that I cannot believe it to be real. I believed this, then that, felt this, felt that. It follows that what's come before and what will come is mist before the morning sun. Much like flying through clouds. There they are, thick, but once on the other side you realise you went through nothing. We are really clouds of images and feelings. And we convince ourselves they are the centre of ourselves. But they are shape-shifters. See them come, see them go.

We are made of nothing. This is freedom, sitting on a balcony, spelling out a word.

HERE WE ARE, Professor Gang and I, with speeches in hand, graded for content, waiting for Fred. He is late.

Ji-hu, who is unravelling by the day, stopped Fred and me in mid-stride and asked us to be judges at a speech competition. He looked terribly apologetic. The committee of this national (I think, couldn't follow him) school competition take themselves very seriously and asked the university to supply the judges for the final round. Also, Ji-hu tried to impress upon us that Professor Gang – the one who appointed me – will be the third judge, which is further proof of the standing of this competition, for which the prize is a few months abroad at a school. But of course we can be wrong about it all. Ji-hu is worse than ever. "You know, I don't know exactly, just nowadays, because you know, when I ask them I can just have a difficulty, maybe except for, I hope you know. How can I say, how I mean is now a days."

How I mean is that Professor Gang in her formal court shoes, blazer, stockings and frilly blouse, may just explode. The competition people have sent a car with driver to collect us. She looks at her watch again and in the same eye-swoop looks disapprovingly at my beautiful new clothes. (Karen Bruns sent these to me – bless her lovely soul for it.) Skirt, sandals and a little top, which covers my shoulders, over another top, which covers nothing. I should have learnt from Hilette to wear clothes that form an armour. But not only am I too summery, I also suspect I have a dash of food poisoning. I feel so bad I can hardly manage a smile. But here comes Fred. With ungraded speeches. He whispers that he has the runs. He ate too much chilli last night and he's not a well boy.

Professor Gang walks around the car to the back. She says Fred is to sit in front. I am to join her. The young Fred, the man, of course in front. But I know I'm too nauseous to manage a conversation and I take the front seat. Her back becomes a trifle more rigid.

We arrive at an impressive building with a fancy auditorium. Everyone is already seated. Here come the judges, all eyes on us, and we smile our way into the carpeted and upholstered maroon-red auditorium. We descend the stairs and take our seats in front, where we have water and sweets. Professor Gang goes in first, then me and then Fred. Fred is halfway down to his seat, but changes direction and runs out to the toilets. Professor Gang does a double-take. "He will be back soon, Professor," I try to placate her. And he is. We sit, ready to start, but Fred is up again and up those carpeted stairs and out. Professor Gang now sports a frown.

"His stomach," I offer.

A terrible feeling has come over me. Swallowing is not going to help indefinitely. Like a shot I too am up those stairs. I cross Fred on his way back. I run as fast as I can, but at the top whatever is poisoning me comes out in an impressive arc. Professor Gang has abandoned self-restraint and has run up behind me. A concerned circle has formed around the judges. "I'll clean up," I say. No! Just get this judge herself cleaned up, others will wash and scrape the carpet. I, meanwhile, run at full throttle to the toilets while a fresh bout is working its way up. Professor Gang is hot on my heels. She's not going to lose her judge. I finish and wipe my clothes and emerge. Without the top that was to cover my shoulders. I walk down the stairs. Back in our seats, but Fred is gone. By now Professor Gang can't sit anymore. She turns around, in full view of the full auditorium, and prays for Fred's speedy return. And here he comes, two stairs at a time.

We take up our papers and wonder what the hell we're looking at. It's all in Hangul. Professor Gang has realised we don't know Adam from Eve and explains which marks for which categories must go into which columns. There's presentation, content and so on.

Suddenly the whole congregation stands up. There is complete silence as all right hands go to left breasts. We duly follow suit. All sit down again. And suddenly I hear my name. My God, man, what's going on? The speaker's hand there up on the stage goes out in my direction and I gather I'm being introduced. I stand up, turn around and bow deeply in my unpleasant aroma. Fred hears his name and does the same. And up goes Professor Gang too. Yes, we did the right thing.

Professor Gang bends sideways and whispers that our judging today will be democratic. This means that her vote won't count more than ours. And up they file. Ninety per cent of them wear glasses. But what's baffling is that after a number of individual speeches a group gathers on stage and bows. By the fifth group Professor Gang remembers to tell us that we also have to appoint the winning group. We wrack our brains to remember the best one so far. Fred is really useless. He gives almost identical marks to mine. "I'll just follow you," he says. And so we battle on, and finally it's the end.

We have now heard primary and high school kids on a set number of topics. The horror of the separation from North Korea was a popular one, and there were heart-rending accounts of split families. One guy's grandfather goes to the border every year and stares across in the hope of seeing his relatives. The pros and cons of plastic surgery was also a hot topic. Many are in favour of this, since beauty will more readily find you employment and give you standing. And then there were beautiful phrases like this: "I wrote my strong feelings into smooth words." They were all so well prepared and earnest. How can there be a single best one? But we tally our very similar scores and one little one, who was just marvellous, comes out tops.

"Very well," says Professor Gang with tight lips, "but the winner a young child! We should choose a student from the older ones. But this is democratic."

And so a little one wins. She's called to the stage and there's unenthusiastic clapping. I realise we made a mistake: not only is she young, but she's also a she. Yes, the wrong one won.

Outside, and there's no car to take us back. Fred and his bowels are going on to a party. I'm the sole company of Professor Gang. We walk forever to a bus stop. Professor Gang gets on the bus and finds a place beside someone else. We have disgraced the competition.

Our PhD is nowhere to be found. He made a midnight run, he's out of Korea. How he must have plotted and planned, perhaps took a night train out, so as not to be seen and reported. In his wake there is pandemonium as his room is ransacked. I find a Brahms CD and feel kind of sad for him, but also happy for his liberation. Long may it last.

Anyway, one man's death is another's bread. He was going to go with Leona, the new Claire and Mae and Paul to a pansori performance, which is a kind of traditional opera. Since Leona is currently in deep hatred of the Frog, and Miss Priss wants to stay in her air-conditioned room, the choice fell on me. I declined, but more as a knee-jerk reaction because I automatically keep my free moments for writing. Then I came to my senses and accepted the invitation.

We have to miss the last class of the night, because the show is in another town, we had to get permission from Ji-hu to make up the classes. All settled. We have our overnight bags and are sweating away in Leona's car. First we stop at Admin. I'm so excited that I forget to be smaller than I am and blurt out to Mun-hee that we're off. He is shocked, but I assure him we have permission from Ji-hu. Nevertheless, a little bit of foreboding settles in me.

We eventually stop at a traditional house that's a B&B. Mae and Paul are already settled and the three of us lay out our bedding on the floor. We are sardined in. There's not an inch to be spared either side or between the threesome. And off we go to the show that can take up to five hours without a break. Ours is an abridged version.

It is completely bizarre. There is not a single known thing it can be compared to. Dae-ho told me pansori singers, if singers are what they can be called, have to injure their vocal cords. They're trained from when they are four. It sounds like spoken/sung screeching and moaning with injured vocal cords. Musicians, all in traditional wear, sit crossed-legged on the floor of the stage to the right. The singers stand in the middle of the stage. Unidentifiable instruments – percussion of some sort and a drum, which hits a note now and again, 'accompany' a character or two to the non-beat of their tortured, emotional narration. The drummer grunts a sound from time to time, as does the audience. It's a cacophony of sound.

The kids told me there are five main stories and each one dramatises one of the five Confucian virtues. They're about dragon kings and cuttlefish, tortoises, under-water palaces, a courtesan and an aristocrat. They are parables of love, goodness versus greed, filial love, sacrifice and healing. I don't know which one we're seeing. It's ugly beyond description and the most fascinating thing I have yet experienced in Korea. It's true emotional outpouring that touches me deeply. I'm absolutely spellbound.

After the show I feel so elated that I talk non-stop on our way to our bedding on the floor. The others are a bit surprised. They have come to know me as someone who says little. We don't have a peaceful night, sardined in, and what with my talking in my sleep. You have to express yourself and if not in the day, it will come out at night. In my sleep I am loud and desperate and aware of how I struggle and strain to get words out.

Come the morning and we're ready for breakfast. I never thought a Korean breakfast of rice, fish, kimchi, garlic, side dishes and chilli could be so nice. Although I'm not really here. I've hauled out a stock fantasy.

I was captured by a rich man's son and am now in a dungeonish place. No one can find me. (I suppose it's the need not to have to function anymore.) My circumstances are dire. I'm bound to a wall and am emaciated and hardly coherent. (The external horror reflects what's going on in my internal world.) Marko comes – I miss him so much – he comes and doesn't know how to find me. But then, and here is the ingenious part, we communicate by telepathy. He follows our magnetic energy field and there he rescues me. (This part is self-explanatory.) On the more practical level, the rich man enters. In exchange for my not laying a charge, he'll pay me. Enough, of course, to last a life long. And somehow he'll have his son supervised so that he doesn't do it again. (I'm glad that I still have a social conscience.) And there, without having to set foot again in any class I fly off to my life of financial security under the SA sky.

I eat some more kimchi. Perhaps it's the unpleasant smell that makes me think about the end of my book again. I have a horrible feeling and it won't leave me. I am afraid. Nonsense,

I tell myself. How can writers fear their own writing? Besides, the end is written, there's nothing more to be said. And not all the symbols need to show their meaning. But still, why is Birdy there, this disembodied energy who is not a person or an object. And the pulverised dog Hilette keeps seeing in the road. And an image that keeps on recurring: Hilette parting her hair, trying to see her scalp. There's a miserable feeling about her scalp.

A book can go on forever, I know that, and one must finish it and stick to that. I can still reason with this, but the terrible pressure Hilette feels in her body – that force that compresses her insides so that she wants to escape from her body – has now lodged itself in me. There's an urgency in me that threatens to force me into something unknown. As if I, too, have to uncover some mystery. A pity I never found out what Hilette keeps hidden from herself. I had hoped it would become clear at the end when she stands in her dead garden after she lost her grip on reality at her inaugural lecture.

And why do I even allude to her childhood hardship? There's no detail. It's vague and doesn't take the story any further. Though perhaps it's good to know what informs this woman. Yes, but definitely not the detail.

I navigate another heap of fish and rice on my chopsticks into my mouth. And put a disingenuous smile on my face.

It's impossible to suppress the big question any longer: go home, or stay?

If I stay, I'll miss the publication of my book.

But it's dawned on me that I won't be able to rot away in Korea with its bows, silence and secrecy until I've built a pension, which clearly will take forever. But at the same time I'm far from free of the conflicting emotions of being white in South Africa. Hilette keeps me very much grounded in this.

A good time to go back is September next year, which is about a year and a half from now. By then Marko will be through with his undergrad and I'll have Victoria's pension.

Home. Even though SA is about to tip into the ocean. That's where my heart is and that's where emotion is not hidden behind politeness. I suspect the misery is not because I'm in Korea, it's simply because I'm not home. This place is not what formed my DNA. It is foreign, foreign. Here I'm in either one of two conditions: my heart is breaking, or my heart is dead.

And it's important to go before home is not home anymore. Get out before you flat-line and life is just going through the motions, before living cut off from yourself becomes the norm. I want to feel normal again, semi-happy, or semi-unhappy. Cindy says she doesn't know what normal feels like anymore. She, like so many others, has been here too long. She has nothing to go back to. She has no friends and no contacts.

But here, although more complicated, life is much more interesting.

I'd been ordering lunch from that lovely woman who teaches me to read. And then suddenly lunch was not delivered anymore. I phoned again and said the few sentences I'd been taught. The woman said some stuff, which I wrote down. I showed it to Hye-mi. She got the slightest of smiles.

Me: Anyong haseyo. Daehakyo. O beak ship o. Hana bibimbab.

Woman: Anieyo.

Me: Gamsamnida. Anyonghi kyeseyo.

This is what went down:

Hello. University. 515. One bibimbab.

No.

Thank you. Goodbye.

Hye-mi phoned. They couldn't deliver one dish only as they used to. I had to order something with it. Okay, this took some doing, but then again, how easy it is to get that lunch delivered.

You go through the 'conversation'. Only one word needs to change: bibimbab, boribab or sundubu, my other favourite dish of tofu and a floating egg in chilli soup and three clams, and rice. You walk down the miles of stairs, open the front door of the dorm and put a brick in front to keep it open. Back up those stairs. Wait ten minutes. Up comes the scooter on the hill and parks next to the opening in the wall. The deliveryman knocks on your door, you open, smile, bow, he comes in and puts a container down on the floor. You give him the money (little, it's cheap), bow again and turn around, switch on the TV and feel comforted by BBC's jingle. You unpack the container onto the ball and claw table and sink down on the floor, still in comforting BBC, which announces the news. The world opens and you are not in a foreign country on a distant continent.

Next you marvel at the cleverness of the dented and battered food container. It is a closed rectangular tin contraption, about knee high and the width of a big round plate. On top is a handle for easy carrying. And easy it has to be, because the deliveryman does many of these deliveries within ten minutes of ordering.

The container is a perfect hot oven. It is opened in front by pulling the front panel up and out. It has two tin shelves, making three levels. On the top shelf are obligatory kimchi and radish pickles and unidentifiable pickles on a long plastic plate covered with cling-wrap. Also stainless steel chopsticks and a spoon with a long handle for soup. The soup of various weeds is on this shelf too, also covered with cling-wrap. It is delicious. The middle shelf has the main dish in a cast-iron bowl on a cast-iron saucer thing. It is very hot. The raw egg on top of the boribab or the floating egg in the sundubu cooks away. Next to this is a portion of rice in a stainless steel bowl, the same size and shape as in all the restaurants. The floor shelf has a big plate with mostly red chilli paste and something mixed in. Also cling-wrapped.

You sit there and eat in the comfort of BBC, but it doesn't work. The most pressing question of all won't stay away. How can you give all this up? You think of the safety, the affordability, the light energy that carries unpredictability and chance. You ask: back to SA with its race consciousness, where you live in fight or flight?

And consider this: I have been thoroughly broken in. I only have to go on and on. On the other hand again I don't need to hate this place to leave it. All I need is to want to be back home more than I want to be here. But on the other, other hand, I should be responsible and stick it out.

Oh God help me, I want my people and the veld and the light and our high heaven. But. According to the UN's Human Development Report, which ranks countries by the desirability of life there, South Africa is 121 out of 177. Korea, no matter how strange the ways here, functions smoothly and offers its citizens a better quality of life in terms of health, education, security and so on.

On the other hand again: perhaps I feel crappy just because I'm me and not because I'm not home. But hell, I can't very well miss the publication of my book that I struggled with for so long. It would be suicide.

Never mind anything, Jesus God help me, how will I earn? I must be mad to even consider going back. My heart may be home, but I don't have enough courage to face the uncertainty and lack of opportunity. I can only go back when I have that courage. In my decrepitude. Yes, stay. And think of the positives. How happy the writing class was to see me after the holiday. How they brimmed with excitement, no one could miss that, not even me, who can't believe I can do one worthwhile thing. Their eyes shone, they were translucent, I could see through them into the workings of their being.

They wanted to write about a story I had told them, which I couldn't remember. Apparently as a little girl I went into a deep forest and came upon a stone house leaning to one side and there was a strange sound coming from the house. So the class was full of sound as they made it. The story went on, because as an adult I went there again, and again the same sound. And that's what they wanted to write about. The mystery of that house in that forest. They fell right into it. How they bowed so naturally to the discipline of writing. Silent, not disturbing one another. Submitting to your story. And not caring about the right English word, just write. Make a line if you don't know the word, or stick a Korean word in. Later, you go back and fix the thing. Later is a different process.

How earnest they were. The air was electrified with their beautiful endeavour. And that's when I thought I could see into their being.

And really, think of Dae-ho and the beautiful places he's taken me to. The far-away mountain where we walked through tall, bare, upright trees. Down there, in the forest of bare trees, we were in a magical land full of silence and we looked up into the heavens, and felt forlorn, yet part of the beauty. And from us radiated our humaneness and all difference fell away.

And there are Sam and Julia, in their marital silence, who

take me all over. A tea plantation, a lights festival, another festival to celebrate something I'm unsure of. And, of course, grand restaurants with exceptional food. Every morsel here is a delight.

Also Hye-mi and I get closer every day. She told me a dream that had left her shaken. "Ghost come to me. Ghost is like passed away person. There is no god for Koreans. There is ghost. Like toilet ghost or kitchen ghost. So if you have relationship with them, ghost will come in your dream and advise you. And also you must do good things. When it is the longest night of year, you make purple stew. You throw purple stew around the house so ghosts won't come into the house. Ghosts don't like purple."

Now what's all this? If only she had better English.

She has a boy she's keen on, but this is not really permitted. Not only does she need to be a virgin, but she should not have much dating experience. This way she'd be a desirable marriage prospect. But, she says, she doesn't do aegyo very well. Aegyo is the way women turn themselves into plaintive girls. Like when a little girl nags her father for permission. The voice rises and wobbles, the head tilts, the mouth turns down ready to cry and the eyes are full of pleading and hope. This is the way to a man's heart and permission. It's also more complicated than that. Aegyo is at the base of the power relationship between male and female.

"Men pay for everything and give present," says Hye-mi. "Woman give aegyo and she get benefit. It's like exchange. Men like to hear aegyo, it makes them feel better. They want to protect and care like for a child. It is like copy children's style. Men feel: I'm stronger than her, I can care for her. It's like woman is a child and shy. Man want to feel strong. If you speak in aegyo it makes everything easier. Like the man will carry your bag. Also, women have aegyo in their blood. It is their natural ability. Woman makes everything easier this way, because she doesn't change the power. But now things are changing. Equal power because of education. Before we are farming people and men were stronger than women."

Hye-mi reckons about seventy per cent of women still do aegyo. Aegyo makes her uncomfortable, it's manipulative. "It's woman trickery, like say she's not hungry or doesn't want more food when still wants. Because woman should eat not so much. Then you trick the man. He believes you are kind, submissive and like a woman he likes."

Her mother wants her to try, because it's easier to be a traditional woman. "No, it is too hard, I am uncomfortable. I don't want benefit from man. I don't care what man think of me. My friends need man's interest, so they worry about small thing like what they look like. I think it's very foolish."

Do men still like her?

"Men not threatened by me, because I am still friendly to them. If I'm very interested in him, he still think I am concerned and care for him. Just a different way. Submissive."

Submissive, yes, as Westerners here become. Leona sitting here next to me on the floor in the aroma of the breakfast kimchi leans a bit forward to see my face better. The face that has been sporting the same inane smile for heaven knows how long I've been lost in my stay or go problem. I take the smile off my face. I get up. I bow. Quite why I don't know since there's not a Korean in sight. And I take myself and my pressing question outside. How can I leave? A different Korea is opening to me. I'm learning so much. From my darling Hyi-mi and lately the silent university students. They have become a treasure trove of information. I now have the answer for one of the many puzzles here that has so far eluded me. You use the honorific for older people and men. They are above women. If a woman is older and higher in rank than a man, she will still defer to the young man, but she won't use the honorific.

The students also explained clearly: there are five 'provisions' of Confucianism, which govern Korean life and have kept this society together for millennia. The first one is trust between king and followers. Now it is between the people and government, or between junior and senior ranks. But the downside is the focus on success in order to advance to a higher rank.

Second is that there should be closeness (they couldn't get the right word) between parents and children, and especially between father and first-born son. It's a family-valued society and family is the basis for everything. The individual is not important, therefore one should overcome the self. Children should lead a life parents can be proud of and that is responsible. Responsibility is determined by one's place in the hierarchy and one's gender. It is paramount. It ensures harmony in the family.

The third is a distinction between the husband's work/function/position and that of his wife's. In South Africa we are not so exempt when it comes to patriarchy, but we can break free. Here you disturb the harmony of the family if you rebel and therefore of all the families that form the big Korean family. And the proud national identity, which won't be sacrificed.

The next provision is critical. It states that there should be 'order' between younger and older people. The good side is of course respect for older people, but, as they say, "Side effect is the young should follow beyond their real motive. Sometimes is bad. Seniors oppress young and young too timid and don't have confidence. But also changing little bit. In past knowledge wasn't easy to get. Now is all over. In past senior was wiser, now not to say. Now old depend on young's knowledge. It is tricky situation."

The last provision is that of trust between friends. "To get trust you must devote and sacrifice. You must loyal and truthful. Good value you learn from childhood friend."

The students are in two minds about the linear hierarchical power system. Men and fathers and eldest sons have the power, but they have to support and care for the others. This places a lot of responsibility and pressure on them.

There is pride and patriotism here. They have come through unthinkable hardship. Their foundation must be sound and strong.

To go, or to stay.

For this there is no answer.

GRETA AND JEREMY, the 'professors' who went to the Christian university, have been sacked and gone home. Perhaps they're better off. I hope I am also better off. I have been to hell and gone with my leaving or staying question.

I am leaving. I could not make a decision based on the facts I presented to myself. In the end I acted on something unknown. Perhaps most 'decisions' are not that. Instead, what leads you is a sort of force, which is not based in reason, nor desire. Whichever way, I'm going next September, which is when my book will be published.

How will I stomach the fear and blast my way through the inaccessible world of little opportunity? Nothing to be done now. All I can do is sit hour in and hour out and fix that manuscript and bear Hilette's terrible pressure in my body.

It's coming, it's coming. I hear this. It wakes me up at night. It's coming. What is coming?

In between this foreboding of something terrible to come, I've been contacting people who may help me find work in SA. I've also been scouring the internet and I even made contact with a recruitment agency. On reading my CV, they said that I can't be filed in any category. They have no way of dealing with someone like me. But there is one man I know through publishing who said yes, he can, without a shadow of that damn doubt, find me work in the SETA world. This Sector Education and Training Authority, it seems, regulates skills development in every economic sector, like banking, manufacturing, agriculture, and so on. All I need is to do a short course and I'll train trainers who teach people various skills in various fields, with the aim to have their experience and their updated skills formally recognised.

So all is good. Except that the two, and by now I've learnt – young – publishers don't answer my emails. On top of this people left right and centre warn me about reverse culture shock, which can be as bad as what I suffered when I came here. The same horror again? Nonsense, I say to these prophets of doom, there's no such thing. Besides, my old habits have been successfully transformed.

I am so buoyed that I've taken myself to a department store to buy a winter jacket. It has to be filled with down. Duck down. I want none of this synthetic stuff. But the man at the men's department (I'm too tall for the women's department) doesn't understand. I have made him feel the stuffing of many jackets and indicated in no uncertain terms with crossed wrists and a strong anieyo, what I don't want. He still can't make the leap from synthetic to down. But the giant won't be deterred and she takes off, becomes a bird in flight. "Tjirp-tjirp, tjirp-tjirp," I make as I fly around, arms flapping, jumping in an effort to be airborne.

The man's head is now cocked to one side, his eyes look past me, he's thinking. But no joy. By now I am panting. I go and stand right in his sight-line. I start plucking feathers from all over my body and take one at a time and blow the invisible thing high up in the air from where I make it waft and fall slowly to the floor.

"Oh," drops the penny, "duck down!"

See how everything goes right. There's even an email from the publishers. They don't want to publish in September, but February to be ready for a festival. They assure me that if I miss this promotional opportunity my book's as good as dead. If I go in February at the end of the academic year, instead of next year September as I had planned – which is possible since they give six month contracts if you request that – I'll have six months' less income and Marko won't be done with varsity. And his plan to get part-time work is unrealistic. It's impossible for an archi student to earn on the side. They work non-stop and do all-nighters weekly. September is the sensible option.

I decide to go home in February, but I don't tell anyone, in case something goes wrong. I don't trust them.

Now we have to hurry up. The publishers must find an editor quickly. But they have gone offline again. It's to drive me mad, as is the nausea about the end of my story. Although it's done and dusted, I don't feel free of it. I'll just have to bury this in my insides.

It's coming. It's coming.

I hear this. What is coming?

This worries me and also my birthday the day after Christmas, which is when I'll reach the cut-off date: fifty. When the best of life has come and gone. The sexless age. The dead age, though I'll be even deader if I let this day come and go and do nothing.

Another worry is that I will have to take back into myself all that's become dormant here. Plus, who am I now? They say when we go home we're never the same again. Lizards lose their tails, but grow another. What kind of tail will I grow? Never mind. The man said, without the shadow: he'll find me work. But what if he doesn't?

Spontaneous death, miraculous combustion, please let there be death. Let this cup pass me by altogether. God help me I can't anymore help me intolerable shut the fuck up you have to get Marko through I'm only small I can't live in the world I can't how will we survive please let me die it's long enough now it's too long please just let me die.

I have packed my summer clothes and Lesley's pan, way back from Gweng-song, in boxes. I have chucked the Clarks practical sandals, the right sole of which has been walked through to a sliver, in the bin. And some things will have to stay behind. I can carry one box at a time to the post office. Only three trips. Just let me die. Only the post office won't accept my boxes. Three trips back. Spontaneous death, it's not so bad, don't fool yourself, the end of the year does mark the end of his undergrad but there are many more years of feeding yourself. Many more years.

Breathe, just breathe.

Hye-mi took me to the post office. They explained that I have the wrong boxes, they are the wrong size, they are not official, and they, they have only boxes for airmail. The surface boxes can be bought from the post office in shinae. We went there and they assured us that their surface boxes break. I cannot use them. But *they* will accept my own boxes, they will overlook the fact that they are not official surface boxes, and they will post them.

My nerves were finished. There was too much talking, incomprehension, it was a tennis match, my head turned from Hye-mi to post office worker to back and forth. My migraines had disappeared, but now one is brewing. I can't sleep so well, I eat too little, my pants fall down. But I now have the measurements of the boxes they will accept and have been to the restaurant where the nice woman teaches me to read. With no language between us I got two boxes of the right size from the alley behind the kitchen where a dog was chained. And I took a third ever so slightly too big one. The woman suddenly stood up from where she was bent helping me find boxes and looked earnestly, and for a long time, into my eyes. When there's no language you have to communicate with every fibre in your being. There were such beautiful wishes in her eyes for me that I started crying and I pressed her hand to my cheek. And out came her only two English words: "Happy Christmas". The beauty of two people, across the divide, being human together.

The boxes now block the entrance to the bathroom. I'm just going to give up for a while.

ALMOST EVERYONE IS on holiday. It's the 24th and I'm going to buy Christmas food for Claire and myself at the big supermarket way down where all kinds of seaweeds are stacked from floor to almost ceiling in a section all of its own. There's a lovely feeling all around, just snow and silence. And that wide feeling when things come to an early close.

I've stopped off at Dae-ho's. He wants to give me my birthday present. He's on the floor working on someone and indicates his tea table where my present is. Waiting for me is the most beautiful painting on rice paper with Chinese calligraphy. Chinese is like Latin for us: the origin, he says. I rush over to hug him. He stays as he is with his right arm still on the woman and turns his body to me. His left hand shoots out behind him, close to the floor so that the woman can't see it and shakes my hand, preventing me from hugging him. It strikes me he's broken many taboos for me. The walking together in the street and the chatting. Brazenly, with a foreigner, disturbing the harmony of the group. How I love him.

Will he have Christmas, I ask him, since I haven't seen any signs of Christmas, except fewer people outside. No beans and veggies spread out on the pavements, only closed shops. No, he says, he won't have Christmas, but Jesus was a special person and he'd like to congratulate him on his birthday. He is such a generous soul.

The problem with Christmas is, even in our more mature years, that it's spoilt by vague expectations. Now what expectations can two lonely women in a small room in a Christmas-less country have? Claire and I had a super lunch. I got a Russian king crab. It was a hell of a big thing. And smoked salmon. For four lemons I paid more than for the crab. I also got, impossible to believe, cream. And good wine from Chile and Argentina. Claire scouted for a cake and came back with an upright dark little thing decorated to the nines with two Father Christmases, one climbing up a ladder. It tasted like cardboard. But hey, we had cake and cream in Korea. I missed Marko. Even though he Skyped.

Today, though, is another matter. It's the cut-off day. I am fifty years old. Vibrancy behind, blandness ahead.

We're at a restaurant at a floor table. It's much more intimate when knees touch and faces are close. Words don't take that second or so to travel from ear to ear.

We're a strange lot. There's Claire and Dennis, whose Asperger's has disappeared for the night. Sam without Julia, who is in Russia again. He's in his element. Hye-mi, who must feel out of place with the older people. And clicking Cindy. There's also a prof in English who's married to a Westerner. I've been to their house a few times. She's given me a beautiful publication of JM Coetzee's lecture and acceptance speech at the Nobel Prize do. I've been going on and on about him. He is a South African root – straight down to that core. Plus, he is a master.

Dae-ho didn't come. Perhaps a group of foreigners is not for him. I'm surprised not to be upset. I must have learnt, while I wasn't paying attention, to be content with what is.

I miss Marko!

When I go to pay, they have already done so.

We go to Elvis's bar. He is melancholic and plays records from his staggeringly large collection. I don't recognise myself I'm so jolly. I've given myself to my old self. I dance with whoever is available or on my own and before I know it I've tackled a pillar and am going at it. My leg extends flat against it, right up to heaven, my back bends floorwards and that pelvis moves in all directions. They are gobsmacked. The silent woman!

Back home and there are lovely emails from my friends. Hazel still wants us to go to Zanzibar when I get back. She even has some kind of itinerary ready. Adel has entered a more sedate state in preparation for Buddhist contemplation of the coming of the new year. I can't quite figure out her message, but Janet wrote to say she might join her, so I suppose I have it right. Dorrian is in Bain's Kloof, floating in the river. She saw Marko before she left and he is in good spirits. And she has the champagne on ice for when

I get back. To Helena's love of whatever she tackles there's no end. She's at the coast surfing and rowing. She's got a stack of *New Yorker*s for me and can't wait for my return. My friend Anna, the psychologist, wants to know whether I feel conflicted about coming back. And she apologises for only now sending a picture with orange in. From way back when I wrote the letter home and craved orange. There she and her husband sit in a field full of orange flowers. I'm going back to a very beautiful country.

What a happy day. Perhaps fifty starts the day after.

But the jolliness continues. It's the last day of the year and Claire and I are in freezing Seoul with its ten million people. This is the other Korea. It's very First World, exceptionally impressive and prosperous, though still restrained.

Here there are signs in English and we find our accommodation easily. It's a traditional house, built around a courtyard. We dump our stuff and off we go to a Van Gogh exhibition. It's disturbing. His surfaces – floors, the ground – seem to heave and strain to control a force that wants to break through. We have hardly digested this than we stumble upon a tucked-away room in a grand shopping centre. The room is full of paintings by Picasso, Miro, Klee, Dali! There's no security. They can't possibly be originals. But how great to expose people to this.

We head towards the historical belfry, Bosingak, where the festivities will be held. It dates from something like the 14th century. It was used to tell the time and the opening and closing of the city gates. It's on a plot of open ground with trees on two sides. The traffic's blocked off and there's a quiet expectancy as hundreds of thousands of well-dressed people, each with a Korean flag, make their way to the belfry. Nearby is a temple with multi-coloured prayer lanterns. They are strung horizontally in rows from rafters beneath the roof of a large outside area. In a devotional atmosphere women in traditional wear are busy with preparations. And suddenly, there is the shock: a huge blow-up doll, lit from the inside, is curled around a temple pillar. It's not a mythological or religious creature. It must be a character from some comic strip.

There are lights wherever you look. One entire skyscraper is covered in blue and green lights that form a Christmas tree. White lights spell out Happy New Year. In English. Just to the right of us is an informal band playing traditional instruments. It has a smack of the pansori.

There are six thousand police, but why they're here is unclear. No one drinks or is disorderly. And they look as if they won't harm a fly. They're so young and cosy in their thick jackets and padded hoodies.

We're nearing midnight. There's a stage up at the belfry with entertainers. Everything is displayed on an enormous TV screen. Five people in traditional wear, one of whom is a woman, have stepped onto the stage. They have taken hold of a wooden gong, a gigantic thing that hangs from heavy chains. The countdown has started. And 12 o'clock comes. As they whack the gong everyone lights crackers and fireworks that shoot up into the sky. There is so much smoke the sky is not visible.

And as peacefully as everyone arrived, everyone leaves. Not a piece of paper is left behind. We walk back to our lodgings through deserted, safe streets and fall into bed. And wake kind of refreshed, since we didn't have a very warm room. We get dressed and take our luggage to the communal room.

"Who is this strange man?"

The man sitting in the communal room in the morning light is wearing a red jersey. He's rather small, short, fair-haired and somewhat weathered looking. He has a strong jaw and prominent cheekbones. His feet are pulled up onto the only chair in the room. He has no idea how wrong this is, he doesn't know to suppress himself, he is not an English teacher in Korea.

"Strange or not, Claire, I'm going to talk to him."

Seb. He's a Scandinavian photographer, apparently with many books to his name. He's just come from Southeast Asia where he has been photographing temples and monasteries.

Right away we are all comfortable with one another and we plan to spend the day together. Can a day in Korea be so lovely, because Seb has the best sense of humour. And there, on the pavement, outside a shop that sells enormous contorted ginseng roots floating in water in bottles, a long-forgotten thing happens. At first I feel: what is this strange vibration in my throat? It's familiar, yet also not. It's a strong earthquake kind of thing, which erupts, fills my head, makes me bend double, racks my sternum, pours out of my mouth. What the hell – I'm laughing! Seb has us laughing and talking and waving our arms, and we have our heads high and feel equal to Koreans. We laugh our way through the streets of Seoul right into a mixed-race part of the city. It's a bit seedy, it's the shadow side of existence. We're right at home.

In front of us is the Mobile African Restaurant, announced in neon letters. From it comes African music. It's a square little room with grey, oil-painted walls. It smells of a paraffin heater, mixed with the smell of dried squid. East and West have met. Behind a curtain is a woman cooking. The steam fills the place. No, she says, she doesn't like this country and she doesn't like standing here all day long and cooking for the men who are on the public side of the curtain. They're from Nigeria and work in a textile factory. How did they end up here? They're not so sure anymore. But the money is so much more when it gets home. We understand each other.

We shell peanuts and drink beer around cheap tables and on makeshift seating. We talk and shout and are silly, silly. We stumble out into the freezing cold. A toddler sits peeing on the pavement, his mother comes from behind the curtain and scolds him, snot runs from his nose. Bring it on!

We stumble back to our room and get the cold night over and done with and face the morning, full of little sleep. Seb's come into our room. He'll be in Seon-chang in two days, he says. He wants to photograph the temples we described to him. He is serious, it's not yesterday and he's not laughing. He looks and looks at me, and kisses me goodbye. Gently, in my neck. I stare at him open-mouthed.

We dump our bags in the communal room. He's off to a meeting and we to coffee shops. When we get back I go to the communal bathroom to brush my teeth. Outside, there's Seb. Claire's back is to us, not a thought passes my brain, I kiss him. There we stand, our bodies miles apart, one short, one tall. I come to my senses and try to straighten my back, he lifts up onto his toes, his lips are stuck to my mine like an anemone. All the way up. Goodbye to chastity. At fifty you know.

I met Seb at the bus stop. Claire couldn't come, which was just as well, because I had already decided. I took him to the nearby yeogwon. We all stay in those love motel things with their rubberised curtains, cut in strips, that hide the cars parked there.

I was a bit shy. Nevertheless, things progressed nicely after the initial sitting on the corner of the bed while he erected some kind of travel hi-fi set. When he turned around I was still somewhat frozen there on the corner, but it evaporated as soon as I voiced my predicament. The predicament being that I was driven mad with clogged-up hormones, but overcome by shyness I hadn't counted on. Of course I wasn't too honest about the hormones business. It wouldn't do him thinking he was to be a sluice. And, I have to admit, there was a real attraction, in spite of our mismatched physiques.

Seb turned out to be a sort of yogi with unusual manoeuvres. All the years floating around in the East, meditating, doing yoga and no doubt having one splendid loose-limbed Eastern girl after another succumb to him had transformed him from the expected into the exotic. God knows how long it went on. It must have been quite a sight: the tall woman, the short man.

Of course we couldn't stay in that sordid room with its ghastly sexual history and what with S&M sounds coming from next door, so we dressed in our heavy winter jackets, boots and beanies and whispered our way down the stairs. Perhaps we felt we had crossed the boundary of decency.

Outside, day was relinquishing itself to night. It was grey and overcast. Or was it the intense cold that had robbed the light of its colour? Whichever, the freedom I felt made me laugh and not notice his arm around me as we walked down the main road, cloaked in the cold in our private little world. I was happy then!

We spotted one of the murky bars whose windows were almost in the road. Not thinking, we chose a spot against the window. We were all too visible there and all touchy-touchy, feely-feely. Then I came to my senses and moved, so that I was sitting this side of the table and he that side.

Seb was confused. He didn't understand the dos and don'ts of Korea. And I, well, I sat there in a state of great longing and self-control.

We talked about the balance he maintains between home and the East. This is the way in which to go out into the world, I thought. Not what we losers back home do. We, with our weakening relationships, our sense of our country fading, our sense of our diminishing former selves incompatible with our sense of our present infant selves. We, who live in deepening duality. It's a chasm so profound that we are but half-beings. If godliness is a state of oneness with the self, then we are beyond redemption. And yet, there is something emerging in me: a stillness beyond my mute way of being. It is fragile in its infancy.

Such were my thoughts as new waves of hormones catapulted me into spontaneous bouts of laughter and happiness. In spite of Korea or, perhaps, because of Korea.

He's moved into my tickey-box room. The designated spy is Cindy. She has been tasked to find out as much as is womanly possible about my suspected affair. But I stay frustratingly vague. A strange man wandered into the dorm the other night. Do you know him? Yes, I said, he is my friend. Yes, we are having a good time. Yes, he is short, meaning it's not so obvious whether we're indulging the flesh. Damn, hell, the signs add up either way: they are, they aren't. I won't be surprised if she's been posted as sentinel outside my door to listen for sounds that can confirm their suspicion that the fifty-year old transgressor is at it, blatantly, in the dorm.

It's a cosy affair here. I call him Down Under on account of his nest of bedding on the floor, on the hot ondol. It's wider and softer than mine. At times he goes off to temples and stays away a few days. Just as well, because I've been sleeping very badly. 'It's coming. It's coming.' This is still waking me up. It alarms me so. What on earth is coming?

But tonight, oh, tonight, he's back and I give not a damn about whatever is coming. I've just finished teaching. I was mad, mad, Teacher's gone crazy, she let all out, no toning down. Up that hill I went, no exhausted shuffling to room number o beak ship o. And down the hill again with him. We're going to see Dae-ho.

In the taxi and I feel vaguely embarrassed because I'm showing off my Korean words: juseyo – please, wenchok – left, orenchok – right, jogi – there, yogi – here, and the cherry on the cake, olmana – how much.

There are many shoes outside Dae-ho's door and inside an array of people. An ex-judo player and sushi chef is sitting in sumo wrestler largeness. Dae-ho's junior from Seoul, who is also his student, is there. Seb bows deeply as he greets Dae-ho. Everyone is a bit uncomfortable. This is not Japan. There's no need to bow so deeply. But then we have a demure Korean laugh and the tension is broken.

We sit down for tea. Dae-ho calmly indicates something to the student. He gets up and turns the music down a notch. Seb keeps on bowing deeply, now with his hands together in prayer, oh, for God's sake, but I keep on beaming. Dae-ho makes tea that tastes like grain. He doesn't know the English word. We drink from the new cups I gave him, they took me weeks to choose. Dae-ho indicates something or other and the student gets up and starts doing yoga in the back. The sushi wrestler has chosen a serene face for this time of English incomprehension. Dae-ho's 'girlfriend' and her son have come to visit. I haven't the heart to tell him a girlfriend is a romantic thing. They hand out those fishes with the bean paste inside.

"Is time for dinner now?" And in the flow of the flow we put on our shoes – Seb takes so long – and waft downstairs. We cross the main road and enter the side streets, walking and talking, we're a loose, relaxed bunch who can't really communicate on account of the language issue. But life is light. And there are no robbers and thieves and guns and we are soft under the trees, which the moon colours a light green.

"What do you want to eat?" Dae-ho asks me.

"Hanjeongsik. Seb would like this." It is a full-course meal of savoury side dishes. Something like twenty dishes. Grilled, boiled, steamed, fried. And also a main dish or two.

The yellow linoleum floor in the hanjeongsik place is warm. Do we want soju, beer? We get soju, and beer for the girlfriend. And the many small dishes start coming. An old woman with lots of cartilage in her enormous nose is frying pajeon in the corner on a rickety table. Pajeon is an unrolled pancake kind of thing. It's not light, but it's not tough, also not thick or thin. It's, well, pajeon. Imbedded can be octopus or various wild weedy things, which are normally parboiled and seasoned with sesame seeds and oil, garlic and green onion. We laugh and our eyes glitter and Dae-ho is neatly between Seb and me.

"My girlfriend likes you very much," Dae-ho tells me. "You're the same."

"The same?"

"She is also ..." whisper "... divorced."

"How come she has her son then?"

But before he can answer the cartilage woman brings more pajeon. It's 'service', on the house. It's the best pajeon in Korea.

"The pajeon's good," I tell the girlfriend. "The best in Korea. Better than anywhere else." But there's no comprehension.

"It is much more good."

"More good? You have good English, madame," says Seb.

"Man, they don't know better and best. More good. They know it's the best good."

And so we finish and drift back across the street in the dark with the glare of neon lights and down a neonless alley with the light green trees just above us, and into the tea shop. And there is the heavenly creature in her fantastical wear. Dae-ho and girlfriend go to a corner that is kind of obscured by a display of teas and cups. She's on the floor and he's treating her back. "He works wherever the need is," says Seb. He's deeply into the idea of a guru. Me too. "For Dae-ho it isn't work. It's like breathing." More people come in and sit at a second table behind a screen. How will she serve us and them at the same time? I see my gap: "Can I do this?" And as if it's the most natural thing they accept and look forward to my service.

I try to arrange myself into a regal position as the tea shop lady does, but grace is missing and I'm not in silk and my made-in-China T-shirt is just that, and getting the jerkiness out of movements, and growing long arms, is more difficult than you would think. I reach across the table, but it's all too far and my bum lifts up ungraciously. We all begin to laugh. But I pour, randomly, and Dae-ho has to instruct me what to do and not do, which will take eons to perfect.

The tea shop lady meanwhile has brought delicate snacks of lotus roots in vinegar coloured with flowers, and small twigs with which to eat it. She can't take her eyes off Seb. "He looks like Barbie doll with his wild blond hair," translates Dae-ho. It's a much more good evening even though I've flopped down on my bum, exhausted. All this gracious erectness takes it out of you.

Dae-ho and I leave, but Seb wants to stay. We stroll up to the dorm through deserted streets. The hastiness in me has gone. Dae-ho laughs, with his head back. We are both free of pressure, of the past and the future. We walk past the place at the river where we sat after one of our lunches and faced the fact that we're slowly saying goodbye. It is an ugly spot, but even this is transformed tonight. The light energy of the East is all around us. The moon shoots down stars, they flicker as we chat and chat under the softest trees, the gentlest friendship.

I wake up sobbing. Down Under, who leaves today, lifts himself and touches my head.

When there's no relief from sorrow it compacts and tears dry up. But with the Seoul trip, Seb's loveliness and all the laughing I've broken through the crust and I feel the love for Dae-ho, the restaurant woman, the tea shop lady, Mae, Hye-mi, Sam, dear Sam. And myself, at last. And I cry for all that's been, for the life that lies ahead – the wonder and the fear – for being alive. But most of all for the gain of Dae-ho, and the loss.

Five more weeks. I'll never see him again.

IT'S COMING! Karin, get out of bed!
　　Hilette is here. She's going to.
　　The breath.
　　Listen! The breath breathes. Hiiiii-huu, hiii-huu.
　　Hilette, what do you hear? What do you see?
　　Down, down on the dark of the ocean. Hilette is going home. She did well delivering her inaugural lecture.
　　The breath breathes. In the car.
　　What do you hear, Hilette?
　　His tongue did a-come, Maama.
　　It licked inside my birdy body.
　　Karin, stop it! Stop Hilette from hearing!
　　She walks past the dead garden. Opens the front door.
　　Hiiiii-huu.
　　The breath goes through the living room. Waits. At the kitchen door.
　　Karin, shut the hell up! You know all you need to know about Hilette.
　　Her name is called. It is a ball that hops. The little girl comes running through the kitchen door. Her hair bounces lightly. Her ball hops, up the stairs. The breath hears the child's sounds, Hilette follows the breath that breathes, hiii-huu, down the passage, the breath goes into her brother Boetie's room. The girl bounces like her hair, all the soft little bones, under her soft skin, the door shuts.
　　Birdy!
　　For God's sake, Karin, there's no need to let Hilette walk down a passage you dreamt up, in a house you dreamt up.
　　The breath.
　　Hilette, run!
　　Birdy! Fly away! Birdy!

Hilette's heart breaks terribly. And she doesn't know why.

His tongue did a-come, Maama. It licked inside my birdy body.
Why, I'm a-floating, you don't catch me
Maama Maama
Hilette sees, she must be asleep:
The child floats horizontally, there, up there in the sky, her ancient little face turned up.

> Her hair pulls her neck, long,
> and the ends hang in the sea.
> Her knees are snapped, they lie apart.
> Her velvet body, is stiff,
> Steel, like the tongue of the fish.
> Maama, why you don't a-catch me
> It licked inside my birdy body.
> Maama.

My heart breaks terribly. And I don't know why.

The piet-my-vrou. Calls again. The girl bounces like her hair, her skin is soft, the door shuts.
Birdy!
The breath stays at the door. Listens. A small voice, cut short. The door opens. Oh, there goes Birdy's ball.
The breath looks. In the passage.
Hilette pulls her body behind her on the floor. Away. Her hind quarter, there, down there is stripped. To the bone. Bone white.
The breath hears. It follows. It sees the child walk into her room. Sits on the bed.
Little girl. Girly, small.
Oh no, not any more. What kind of child grown thing is here?
The child becomes abominable. Her hair grows and grows, it pulls her head down. The hair must go. The child sits a hollow in the bed, the woman sits with her thick thighs. A crater through the bed.
Passages, they are for worn out life.

Hilette walks to the unoccupied room. She remembers her birdy legs and her soft-soft skin. How cold and daylight cruel the world. How warm, and dark, her brother Boetie.
Time comes, and time goes.

In whose arms can Hilette cry? In whose arms can I cry?
"It's coming." I hear this. And I am afraid.

Hilette hears her lover come down the street. That ridiculous man. He walks past the dead garden and climbs up the stairs.

"Klaus, how lovely to see you. This way, darling."
This is not love. Sounds on a tongue in a room. Despair cloaked as ecstasy. Never forget in what you have your origin: pain, around every cell. *This* is love.

The appalling things that were done in the room.
They throw her in the passage. Girly girl.

Love, that's the word she feels for Klaus.
This is what she must do, for Klaus, a big plate of vegetables. Here she goes down the stairs. Her legs stumble. Into the kitchen, where will her help come from? From Boetie, vegetables cut for him.
Hiii-huu yes-yes-yes. The knife is heavy. Cut. Miss the vegetables.
At her ear, the breath, what do you feel, Hilette?
Billion drops of rain. Sharp, inside her body, shatter her inside. Hiihuu, hush. Cutting vegetables for Klaus.
Her hair hangs over her eyes. The child's hair always hangs over her eyes. The hair must go.
Cut!
Too close. It hurts. There goes the hair.
Yu-yu-yu-hii-yu-yu-huu-yu-yu-yu-yu-hiihuu.
Rotten smell on the head. Cut, right through. The scalp. There is the thing that drags itself, pulped dog thing. Red intestines. Her hind quarter, there, down there is stripped. To the bone.
Hushsh, fresh vegetables, Boetie's eyes shine. Birdy on the bed, on the body bed.
The sun shines and she bounces her ball high for the birdies, Boetie calls, he has a friend, yay, Piet is also here. Stupid thoughts.
Hilette, look!
A small puddle of blood. Hushsh.

They catch her they catch her it's all all, won't the pumpkin cut today! Look, now you hacked the thing. Hushsh hiiihuuu, shove the knife into the pumpkin thing. It bleeds so much.

Hilette, look out! The finger is red. The sun shines through the finger is red, pietmyvrou. Piet, maak gou!

Boetie shuts her mouth, here comes the feeling, the fee-eee-ling, in-out-in-out-, in her noony, the feeling goes into her tummy, Boetie-piet-maak-gou-on-goes on on in-out-in-out, bounce the ball stop, yu-yu-yu-sharp. Kick. With the heels. Piet, hurry up!

The finger, is red, they throw her in the passage, her legs flop, frog legs that lie wide, what is it that happened, I, I-I-I, I don't know, goes o-o-on.

Boetie and Piet. She has to run away, she will take the knife, stab, just stab the pumpkin thing, look, it gushes.

Up there comes Boetie. He says she mustn't stab her hand. Boetie. He looks so strange. He has a big tummy and he has lots of hair on his body. Hilette saw Boetie so long ago.

Boetie! She throws herself into him. He pulls away. He's going to throw her in the passage.

Oh no, not again.

Now I am.

Push my finger into you. It is sharp, under your tummy, you can't see how sharp is my finger going in, red, in. Your legs are red.

Lie against the wall. Your eyes are here, brown, Boetie. Boetie brown eye, Klaus green eye, Boetie and Klaus, we sit against the passage wall. It is dark, Boetie plays with me he loves me it is warm –

The woman sees herself. The abhorrent monstrosity. Lies against the passage wall. Next to the lifeless man.

The woman sees.

The *woman* doesn't see. No.

I see. *I*.

I feel.

The terrible pressure has stopped. The life-long pressure. It is calm.

I see at last. And I accept.

Shines the new moon. I look down.

From my navel sprouts a shoot. A baby long-neck shoot, look, the brave little leaves. Wave lightly on the tip.

In the new moon.

Neither with hope, nor with fear.

※

Hush, hush, I tell myself. Where will your help come from? Hazel, Hazie, I phone her. I want to say I have at last found the real ending for my book, which replaces the one I was all along uncomfortable with. And that so many mysteries are now clear to me. Who Birdy is; the significance of the piet-my-vrou that Hilette kept hearing; and Hilette's need to cut off her hair, which hid what she kept out of consciousness: her abused body she experienced as a pulverised dog.

But I find my mouth won't form the words, and Hazel, so sensitive she is, hears the unsaid distress and takes me back to happy times.

That midnight we went down to the beach and swam deeper and deeper into the black sea near the rocks. How alive we were with danger mounting in each breaking wave. And when we came out the sea had swallowed her clothes. Her naked ducking and diving back up the hill to the house. And all the John Collins drinks – with two cherries – her Ernst would feed me. The mad, happiest Sundays on her veranda; the mounds of crayfish, enough for little Marko, who'd eat for three. And her relief when after lunch she could stay behind on the veranda. Ernst, who'd had a stroke, would shuffle us to his study with the old kelims, paintings and the sea in front. He'd sit behind on an upright chair, next to the hi-fi, and I to the front, in the comfy chair. With his lame hand and not altogether good other hand, he'd play Baroque, Classical, Romantic, sopranos and tenors. Piano, violin, cello, and when we emerged Hazel would be slouched in her chair, her feet up on the table, staring past the horizon. My friend, she's brought me back from there where I was lost in my horror.

I HAVE AN editor. I wish I could discuss the end with her. It upsets me so. But I don't know her well enough to throw a barrage of emotion at her. She is sensitive to me and respectful. I feel like saying to her it's just me. You are screwing with my identity.

I sent her the manuscript with the new ending, but making clear that I'm still reworking it. Working on this has been draining me. First, there's a time constraint. We have to get the manuscript off urgently. Those publishers need to get page proofs to me some time before I leave so that I can work through those proofs.

But I can't allow this urgency to prevent me submerging myself in the unsettling emotion and experiencing it anew every time I work on the piece. At the same time, I must keep a sharp brain with which to judge the placement and necessity of every word, show the logical progression from suppressed, unconscious and illogical content, to the conscious realisation of it. And this by allowing emotion to carry the piece. Then checking, throughout the novel, to see if the end now perhaps contradicts anything that comes before. In other words: literally picking up the novel and starting at page one. I know I should focus only on this, but I just can't help, for instance, moving around a misplaced comma here and there. The magic as the feeling and rhythm change right here in front of your eyes!

This, shot through with teaching and showing a well-balanced face to the world. But I'd rather not be doing anything else. Sleep, perhaps, since there's little of that going on.

And – from the sublime to the ridiculous – the editor has now got herself hung up on pheromones. Does this exist? God, man, it's fiction, I'll make Hilette *assume* there is. Problem circumvented.

Everything is happening together. The publishers have started sending covers. I should be glad, but it hampers my process. And those covers are inappropriate. There was even one of a naked, voluptuous woman lying on silk sheets on a Liberace bed. For my Hilette?! She's the most uptight being. Both Helena and Karen Bruns now send covers, which I send on to the publishers to point them in a direction. The direction has been staying lacking. I don't have a good feeling.

Neither is the feeling good when our Head Girl tells me my contract won't be renewed. Never mind that I'm not staying, it's a shock.

Her hands are clasped behind her head, elbows out, she stretches backwards, there's a triumphant smile on her face. Why, I ask. I miss classes, she beams. She must be referring to the one class she, Claire and I missed when we went to the pansori show. The evening I blurted it out to Mun-hee. You did not correct them, Head Girl? She doesn't answer. Dennis's contract is not being renewed either, she beams in her backward stretch. I'm still okay, I'm going home, but where will Asperger Dennis find another contract?

Everyone is free to make an appointment with the head head professor, whom we never see. HG tells me it's really not necessary that I see him. I make an appointment. I want to know what's going on, or has been going on behind my back.

"Watch your back," Dae-ho told me after he had met Leona.

What an impressive man, the head head professor. Perfect English. Open manner, engaging.

"I believe my contract's not going to be renewed."

"Who told you that?"

"Leona."

"I told her that is not the case! I wanted to hear from you about missing classes."

There you have it. Between snake Mun-hee and politicking Head Girl I had left my back wide open.

"You have good reports. But a mother complained about you three times."

"I only know about the one complaint."

"You weren't told about the others?"

More politicking. And I wake up. Now is the time to defend myself and blow my own horn.

"That child suffers from attention deficit disorder. I get along well with the others. One mother begged me to teach her child in the holidays."

I can see he feels angered by what he was told.

"Send me her contact details."

We got the unsavoury business over with quickly and then spoke about literature, publishing, the psychological effect of being here, different cultures. It felt like talking to someone back home. We talked about the insularity of a foreign community, the lack of stimulation, the vacuous conversations and how unengaged we become with the world.

He started talking about loyalty, also between friends, and I knew he was referring to the Head Girl. He must have been shocked. Koreans have such loyal friendships.

I had better take note: the world I am in does not single out loyalty as one of the most important values. I believe I stayed loyal to the little intimacy I did share with people. I did not gossip from one to the other, but, as Miss Priss pointed out, gossip means nothing, everyone gossips. My loyalty issue is a strength, but it is also my demise.

The hour or so with the professor was a highlight. We, the English teachers, function in a substratum. There's a whole Korean population out there we know nothing about.

As is clear with the stories Seb came back with from the temples. Not all the monks are pure within and without. One, a high-tech monk, has naked women as a screen-saver. Another shakes off the monk's robes at night to emerge dressed as a 'businessman' and then hits town in his 4x4. He and Seb spent a memorable time drinking the evening away. Dae-ho also said there are criminals who flee to the mountains and hide as monks.

I walked back to my apartment feeling good after the time with the prof, to find the page proofs in my inbox. But bloody hell, after I had worked myself to a standstill to get my edited manuscript to them, they went ahead and set the initial manuscript I submitted to be considered for publication. I'll just have to get the right stuff through their computers and keep good focus since things here are not calm.

Ji-hu is now frayed to the bone. He's resigned, but still barges in, gives a little bow and uses his fifty best English sentences to give us incomprehensible commands. Oh, Ji-hu, we're almost at the end of the academic year and we really can't understand you.

I, too, am fraying. I have really bad judgement. I got the teenagers to write an intimate letter in Korean that I want to give to the restaurant woman. How alone I felt and how she comforted me without knowing she did. How she made me feel at home in her restaurant, which was almost like a sanctuary. How I loved being taught to read. And how loving she was to a foreigner.

I am now also constantly clapping hands. For every half-okay English accomplishment English Teacher claps those hands of hers while tears fill her eyes. Well done, she applauds the stunned learner. I'm past emotional and perhaps as a result am deluded, but even if I get those publishers to connect with the book it's too late for the festival. The publication date will have to be postponed. They are adamant that all is possible. Then I should get the right proofs *now*. Before I embark here in two weeks' time and perhaps hit the Bermuda triangle, I don't know what waits for me, I'll be offline. They don't answer. What a surreal time, a kind of limbo. I'm not here in Korea; I'm not there in SA. I can't imagine SA, I can't see Korea.

And the goodbyes lie ahead.

TODAY, THE DAY after Seollal – the lunar New Year in the Land of the Morning Calm – is the day I'm saying goodbye to Hye-mi. I'm waiting outside the dorm. Here comes her fancy little red car up the side road. She's taking me to her home.

While she drives us into the most beautiful mountains my prejudice against ugly Korea starts slipping. We come to a real house with nothing but mountains around us and a dream view of the sea. To have *this* in Korea.

Her mother is outside to greet us. We bow our little bows and step into a furnished house with overly large couches, an enormous TV, a first-class kitchen and a long dining room table stacked with food. In the corner of one of the couches sits a friend of the mother's. Hye-mi whispers to me that she is depressed. "Because she is abused woman."

Oh, this protracted farewell, my heart's breaking, I eat all the fish, all the bulgogi, all the roots, all the best food I've yet had in Korea, but nothing helps. Our sorrow mounts and mounts, it makes us silly. There's a heavy hula-hoop. I grab the oversized thing and try. The mother shows me how. Her little body hardly swirls, but she keeps the hoop up. We laugh and laugh. The abused friend sits in the corner and stares ahead.

And now I grab my camera and start shooting. Mother and Hye-mi, Hye-mi, mother, and we look at the result after every photo. Cries of shame and of pleasure. Hye-mi now has her formidable camera in my face. "For God's sake, Hye-mi, don't take me from so low down. It's not a flattering angle when you're fifty." Hye-mi jumps on a chair to give her height. "All women are the same," she says in perfect English.

It is indeed a day of women. Hye-mi's father stays hidden in his wing of the house, but as we're about to leave a bottle of Johnnie Walker Blue appears. "My father says thank you. This is his gift." Her mother now piles into my hands fruit of all kinds – the best gift they can give – and small packets of green tea she made herself.

So here I got the best food in two years and I met a Korean without reserve. Just trust and warmth. We hug goodbye like long-lost friends and the mother has a wide smile as we drive off.

It's quiet in the car. The sadness underneath the jolliness is rampant. Close to the uni we get to a tollgate. The woman in the cubicle is in full traditional dress for Seollal. Both Hye-mi and the woman are astonished as the Westerner takes photos.

"Karin, I have not thought this ever. To take photo of the woman!"

And we're driving up the side road to the dorm. All too soon Hye-mi has parked and we are outside the car. I have her head in my neck, my hand in her hair, hugging her head, stroking her back. She's clasping me tightly around the waist.

I'm kissing her silky cheek. Little kisses, little kisses for Hye-mi.

"Hye-mi ..." and now her face is between my hands. "Hye-mi, in your country you can't be friends with an older person, but in mine we follow our hearts. You are my friend, and I am your friend." Yes, yes, her head nods up and down.

The streetlight is soft. The brown of her small eyes, that side of her white-rimmed glasses, shine. No tears will spill over. It would be too unrestrained. But they stay so moist and I see the best of thousands of years of culture in her eyes, loving me. And I see the terrible hurt of this farewell.

And so I start to talk more, but find nothing to say, and now she's kissing my cheek, kissing, kissing. And all that's left is to turn and go through the opening in the wall. Hye-mi gets into her car. I wait for her to drive off. She waits for me to walk, away from the opening. And I walk. I look back. I wave, a straight arm, I walk, and now my hand is not visible anymore. Hye-mi drives off.

It is indeed the most painful time. Sam and Julia have taken me to a place where the pork melts in your mouth. Julia is quiet. She's sad, she says. And can it be? But yes, Sam has tears in his eyes. My God, man, this is all unbearable.

I phoned Mae. That warm heart of hers.

Tomorrow I leave. Five am. Dae-ho will fetch me and take me down the side road and into the main road and two blocks down to the bus depot next to the tickey-box of a stationery shop and the shop with the plastic things stacked from floor to ceiling. Then I will start the journey back. To where I belong – this is not certain anymore. I am aware of what I'm leaving behind. The hustle and bustle of this unfathomable planet in its own cosmos. All will be behind me and I don't know how to accept. What will time do to me and the Korea I so struggled with and came to love? Will it settle in me, until the end of my days, tainting me with the loss of it?

There's an atmosphere of an ending. Most of the foreigners are leaving the uni and I've said goodbye to the students, bowed, smiled, and kept myself in check so as not to be too unrestrained. And I've been to Admin. There they all were. Mrs Kim, who came out from back there, and smiled broadly in this country of no smiling. Seo-yeon I hugged, her belly with her boy inside a small mountain between us. Mun-hee, he jumped up, and he too smiled, and he was genuine, I saw it in his eyes. He took my hand and shook and shook it while delivering his parting words: "Nice to meet you."

And then I went down to the restaurant woman to take her my plants and the letter. I suddenly felt so lost and turned around and around: wherewhere came back from the beginning days when I had no language and had lost the me I had known. Before I had learnt to watch what enfolds, watch this being put one foot in front of another.

But now it is now, the last day here and how will I manage? It's goodbye time to Dae-ho. This I know: *you* will stay etched in me, in spite of time. I walk a few metres to the bus stop. This will be my last trip to shinae.

I sit in front, like always, ready for the get-out. Down we go, into the very narrow road with the many power-lines, and the veg and fruit and bean sellers with their wares spread along the pavements. I get off where the bus can't go any further, and past the shop that fixes scooters on the pavement, and now up Dae-ho's stairs. His door is open, there he is on the far side, packing up his studio.

"Dae-ho?"

He is to become 'business man'. He is drained from the energy he spent. He is spent, my Dae-ho is spent, there, in the soft sun through the windows. He smiles in full acceptance.

"Where do you want to eat? But please, Karin, a special place for you today."

"The baekban place."

Unbearable. We walk out into the street in our beanies and scarves and gloves. Dae-ho has a long black woollen coat. He looks so smart for today, so smart, in the endlessness of the universe. We say nothing, the winter light is our sorrow, it is in the cells in our souls.

"This is special day for you, Karin." We sit on chairs, special day for me.

"Dae-ho, say again. I must record you. I must have your voice when my ears want to hear you. When I am old."

He laughs his laugh, down his throat, and his tongue peeps between his teeth. "Karin," in his lilt, "this is so, there are two ways to live, to make a best friend on earth. First thing is what I learnt from my friend. Second thing is who I to call my friend. That is all, you know. Cheers." He looks down in unease.

We drink soju with something added. "It makes soju soft." We eat and laugh and so our time here comes to an end. We walk down to the tea shop lady. She takes a photo of us, my head on Dae-ho's shoulder. "We are all connected," he says. "We need no words. But you are writer. You will know when to use your words."

"You showed me a life free from words, where feeling need not be spoken or written, because there is being. This is what you taught me."

It is time to stand up. The tea shop lady crosses her wrists. No, we must not pay today.

"Please tell her I want to buy you the tea that is a hundred years old."

I buy, but it can't be the tea, it is not expensive and I start sobbing as we leave the tea lady behind. Inconsolable, as we walk across the main road to the taxi. Dae-ho puts his arm right around my shoulders. He does this in spite of the taboo of touching in public. And here is the taxi. I throw myself into his body. I sob so much. Thick tears coat his eyes. He opens the door. I get in, I sob, my head in my hands, and the taxi drives off. I wave, he waves, we wave till we are out of sight. Out of sight. Dae-ho with his black woollen coat.

And straight to the kids' building, up the four flights and into the staff office.

"Here." Cindy shoves a bottle of soju in my hands. "Just watch out in case Admin comes."

Admin comes in the form of Ji-hu. But Ji-hu is past registering drinking on the job. He's fallen apart. He cries while he talks at top speed and tells us he's resigned, he'll soon be a free man. But what is tormenting him is the devastating reality of his not being married. How will their lineage be carried on? It is his duty. His parents have found a good matchmaker and paid her a fortune and they are negotiating with the family of the bride-to-be. No, he hasn't met her yet, but he trusts that the decision his parents make will be a good one.

"What about love, Ji-hu?"

There's the slightest pause in his barrage of unhappiness, then on he goes. He just hopes all will go well. As for the woman: I wonder does she know she's marrying a man in the middle of a breakdown? Though one with a hundred per cent TOEIC score. In mid-sentence and mid-tear Ji-hu spins around and is out the door.

I switch on my computer. In the inbox is a cover for my book. It's good enough. I burst into tears. Years of obsessive work are coming to an end. Cindy comes over and I continue crying on her shoulder. Spaced-out Fred offers to take my classes. It's sweet of him, but I want to say goodbye to the teenagers and the younger ones and the writing class, for whom, to keep them occupied, I sucked my thumb dry.

It's a mad day. Kids all over, hyped by MSG, in and out of the office, where the soju flows in gallons. And it's the end. We switch off our computers and the lights and lock the doors. And there's a lost mop in the passage. Which I touch.

At home I pour my last cup of soju and there in my inbox, heaven of mercy, are the proofs. But. I get up for another cup. Sit down again. This is a disaster. My paragraphs have all fallen away. The pages aren't the same length. And what's with all the typos?

I can sit here all night long and correct, but it won't be time enough. I make a general list of what's wrong and what they have to look out for. If they follow this, all may still be fine.

To offset this Hye-mi has sent mail:

> Yes!!!!!!! I'm drunken!!! Can you believe i can write English!!!
> I was wrote many things, but because of my drunken it's gone…terrible!!!
> I just want to say I love you. That's all. Do you know? how much you are in my heart. Whatever i do, I always think about you. It's up to you believe it or not, you are like just my mother. Emotion mother. keep in touch or not, it doesnt matter. Alwwways in my heart.
> After i get my mind, I'll wirte again.
> love, love, love.
> Hye-mi.
> please forgive my wrong grammar! I have a lot of thing to tell you!

I stare at her mail so long my screen-saver starts and one photo after another comes up. Look, Korea is beautiful! Why could I not see what I see now?

And I know: it is the gentle light that moulds itself to your being I'll miss, it is this light that says, ssh, ssh, it is all unbearable, but you are safe, look, you are in a human form, all of you is here.

I close my computer. My bags are packed. They stand in a neat pile on the plastic wooden floor. A last few items remain. I reach for my tin pencil cases, but my hand stops and hangs mid-air while I read what's printed on them:

> And now good morning to our waking souls, which
> watch not one another out of fear.
> How could I have known that you'd ever
> back on the memory of for love all love of other
> sights controls, and makes one little room a universe,
> yes, that would be us.
> English is very well
> dream come true.
> Sneak off.

And this one:

> Precious in my love
> Happy Virus
> Sweet Food
> A season when a dream would come true

I stand in awe: Korea is really a story of triumph, and of hope. I take my cup of soju and open the sliding doors. The stars light up the bird's nest in the tree to the right. The vegetable patches shimmer, ready for tomorrow. The neon crosses shine in the distance.

It is as if a bolt of electricity shoots through me: everything that happens is sent by God, the energies, the universe, for a reason, and I'll be guided through it. These fancy flights of the mind are an illusion. In reality there's only cause and effect and can *you* transform hardship into a life-giving positive? There is little dissatisfaction to live in the excruciating simplicity of it. And there is harmony. Until this belief, too, changes.

To get to this still point. This is what the process was about. These two years I spent standing on the outside, observing myself and the world; letting go of certainty and all that was I. Just accept, says Dae-ho. I go back inside and take out my Eliot book. Ash Wednesday, which I interpret to suit me, draws me:

> Because I know that time is always time
> And place is always and only place
> And what is actual is actual only for one time
> And only for one place
> I rejoice that things are as they are and
> I renounce the blessèd face
> And renounce the voice
> Because I cannot hope to turn again
> Consequently I rejoice, having to construct something
> Upon which to rejoice

With my stillness I climb into bed and kiss my bird goodnight. He too will stay behind and it is fine. There are men in the showers. They spit and chat. They won't disturb me. I've learnt to sleep through their noise.

Through the window shines the neon light.

HOME?

THIS TIME MARKO decked himself out in matching colours for the great mother-homecoming. We've driven up the West Coast, where Hazel is with her abundant heart and food and merriment.

"My hartjie," and she hugs me and keeps me right there next to her heart. She takes me outside. There is my Jasper dog's grave. She has honoured his life and my love of him with a cairn. Jasper, I think, I can't mourn you now. But I will come back to you, my most beloved love.

She runs a bath and I sink into heaven. How can this be reverse culture shock? A shock, sure, but of loveliness. We laugh, because there's so much foam. Hazel's got our Zanzibar itinerary, which is where we're going after the launch of my book. I lie in this bliss for a long time before I join them on the veranda with the sea in front. I'm so happy. My son is here, we're drinking wine and we're going to eat Hazel's gazpacho. So much talking. It is impossible to follow all their words. Marko says in his gentlest voice:

"Mams, what's wrong with you? Your gestures are exaggerated, they look like sign language. We don't need to see what we can hear."

"Is it disconcerting? Am I?"

"Yes, Mams, well, no, but you don't make full sentences. You start halfway through a sentence and then that doesn't have anything to do with what we've been talking about."

But to me I make sense. I talk to the silence in me as I have been doing for the last two years.

"You are a bit strange. Out of the blue you just said '... intense colours of the gazpacho, sea is brilliant'." He looks across at my friend. "Hazel," he whispers, "it's not normal."

"Marko, my boy ..."

My inability, this silence, is beautiful too. We can hear the magnificent expanse of our African night. There is an owl sitting right in front of us. He looks straight into our eyes. After a long while we go to bed and I sleep, half aware of the rumble of the sea.

In the morning there's more of Marko and Hazel and their lots of talking and my lots of silence. Dorrian phones to say welcome home, but I struggle to express how I appreciate her call. I wonder how I'm going to cope when I have to see the publishers. I wonder whether I can still drive.

But drive I can. I stop at a shop. There is a huge woman with a sarong tied around her boobs and bra straps over her shoulders. She's singing and moving her big hips. She's given herself to her moment of joy. No one bats an eye. This is Africa. We are loud and beautiful in our unrestrained expression. And it hits me: I'm home!

But at the publishers I sigh as I get out of the car. How am I going to match their ebullience? They are outside in the brilliant sun. The publisher with whom I first signed up is there – she is a matriarch and I had faith in her – and flanking her are the two young ones who have since taken over. There are other people, too, to help make this a festive occasion and there's a lot of 'hello, hello', hugging, high voices, and general goodwill. I struggle indeed and now here comes the book and the sound of a camera clicking. The cover looks good and the blurb on the back, oh hell, impossible to read. Both the colour and type are too faint. The camera clicks again and I spot a typo. And they used cheap paper. A typo on cheap paper. I smile. A glass of champagne is put into my hand. One typo is not so bad ... *Any* typos are bad, all eyes on me, I have to say how happy I am, I do, now a sheet of paper finds its way into my hands. It's the proposed publicity. It is seriously lacking. Whoever sucked this from a thumb has no clue, no use talking about it now, the matriarch flits past and says you were already gone, we could not verify, we were not sure about some paragraphs, the printing schedule. I look up, the sun is behind her, I realise it is the time to smile, which I do while she wonders aloud – for a brief moment – why I came to them, I could have gone to a big publishing company, I must have had my reasons. Yes, I had my reasons, I want to say to her sun-obliterated face: you were going to rework this lot for the stage and get me onto it. That's what you said. Remember? But I don't say, and she doesn't remember and she's off again. They are really very hospitable and what's wrong with me that I feel outnumbered?

Then it's lunch around a long table and paterfamilias asks what my wish is for this book and I take the plunge and say with the funding you have access to and your expertise and contacts you're going to rework it into a play and get it onto a stage. Yes, what a good idea, but *I* must first get this into a script and then there are competitions I can enter and via this route take it to the stage. I wish I had a lot of fat on my frame: I would not feel the slight breeze.

The afternoon is at last over. I did not live up to the jolliness. I've forgotten how we South Africans participate in our hospitable and energetic way. Until we drop dead.

But on I go. I have to select the passages I'm going to read at the festival – the important festival I simply *had* to come back for.

I find more typos, stop paging through the book and go only to the passages I've decided to read. How will I get onto a stage and read when I find it strange to feel the vibrations of my voice? I take to the deserted streets with their shut-up holiday homes and the sea everywhere. I force my voice out, yes, I can.

Back at the house Hazel is on the veranda. Her cancer is back but you can hardly see it; it's not aggressive and is contained. She's on a new kind of chemo that is much gentler, although it affects her feet. I make her sit down with her feet first in water and then on my lap. She has such beautiful slender and delicate feet. As I oil them I realise how lucky I am to love her so and that ageing has its pluses: we have a history together. I know I exist, because Hazel is here and she can say, this here, this is Karin, and I, Hazel, know her, because I can attest to her life's comings and goings. And I know, because I've known her for more than twenty years, that she doesn't mind my voicelessness; that she still loves this changed creature.

Though not so changed that I can't see the great festival is going to be a disaster. In terms of numbers at least. The promotional info had almost nothing about either me or the book, only a line or two about the matriarch, who will do the interview.

And sure as hell, but for Adel and Janet and two of Adel's friends she's commandeered to increase the numbers, and drop-dead gorgeous Anna (how does she do it? She's shuffling towards sixty), only five people are there that I don't know.

Just as well. My reading is sub-standard. The world is so loud, my tongue won't move. Much like Hilette at her inaugural lecture. The matriarch asks good questions, but I struggle to rise to the occasion. Anna there in the audience asks relevant questions. I wish she'd stop. She makes one last effort at properly formalising this 'discussion and reading' and then I can get off the stage. There's a lot of hugging. We part, they in their happy jolliness and I in my muteness.

Just accept. Even though I have forfeited six months' income that would have seen Marko comfortably through his course.

Bloody hell, just accept.

"DEARIE," SAYS JANET.

Her rental cottage in the southern suburbs which I have for three months is spotless, with only a door separating us. It's very early. She has opened that door with a flourish. She is dressed and wishes to wish me good morning. I, on the other hand, lift my head off the pillow, look at her with incomprehension and feel deeply disturbed.

"Goodbye, I'm leaving for work."

Not even in Korea with its absence of privacy did this ever happen. Coming to think of it, I had perfect privacy in my isolation. Few social codes altered my behaviour, since I didn't know what they were. My inner world was unsullied, I could sit still, nun-like, and let a country's comings and goings wash over me. There was no need to have an outer casing of hardness to shield the inside. I became soft in the Korean air. Here, on the other contorted hand, everything forces its way into you. Overheard conversations, gestures, innuendos, the subliminal messages of advertising, everything bombards you and I have lost the ability to filter anything. My defences are gone, dissipated into the Korean air.

Surely 'Dearie' won't continue forcing herself into me like this, though she means so well. Everything, everybody, go away! I do not want to be seen. I miss Dae-ho! But he, too, has dissipated into the Korean air. He never existed, sundubu and bulgogi never existed, what exist are cheese, cream, butter, nausea, loud voices, too much. Marko comes for supper often. He is jolly and happy, his mother is back, we talk, cook, all in the tiny cottage, and Dearie's dog barks constantly, her phone keeps on ringing.

The softness is fading, obliterated by an isolation and an inability to communicate with all these friends-become-strangers. But I try hard to connect and join Dearie, Adel and some others for meditation. We sit on cushions. Some just can't and perch guiltily on chairs. Adel is in front operating a recorder. We listen to a guru, in this case a woman's recorded voice. We are in double awe: wisdom *and* a woman, and we are elevated. We are wisdom too, we are on the righteous one and only path.

After not too long we assemble around a sumptuous spread, but don't eat. Everyone has something earth-shattering to add to the high level of wisdom doing the rounds. Some can't help it and 'discuss' the one and only who has outdone them in the race to be in the inner circle, to be the right hand of the holy teacher. Not only does she lead the group, but she also has access to the being in possession of the tape of wisdom. This means she is close to the source, elevated.

In essence, how do the Buddhist study group and the Bible study group and the Quran study group differ? But soon, thank God, a brave soul breaks the eating impasse and loads her plate. The rest follow suit. Silence now envelops the munching women in deep contemplation, scheming really: how to fill the plate again without seeming gluttonous. Gluttony and cultivated serenity don't go together, and they must follow the laws of this new religion for which they gave up the religion they were born into. Since that one is outmoded.

All these belief systems. This one brings retribution, that one an endless cycle of living, another deliverance, one promises the end of misery through heaven and another through nirvana. All these people force their being into alliance with some arbitrary truth and belief. How different was Dae-ho, who aspired to nothing, he *was* Buddhism.

What I need to accept is that I am the one who has changed. These people's lives have continued as before. They can't relate to this radically changed me, whom they do not know.

How could they understand the impact of Dae-ho? I had a friend, I would say. He was my healer. He was beautiful. His little boy was beautiful, his father loved him in a way unknown to me. It was beautiful.

Yes, so? they would say.

He is light as air, phew, his essence is gone.

I had a friend. He lives in the past tense now.

Yet I yearn to sit with those I love.

On the lighter side, wherever I go I see unopened sesame oil bottles – Korea Number One. And dusty ginger peelers.

And I now hide in the bathroom till Dearie departs. I hide in the bathroom when Dearie returns. I am done drinking coffee while retelling the day's miseries as an intro to rehashing old pain and old injustices. I have an intolerance to this glue women use to bind friendships. Get on with your own miseries, I am done with mine. In the space of two years they were shocked from my system. They are gone, gonner, gonnest. I have new ones to discover.

Gone, too, is the ability to cut off from my book. I am horrified. I discover new typos and gross calamities on almost every page. The paragraphs are all still gone. A paragraph has a function. It's not an invention to make a page look good. It's a cataclysmic disaster.

I try to think calmly. The measly few copies the start-up distributors managed to get into the shops, this hopelessly inadequate number of copies, will have to be recalled. The book will have to be redone with my checking every word. The book will have to be reprinted. This means financial loss for the two would-be, wet-behind-the-ears publishers.

Frustration is boiling to scorching point. I can't pin them down. The one will talk to the other one. The other one will talk to this one. Yes, they will reprint. No, they never said they'd reprint. The other one said so, did not say so. They will cut out and tip-in the faulty pages. Good, cheap idea, but there are so many pages to tip-in – almost three quarters of the book – that the spine won't be thick enough. The book will have to stand as it is, comes the decision. As it is?! No, the other one never said that. And now they're on holiday. They are exhausted.

I am sick of my compliancy. I have lost the ability to demand what is due me. I come from the East. I am light, light. The vibrations that come from my cells float past all the other trillion vibrations in Africa. I do not know how to stamp my feet into the African earth till it shakes. My God, if I'm not from here anymore, where am I from?

The nightmare continues in this vein till the gravity of the whole bloody thing is realised. The only option is to reprint. And so I work through what has now become a manuscript again. Letter and space for painstaking letter and space. And add in the lost paragraphs and measure the page lengths. In the meantime, I'm assured, the books have been recalled. And while I'm at it, in Dearie's ambience, hiding and not hiding, I pretend it is not my book and I write a kick-ass press release. And Karen Bruns – she of the writing course book and of the new clothes I wore to the speech competition, which came just at the moment I thought my friends had been an illusion – she, Karen, uses her clever brain and sees to it that it's quite perfect.

The corrected manuscript comes back. But the problem is this: if you do not know the programme you're working in you may successfully correct one problem, but that then throws out the rest of the manuscript, with resulting new problems. One of the resulting problems being words broken up in ridiculous places and hyphens in words that now aren't at the end of a line anymore. I mark them all. I stay very calm. They are 'whatever'. I accept. I send my manuscript back. The new one comes back. I work through the thing again. I take days and nights.

I tell Hazel that since the launch will have to be postponed and since I cannot trust them to work without supervision, I can't go to Zanzibar until this bloody misery is over. She cancels our bookings and makes new ones.

The fourth manuscript comes back and fucking hell it's the same old business. I work through it again. Off it goes. Back comes the fifth one, ditto, same problems. I take the horrible plunge and phone the matriarch. We meet. I calmly explain; she calmly can't understand why it's taken me so long to 'report' the problem. She says the two young ones underestimated me. They thought I was some ineffectual old woman floating around in the East. The matriarch is a professional woman. She will take matters in hand.

So I go through the whole process again. Only this time the matriarch is in the picture and every corrected page has to be signed by both me and her. Eureka.

But the problem is, by now the contact who was going to set me up with work, this one and only contact, has gone overseas for a leisurely visit. Money doesn't last forever. And it's dawned on me that I'll have to buy a car. Friends Thea and

Hendrik offered me the use of an ancient Merc. It's very much like my Hilette's. It's a petrol-consuming cream wagon, it runs by the gallon. But I can't really think much further than the manuscript, the printers and the launch.

With a phone call from a friend I think further. He has spotted them, the books that should now be in a pulping machine, in many of the few bookshops that carry them. The publishers are still 'whatever'. They sent out an email, it's not their fault. This is not a case of sending out an email. A phone call is what is asked for.

I want to lament in Adel's ear. But she's become unavailable.

"I don't know what's up with Adel. She's into her pinched voice."

"It's nothing new, Mams," says Marko. He's brought a salsa CD and he's going to teach me to salsa. "I don't know why you're friends with her. She always hurts you."

"She does this, this withdrawing, doesn't she?"

"Yep. Let's move the couch to the side. I'll put the coffee table outside. Your digs aren't bad, Mams. And you've got a great bathroom."

"True, though I'm three feet from a garden wall. Hey, let's get Dearie to dance with us. She looks so chronically unhappy."

"She has no rhythm."

"Oh come on, you can make her feel better. A dance or two. She's probably read my book and it's shocked her. Adel, I mean. She's actually conservative in spite of her seemingly liberated beliefs. She just replaced one set of religious beliefs with another. God's wrath and doomed afterlife is now the fear of bad karma and a bad reincarnation. The Ten Commandments have become the Noble Eightfold Path. Same-same thing."

"Okay, are you ready?"

"Let me go and fetch Dearie."

And Dearie is willing, but she wants to watch first. Marko and I are doing great, though we're out of the salsa and into the bob.

"Mams, you can't lead. I'm the man. You have to follow me."

"Yes, man, I'm trying."

"You always try and lead. Mams, you have to meet my new friend, Oscar Junghaenel. Young chicken."

"Young what?"

"Chicken. He's Swiss. I met him through salsa. He's a fifth year medical student. But he's older. He has a car rental company, he also sells cars."

"Okay. You visited Dorrian often? You have a nice friendship. And she fed you? Bless her. Hey, the launch is going to be great. I told them they don't have to spend so much, but they say they have their standards. Come, give Dearie a chance. She's just sitting there."

The thing is: where to from here? To the quiet acceptance of middle age? The buckle-down, count-your-blessings time. An enforced, insignificant little job. Home at five, exhausted from under-stimulation and over-diligence. Eat, sleep, tomorrow the same. A one-dimensional state of living in what is not possible anymore.

In the suburbs.

No! I cannot let this happen to me.

The tenants are still in the house for four months. Marko won't have finished his year. I may have to move back.

There is still some money.

How long will it last?

I'll find work. Yes, that was the plan. But with the book delay that most important contact – the *only* contact, come think of it – is gone. What if everything goes wrong?

Don't think like this.

Yes, be realistic.

As soon as the launch is over I'll get editing work. I can't edit. Of course I can edit. I am useless, I have no skills. I can work in a café. I don't know how to work a till. Surely one can learn to work a till? I can become a prostitute. How do you get set up? Man, who wants a prostitute of fifty? Surely this is the one area where experience counts. I wouldn't be able to deliver. You are useless.

Fucking hell kill me dead how will I survive how will Marko eat? I'll stay in a ditch in the Karoo but what about Marko I can run an electric cable through a deserted farmhouse window for the computer and wash in the dam it is not realistic oh yes it is shut up now think clearly I don't have a car to park in a ditch.

Forget the ditch.

Just trust.

In what?

The universe.

Don't be bloody stupid.

Well then, accept.

Off to Hazel. She's too worried to phone the doctor.

"Hazie, everything will be fine, you're on good chemo, now phone that doctor."

The doctor's office says: all clear! And Hazel cooks with truffles and stuff and we watch the silent stars and the dark sea and sleep and wake up and sit on the veranda. She's brought a container with nail varnishes and we buff and polish. She emerges with dazzling red toenails. She wonders whether she chose the right red.

The doctor phones back and yes, it's best she come in to hospital. Just to make very sure.

"My hartjie, don't be alarmed. My attorney is coming later today. We should all have our wills up to date, is yours?"

What is this nonsense about a will? See how things work out nicely. Three months with Dearie is almost done. I'm going to stay in a house belonging to friends for a month while they're away in France. And then after that there'll be just one month to fill while I wait for the tenants' contract to end. And this will be filled with the publicity tour in Joburg. If I lingered longer up in the north, I could move straight into the house. For a month until I get a place, or a week until I get new tenants. Or something. But where to with Marko? Tenants don't want an addendum and I'm definitely not going to let him move as he suggested. It's too close to his final exam. And what about everything I'll have to give up? The oak tree, the golden light, the wooden floors? What about my heart?

Man, your heart's a fifth wheel. Phone the hospital! Find out about Hazel. It's routine.

She's in intensive care?! You must have the wrong name. It's all routine. It's meant to be a small routine investigation. The cancer is back and it is all over. It is all over. It is all over.

❦

Dressed in new clothes from Habits for this wonderful launch you wouldn't say there's a spot of anxiety over the future. A spot? You're losing your life and you call it a spot? Bloody marvellous, this launch. They used good paper for the new book. And there are no typos, and the blurb is visible. Thank you, profusely, young publishers, who are getting drunker by the minute. Marvellous. All the many people, such happy reunions. My reading is great, everyone urges me to take to the stage. It's my natural talent, yes, but watch my new natural talent, I'm going to work a till and/or contort into prostitution. What a wonderful evening.

Why did Adel not stay? She was only in, and then out.

I had a quiet moment for Hazel. She is so mortally ill.

I stare into Dearie's garden wall. I'm in no man's land between nothing past and nothing waiting. I am light, light on the wall, said my Pearl. Pull yourself together, said my Hilette. Pull what from where into what? There it goes, the elusive Korean energy, into the African soil.

Staring into the garden wall, I feel the laughter dripping out of me.

Intensive care late at night is a solemn place. They don't mind my coming. What does it matter? Hazel is dying.

But she can hear. Her eyebrows move when I lie to her and tell her this one and that one who had broken her heart, phoned. I may as well.

Down I go in the heavy Merc. Down, down, back to Dearie's.

I may as well, it is three in the morning, go back.

She lies so still. Her eyebrows don't move. Only the heart-lung machine. It forces her ribcage out and in, it is a violent act. Her legs and feet are covered in white stockings. Her toes peep through. She chose the right red.

"Hazel, Hazie, I want to tell you what is in my heart. In my heart is such sorrow. And gratitude. We're saying goodbye, you and I, and you were my cornerstone. You were the one still point in my strange life, this life neither you nor I understood.

"Hazie, without you, how would I have survived? And now, how will I? Thank you for the many years you made beautiful. So beautiful."

The past tense. Honesty for Hazel.

"I'm saying goodbye to you."

And from the outside corner of her eye nearest me rolls a tear. And, slowly, more. And what the hell, I'll kiss her forehead, I kiss her, I kiss her.

I kiss her.

THE MERC'S PACKED to capacity. All my boxes are here. Bless the Korean postal service. I'm lying on the bed, Dearie's sitting, in our sad, wordless goodbye. We know how impermanent everything is, how ephemeral even friendship. Dearie senses her own life wafting through her, how you are a thistle in the wind. I'm a reminder that all is not solid.

And I'm off. En route a beggar accosts me. In Korea I experienced the safety, not only from the absence of guns and robbers, but of intrusion. I was free to merge with the world.

My friends' house will feel deserted, the way a place does when those who have their lives there leave. I'll take my boxes inside; look for the light switches. I'll open the doors, which face a river. I'll wrap myself in a blanket and listen to the night frogs. I'll come back in and rummage through my food box.

I'll be alone and that's what I want.

But Marko has moved in for the winter holiday, desktop computer and all. Has he moved the entire cottage at home? I feel overwhelmed, but it's also lovely to have him here. How he warms up my life. Mams, he assures me, it's very cramped in the cottage what with Jerry who's now joined him. What can I say? Xenophobia has hit Cape Town again and Jerry, the car guard from the Congo who taught Marko French, the Buddhist by necessity who found accommodation at a Buddhist retreat centre, has moved in. He's been dispossessed of all. What I can't understand is that Jerry never lived in the townships where the attacks are. Something like his workshop was there, but it still makes no sense that he is, as a result of the horror in the townships, now homeless.

Also, Jerry calls me Mama and he's won me over. And he looks at me with kind eyes. He sees something in me, perhaps something close to tears. I see something in him: the desperate, exhaustive struggle trying to make it in a society that will never let you in. Because Jerry, his gallant efforts notwithstanding, is farting against the South African wind.

He and Marko are going to start a furniture business. Marko works in wood, Jerry in fibreglass. Wood and fibreglass in the same design? Yes, Mams, you'll see. Does Jerry at least count as black enough? I mean, will he elevate your company to BEE status? No, the Congolese don't count. But what about your studies? You're in the middle of your final undergrad year. He's excelling, I must just watch him. I watch and I'm baffled. He's now also entered a design competition and makes a reading lamp from reusable material. And he's found a restaurant where he's going to wait tables.

I have, meanwhile, established that I need to do a training course before I can train trainers in the SETA world. I've even resurrected an old doctor who's been wanting me for years to write his biography. His stuff arrives, zipped and all, but how can I make his lifetime's notes into a book? Also, I contacted a publisher and asked for editing work, and wrote a CV and covering letter for an internet company that needs marketing material. It doesn't read well. There's something wrong with my style. It's frozen. Or perhaps I'm just frozen in this house of glass in the wettest winter yet.

Enter Marko with Mangaliso, his lifelong friend, and Jerry and the young chicken chap, Oscar Junghaenel. He's a mighty strange creature, a just-short-of tall, thin chap with a lightish complexion. What distinguishes him is that he doesn't have a single distinguishing feature. But he vibrates sky high. He, the medical student, has just come back from hospital – God help us, stethoscope around the neck – and will join Marko, Jerry, Mangaliso and me for dinner.

What a happy bunch we are: Mama and the four grown men who eat Mama out of the house again before they go off to salsa. Jerry doesn't go on account of I don't know what. But he'll drop them off in Marko's car. No, says Oscar, he will need the car tomorrow, Jerry can't have it tonight. I don't understand, I say. Jerry needs to do all kinds of things in the morning and Oscar needs to get from point A to B, but he can't use one of his own cars in the fleet he owns since Marko is trying to help pay for life and that's why he's forever walking and using public transport, and he, Oscar, is in this way saving to help Marko buy a bakkie, which Marko and Jerry will need for their business, though Oscar is not going into business with them, but Marko is going into business with Oscar who will need to sell Marko's car. Correction: it's my car Marko is using. Well, whatever, Oscar will need to sell the car and then use some of the money to buy the two furniture partners a bakkie and the rest to pay for Marko's entrance into Oscar's car business, so that Marko can earn and help but this will still leave Marko to get a substantial loan for the bakkie, he'll get that from Mama. Mangaliso doesn't eat. His shakes his head. But the good news is that Oscar can get me a car for ridiculously little. How come? He gets repossessed cars from the bank and he'll sell one to me at cost. There's this great little whatever with only a few thousand k's going for little. And it's last year's model. My God, get me that car! Mams, let's look around a bit. No, no, what colour is it? Mams, one doesn't buy a car for the colour. Whatever, just get it.

Damn hell, the great little thing got sold just before Oscar could get his hands on it. Perhaps just as well. Best I have a look at the car I'm going to buy. No, Oscar's contact at the bank will show the cars only to him. Oh.

But there is an Audi and there is a BMW. What would I want a BMW for? Your image, offers Oscar, who is now talking to me from the bank's car holding place. Man, I have no image. No, I don't want a BMW. What about the Audi then? I was going to buy that small little thing for little. This is not such a bargain anymore. But I have to decide, Oscar is waiting. I don't know what an Audi looks like. Are they those long kind of cars? There was one parked on our block. They could be. I don't like them. But it's not the same long car. He wants to leave, I must decide. I just can't make up my mind so quickly. Oscar will send a photo. And here it comes. He's taken it into the sun. He has now left.

And arrives in time for dinner. He looks tired. He had a trying day at the hospital. But you were at the car holding place? Before that. Four people dead in an accident, best one drives a good, strong car. Best I take that Audi, but are they those long kind of cars I don't like? Yes, says Marko, they are long, but they are nice long cars. My God, man, what if you, Oscar and I aren't talking about the same long cars? Never mind that now, best I take it. He's doing this all for free and if he's not going to help me get a car I won't be able to ever own one. Boys, I'm buying that Audi. Let's drink to it. Colour, may I ask? White. Let's drink.

I'm in a freezing hole training to train trainers. But it's dawning on me that this SETA system, in which I'm going to make my comfortable living, is a pitfall. If you are going to train trainers you need info you can't get in a manual, but only from experience. Besides, it seems I'm being trained not to train trainers. With this expensive qualification I can walk the streets and look for, basically, teaching work.

If I replaced the word 'train' with 'teach' then this is how the picture looks: a teacher is teaching me how to teach. And not to teach teachers, but to teach lower down: the students doing a course. She is also teaching me about the ins and outs of the SETA world.

Oscar phones. That long white Audi was in an accident en route to the bank's holding place. There's another one though – more expensive – do I want it? Man, I don't actually want those long cars. Well, there's still the BMW. It has leather seats. Oscar, as we speak, I'm being taught how to teach and let me just get to teatime to think it over.

Teatime comes without enlightenment, but the good Lord stepped in and now the latest Audi was sold. Really, there's the one and last thing left – the BMW, and he can't go back there again. Think now: it is a very good car, it has only a few kilometres on, it belonged to an old lady, yes, if I find after a while I don't want it he, Oscar, will buy it from me for his business. Also, I'll be able to sell it for at least double what I paid. It's a bargain even if it's not remotely close to the amount I started out with. But I will have to go to the bank right now and transfer the money. I'm not near a bank, I'm in a hole somewhere and I don't trust this ancient Merc I'm driving. But here I go, down the long street. Didn't my disintegrating Hilette also drive an ancient Merc before she drove the splashy new one she bought on impulse? Yes, that was another nail in her doomsday coffin.

All the money is in Oscar's account.
Hilette bought a red Merc. Colour of the BMW? Don't know.
Hazel, for God's sake. No!

Bloody hell, and now Oscar's still not bringing the car. It's had enough time to go through the test and licensing.
"Why is it taking so long? You said it goes quick-quick."
"My one contact is on holiday. And the new woman there doesn't want chocolates. She wants too much money."
"You *bribe* them?"
"Of course."
"Of course? Good hell ... what do you mean she doesn't want chocolates? You bribe them with chocolates?"
"The women. The men want money."
"For God's sake, you're exploiting the women. What kind of chocolates?"
"Black Magic."
"You give them cheap Black Magic?"
"They like it."
"Oscar, I don't think I approve. How much? How much does she want? I have to go to Joburg on Friday, I have to be out of this house."
What am I involved in? Gender inequality.

We can't get up the hill. There they go: the car dealer cum medical student, driving; the son, next to him; the non-compliant BEE business partner, and the mother, Mama, in the back. She didn't want to drive or sit in front, her nerves are frayed.
It's not a very steep hill. All breaths are held.
"Switch on the aircon. It's stuffy."
"The aircon's a bit out of order."
"Then open the windows."
Only one window rolls down. The others are a bit out of order.
"Mams, just listen to this sound." KFM blasts through the car. "I'll get Fine Music Radio for you."
"Yes, it's very good sound." We're still not up the hill.
"Mams, just look. It has real wooden panels. Inlaid."

Oh wonderful.

"Mama," says Jerry, and takes my hand, "the car is a nice green. And the seats. They are nice."

"Yes, they're a good cream," offers Marko. There's a furrow on his young forehead.

We're at the top.

It's a minor adjustment. Oscar will have it done tomorrow. He has to. The day after this tomorrow I'm driving up a bloody steep hill, all the way up to Joburg.

We're still at the top, trying to turn. But here we go, freeing down in neutral, right into the garage.

"Marko, while Oscar is going to have that small adjustment made you have to clean up your room and all that stuff outside you used for making that lamp. This house will be spotless when we leave. And you'll have to help me with my boxes. They said it's okay to leave them here. These are neat people, just look at the garage. There's space, but my boxes will simply have to merge into the neatness of it all. We'll have to unpack their stuff, pack my stuff at the back, and then repack. And stop that cell phone."

"I have a 'please call me'."

"Yes, you have been running this business happily responding to 'please call me's'. It's the last month I'm paying your astronomical bill."

"It's my future I'm making."

"Your future lies in finishing architecture."

"I want to work with my hands!"

"Then work with them. But finish your undergrad first. In life you can do what the hell ever you want. But finish what you started. Walk away because it's your choice, not because you have no choice."

There was not a single day in all his school years Marko had to be urged to do his work. He was the most responsible child. What's happened to my boy? He has the will of a man, but does not shoulder a man's responsibility. It's a lethal combination and a lethal age. This begs the question: what's happened to me? I don't know I don't know I just can't. The silence, it has dripped out of me.

I MUST ADMIT it's wonderful driving this car. You glide along. I'm on my way to Joburg. Who was the old lady and why was she disposessed of her car? I hope she's not dead or paralysed by a stroke, the stroke I'm definitely going to get. The CD player doesn't work.

"Oscar, what now?"

He doesn't know. And I gave him a lot for his trouble and extra for his cell phone calls.

I drive in silence into the Karoo where I'm to write, quite what I don't know, while I squander time before Joburg. A lot of this has to pass. I do not have a fixed abode and can't hope to have one till the tenants are out.

I wonder why the old lady had the fancy sound system put in?

Karoo done. Two houses left spotless. Exhaustion. Hilette's yearly sleep therapy. For two weeks. Can one have chemicals dripped into one for three weeks? Not dangerous? If not, then definitely three weeks. One's exhaustion knows no end.

I'm back on the road. A light on the dashboard comes on that means 'Imminent Disaster'. Oscar says to ignore it, but it flashes red. A car comes speeding head-on in my lane. I'm onto the gravel, down a semi-ditch. I try to get out, but my legs won't stand so I'm back on the road and pull off into some godforsaken town and drive around. I take to the road again. Am I still going north? I turn back, I stay lost. Two hours pass. Some crying's brewing that wants to come out. I shall not cry. I shall not cry for Hazel. Dead at sixty-seven. What a waste of life. I shall turn my feelings into anger, which turn into chastising the self for having taken the wrong turn-off and who is now lost in the Joburg rush-hour traffic in a suspect place with road-less roads, barbed-wire and chickens. Helena doesn't know where the hell I am.

Two hours of road-less roads and, voilà, I hit the highway, another hour and I flop down under Helena's chair.

"No, no-no."

This here crawler beneath the chair, whom Helena's known for fifteen years, she's never seen like this. A friend of hers rushes over with tranquillisers. A bath is run, a former human being cries and cries and sobs out fifty years' worth of life.

"What's going on?"

"I don't know. I can't think straight anymore."

※

Joburg's a waste. The great publicity tour constitutes one talk. My support base is small, but they're a loyal lot. There they all sit.

It is unbearable to see my brother-in-law in a wheelchair, contorted with pain, which he stoically tries to hide. But behind it he is translucent. It seems that his pain is purifying him; that he is moving towards a space where he will yet be the most beautiful a human being can be, where his spirit will touch all of us. He is already empty of blame, of self-pity and hatred and loves his Lord, of whom he doesn't ask questions. A wail settles in my throat. I cut it short. There's a task at hand. My brother-in-law has read the book. He has some questions.

My father says that once he's heard the book explained he'll read it for the third time and understand. No! You should not have read at all. You should have skipped this book. He's given me a Moleskine notebook. To fill with what? Unravelling?

Helena is sitting slightly forward and she looks worried. She's been very gracious with her guest, who plays housey-housey and who has food ready when she gets home from work. Very gracious indeed, because the guest's problems are demanding. The green car has broken. It's AA and garages.

The whole crowd seem to have a similar look: how could you come to Joburg without a map book? Point is: how could I go and lose the map book of my life? Never mind map-less, there's going to be a week of no accommodation in Cape Town.

I can*not* live with someone. I have to be alone. Forget ditch-living in the Karoo. It came from a temporarily deranged mind who never believed it anyhow. Never mind, here comes a brainwave: Gill and Trevor's cellar under oak trees near my house.

And hallelujah! They're going overseas. Real solitude.

All is well, the BMW drove straight down from Joburg without any hiccups. And the cellar even has windows and they are level with a good, green lawn. There's a shower and a fridge and a microwave in which is made oats for breakfast, oats for lunch, oats for dinner.

The tenants have left my own house a disaster. I'll have to be in this cellar for much longer than a week. Besides, Marko & Co have taken occupation. There's dispossessed Jerry in what used to be Marko's room. Marko is in the main bedroom. Oscar's new car-dealing partner and his girlfriend are in what used to be the study. Oscar is in the cottage. And an American student is in the small room. She's paying rent. And with this, Marko's saved the day.

The agents pointed out that if the kitchen and bathroom were redone the rent would be much better. They offered a fantastic builder. Who destroyed the geyser, but the squatters don't complain. They simply don't wash, they hope the winter cold will freeze their smelly sweat. They are squatters, squatters, I find a pot with mouldy porridge in a cupboard. And plastic bags with other decomposing matter on the floor. It seems they had run out of cupboard space and Marko out of his usual neat ways.

The builders are now ripping out the kitchen. Only the sink remains, which is stacked to high heaven. And here comes a sleepy creature I haven't seen before. Hi, who are you? I'm the owner. Oh.

"Marko, how can the American girl pay rent? This place is a dump."

"She doesn't want more of California, she's come to Africa to have Africa. She's very happy."

"What's going on here?"

"Mams, you can't move back. You won't fit in. We're a nice group together and Oscar is also paying rent."

It breaks my heart that Marko is so concerned about money.

"Of course I can't. Look at this place! What's with all the old porridge everywhere? There's even an egg draped on that mound there under the chair."

"Mams, I have to feed Jerry as well."

"Pap and egg! What's become of us? I'll give you more money."

"You have already. I won't take more."

"Yes, you will. Pap and egg!"

In this frenzy I meet Victoria to discuss how she wants her pension paid. She looks reassuring, but I on the other hand must look less so, because she takes one look at me – she knows me so well – and asks what's wrong.

"It's the house. It's Marko who is like he has never been before. He's no longer neat. And I wonder if he's even clean. What with the geyser broken. And all those strange people living there, it's the car, it's the cellar, it's the whole of this country. It's my book."

Victoria calmly tells me that I've been through strange times before and that I'll sort out this mess. I just stare at her. Where does her confidence in me come from?

"But you haven't seen the house!"

"You'll fix it. That's what you'll do."

When we say goodbye I tell myself to see Victoria's face in front of me next time I go into that house.

I should not be alarmed, says Hettie, the editor of my first book and my most trusted person on earth, but the first review is out. It's an online thing, but many people go there, look, I shouldn't be alarmed, it's a compliment, though bad for the book. The reviewer found the book too difficult for him. How is a book difficult or not difficult? What else does he say? Nothing really. He was reading a crime novel and had to take time off to read my novel and he couldn't figure who the baddy was. The baddy? Mine is not a crime novel! It's about disintegration. He did say, though, that the book could be the beginning of a much needed new Afrikaans literary tradition. But with this ninety per cent of readers will take flight.

At least a Sunday newspaper has come out with a glorious review cum interview, a whole page full. Better it can't get, though one swallow doesn't make a summer. There's bugger all else happening, except some other internet stuff, but that somehow doesn't count. And I bumped into two booksellers. Through whom must they order the book? They couldn't ask the publishers, because there's no telephone number for them in either a telephone directory or on the net. And they don't know who the distributors are. No, they wouldn't, because the distributors themselves don't even know the book's on their list. Plus, someone else told me, it's out of print. But it's only just been printed? Yes, say the publishers, the printrun wasn't too big. Do they not know that you can't have a newly published book out of print? There's a momentum for a book and when it's over, it's over. They'll look into it.

Two weeks later and they're still looking into it. I feel ill. You don't stand by and watch, and not be affected, while years of work is driven down the drain by incompetence. Even so. I have to cut off.

Never mind even so. I should rather deal with the fact that the tenants, Doctor and Missus So and So destroyed my furniture by dumping it into the damp garage. They also destroyed the lawn, and where are the edgings around the beds? Also destroyed are the Rotel sound system; the dishwasher; the washing machine, which stood outside, draped in plastic, in the highest rainfall area in the country; the floors, which have craters cut into them; the blinds in the lounge; a priceless hand-made, vegetable-dyed Persian carpet; the double bed mattress. And they made it clear, through the agents, that if I deduct a single cent from the deposit they'll take me to court. I am more of a victim, because how can I fight a court? But justice doesn't sleep, because friend Cathy, a real hot-shot advocate of the High Court, phones as I'm writing them a letter and she says, No, you can't send that! Send me the information and I'll do it properly. Well, hell, Doctor and Missus, here comes Advocate's fully fledged *legal* document – in law language – and now let's see the inside of a court.

But my nerves are shot. Also on account of the flood that's hit the cellar I'm staying in. What was on the floor is now floating on an ankle-deep lake.

I have thrown out bucketfuls of water and moved the bed away from the wall. I am afloat under garden level. But the upside is that from this position on the bed, where I've permanently placed myself, I can see the green lawn.

Ha, much like a queen bee. There sits the queen in the middle of the floating bed. She doesn't budge.

Oscar has the first audience.

"Oscar, are we still keeping track of what you borrowed and what you've paid back?"

"I paid back that money with the money I spent to have the car fixed."

"To the cent?"

"A little bit more to the cent."

"That means I owe you? But you borrowed again? Wait, I have it written down."

"That was before I fixed the other problem of the car."

"Oh. But the car is not fixed."

"It's on its way back to you. Just some days more."

"Do I still owe you then?"

"Half of what the new fixing will be. The other half was the extra on top of what I borrowed."

"Oh. But hey, you borrowed a third time. It's not on my piece of paper, but I'm sure. It was that day it rained so much and you were in a hurry."

"That was the second time. Maybe the first time."

"Oh."

In and out is bloody Oscar. Lending money, bringing back, car not back, fixed, not fixed.

The bee hovers.

Now the builder has an audience.

"This will be the last time I see you?"

"I will always look after you. I'm your friend, it's better you pay me the final amount."

"I haven't seen the end result yet. I'll inspect when Marko gets his car back from the communal car pool and collects me. It will be after the weekend."

"My men want to go home and have a good weekend. We all worked very hard."

"Have you taken off the geyser money?"

"That was taken off long ago. I did you a favour. The owner is responsible for the geyser."

"Even though you burnt it out?"

"It is not possible to burn out a geyser the way you said."

"Well, it was on and you let it run dry."
"That's not why."
"Oh. I always thought that was important."
"Let my men have a good weekend."
"Okay, what the hell – here. I have now paid everything, hey? I don't owe you any more?"

What a relief that all my debt is paid. Mama's stack of money under the mattress is now flat. I just don't know about that car.

The queen bee can at last get tenants. She must just fly up and away from this bed and into her garden. Jerry can help fix it. But he's depressed, he sleeps and sleeps. She'll be a busy little bee all on her own there in the garden. Perhaps Oscar's business partner can help. He's staying in the house for free. But yesterday when she phoned he paced up and down. He thinks Oscar may have misled him.

How? Is he a crook?

A tummy contracts.

THE WHOLE FUCKING lot must get *out*!
 I'm moving back.
 I'm going to get my son through his final year.
 I'm gonna.
 I'm going to cook and clean and wash and fetch and carry. I'm going to be a full-time mother.
 He's *gonna* get his degree.
 Jerry sensed Mama wasn't going to cook and clean for him as well. Bless his beautiful soul, which has now turned Christian since he's found some church where he'll have various duties to pay for his accommodation. I take my hat off to Jerry's inventiveness; he's resolute and by now he's honed his desperate survival skills.
 We are all sad so we drive in silence to a not so great area where the buses and trains are. Jerry tells us he'll be fine and he'll come and visit. We park, Jerry gets out, knocks on a narrow door squeezed in between other narrow doors, and the pastor opens. He's descended a long flight of dark stairs which stretch up into eternity. They shake hands, Jerry turns around, takes his few bundles from the car, looks at us with love, and vanishes into the dark. Marko and I sit in the car, paralysed, and cry.
 The American girl is now in the cottage with its fresh paint and new tiles in the bathroom. The geyser is working and I'm hoping she'll take to washing her rather smelly body. Now I don't feel bad about accepting rent from her. And Marko, well, he's about to start preparing for his finals. And while he prepares he's going to wait tables. Wait tables?! He has all-nighters constantly and walks around with dark circles under his eyes. I absolutely veto this. Things must just run smoothly here.
 Through my sister's contact I got an urgent little job to which I can walk. The green car with leather seats and wood,

inlaid, is in Oscar's mechanic's garage again and it is now the third week. But I don't mind, I am revved up, I've taken over from a useless trainer and I am training shop assistants to assist. With this qualification these very young women will have earned themselves a spot in/on the National Qualifications Framework in some or other of the SETAS, and won't be better or worse off than before, but perhaps worse, because on some it may dawn that the level of their school education was bad, just so dismally bad, and that they have missed crucial years they can't make up for. I weep and fume inwardly and blame Bengu, the first Education minister, for setting our country on a nowhere road. But still, this is a jol and we do all this stuff they'll forget the moment the course is over. We fill out those worksheets and write the rehearsed tests and debate the obvious and drink tea and talk about their future and their past and they sing love songs to me and we love every moment and one another. They think they understand math's pi (Who the hell *can*? Who designed this curriculum?) – they think they understand, bar of course division; let alone the whole irrational numbers thing. But we've walked all around a shopping centre and now they understand circumference but still put the emphasis on 'ference' but never mind, some things won't change and yes, they can work out how much floor space minus display space, divided by some kind of pi space will give them space in a shop where they'll sell someone else's wares. And for some there is hope and for some just none.

For Marko there may be hope, but I'm not sure. For his final project he's designed a building he was told an undergrad should not attempt. He's his mother's child, he tells me, I put my mind to it, I made my book happen. But I'm rethinking my way of life, I offer. Perhaps it can be easier. I'm not so sure that the ten years spent on the book were worth it. I got little in return. No money, and I live in a vacuum, because no one talks to me about it. All I get is Helena, who says it's upsetting. It undoes the reader. And Brian, who's really taken. (But Adel says he's in love with me, that's why he's taken.) Oh Mams, says Marko, don't worry, he'll make this work, I must just stay out of it, but I can't because he has to build a model of this building he was told not to attempt and he needs extra hands.

It's a hell of a job and you have to cut through thick cardboard and prepare clay by the moundful. From the front door right through to the very furthest corner of the house are pieces of clay, board, glue, pins, drawings. I'm up and down to a special shop to buy more stuff. Time's running out and we burn that oil way past midnight. There's not enough energy to do the rounds so I take to Coke and peppermint Aero and Marko to adrenalin. Also because three proper meals can't be cooked. The kitchen has become the clay-preparing place.

The kitchen, yes, it's not turned out all too grand. The builders were clearly no cabinet makers. The bathroom's okay, but the perfectly good drain is now no longer perfectly good. A plumber will have to unearth the pipes. And the newly sanded floors were used as training ground for a new recruit. The builder's been paid in full because Mama was in her queen bee stage ensconced on that floating bed and allowed the builder to bamboozle her.

But the kitchen is the least of worries. Marko has to tell me to shape up, please, I'm not cutting straight anymore, so Jerry's called to help. Oscar's also here and I must just sign here, this is to release Marko's car, which is really my car, so that he, Oscar, can sell it at a great profit and buy something else at a great profit too.

Since Marko and I have to separate – he's now an adult and I should not hold on, even though it's beyond wonderful to be involved in his life again – since this separating business is the new status quo, I sign. And he'll have that bakkie soon. But is the design and manufacture business for which he needs the bakkie still going on? A bakkie is always useful, he's laying the grounds for his future. While he's laying the grounds Brian has come around and seen the state of things for himself and invited us for dinner.

"So, Marko," says Brian, while he calmly slices a tomato, "a while ago you had a car. Now you don't."

Silence. It's kind of true.

"And Karin, you had money, now you don't."

"The BMW ..."

"Has used up your money, and will continue doing so. Between the two of you you had a functioning car and money."

"You're wrong," says Marko. "Oscar's bought a car with the money he got for the old car. I now have a car in his business that's going to make money."

"Do you have proof? Is this car in your name?"

"I trust Oscar absolutely!"

"Now you have nothing," continues Brian.

Marko and I look at each other. And Oscar's gone overseas. And his business partner who is now his ex-business partner has moved and all I remember is that he was hell worried at some stage.

It's at last exam day and the enormous model, which will get its last finishing touches in the very room in which it's to be examined, has been delivered. And son and ever-helpful Jerry as well. As for the plans for this model, they run into metres and metres of paper and who knows how good they are, he was warned not to attempt it. I am worried, but he's an adult now, I am not to worry, I'm going home. I'm going to sleep. But instead, my hands shake and I can't stand to even approach the house. I can never set foot in that house again. I've done what I set out to do. I got Marko through. My life's work is done. I got him through, many years, my Marko boy is through growing up, he is through university, and now I can be through with life. I need not anymore. I need not struggle, survive, make it happen anymore.

I need not.

I sit on the bench outside under the oak tree there in the lee of Table Mountain. How beautifully strange, there's a world out there far away, it echoes soundlessly and what was that dream of Table Mountain? That it was hollow, but that a mountain like that could never be hollowed out? Very far away, so quiet, but do I still have myself inside myself? What was inside me? Marko. Love, and steering him through the pitfalls inside himself. But all is well and far away because he's through, my part is done.

I need not anymore.

Anna phones and yes, I'll have lunch with her. But when she collects me she drives me straight to her doctor for tablets to sleep, to calm. And takes me to her house. Where I stare at the ceiling for four days and cry, while they pack for a trip, until Marko fetches me with the BMW. And now Marko can't understand, this rock in his life, this mother, what? She's crying unhindered. And more and more and says she can't she just can't go back to that house.

"Mams," and he holds my hand, while he should have it on the steering wheel, "Mams, you'll work it out. You're as strong as a rock."

But the Lord's worked it out because Thea phones and hears the distress and says come to me, let Marko bring you right now then you don't have to enter that house at all. He can bring clean clothing later.

Thea is going to the Karoo and she takes me, my suitcase and an electrical fan to a friend in Prince Albert.

I lie on a bed with the fan at full throttle for three weeks, while my friend cares with pulses and Glühwein. I regain equilibrium. Except for Hilette. There she is, still walking around with her wounds.

Had I not known better I may have suspected my dislike of her was to screen me from her hurts. Which leads to: had I not known better I might have thought I, too, had hurts, which I conveniently dropped into Hilette. Meaning Hilette is full of me. Meaning, Hilette is in me?! Oh no, this can't be. It's too impossible. But if, then only slightly partly, because there is something like imagination and invention. Still, a horrible thought.

Man, no! Your perpetual discomfort has nothing to do with wounds.

You shattered your illusions and now you wonder if the unremitting and pervasive force of the resulting spotlight is so necessary after all? It hardly brings comfort. On the contrary. And with the illusions went any social mask you may still have had. Does the clarity of this maskless life make for a better life?

Staying in the folds, contorting to keep your spot on the social and professional ladder, makes for a less arduous and safer life. It gives people an elevated image to interact with. I went and stripped myself. God alone knows why I deflect all positive projections. The result of this? Who feels great about themselves to be close to the fallible and by that close to their own unlovely selves?

So yes, Hilette, I can't stand you because like most people you lived the lie and hid yourself behind your mask in a system that didn't support who you were. In the end you paid a price for this. I broke out. I pay a different price. Perhaps the price is being me.

That may very well be, but what's important is that things are coming together. Adel is going away for two months and I can stay in her flat in Simon's Town until a flat on the fourth floor becomes available. The flat overlooks the sea and I like Simon's Town. I have paid the deposit plus the first month's rent. I have money left for Glühwein and pulses and so on.

I have also found a new agent, who has found good tenants. The American girl has left Africa. Marko is going to move into a fancy house with Oscar. But in the meantime Oscar has formally moved into the cottage – he's paying, Mams! – and all is well.

The only thing is that Oscar's now had the car at the window-fixing place for four weeks. I want it back. He can't give it back, the windows are halfway up, or down, but definitely not fixed. I want the car with or without windows. No need to get upset. He'll show me the registration of Marko's car. It's not quite in Marko's name, but there'll be a business contract that says it's in his name. I want that BMW back.

But. If I string Adel's vodka-induced half-sentences together, this is what I get: her aunt's going to use her flat. Her aunt has a lover, quite unexpectedly, and the flat is essential for the success of the affair, which could even develop into marriage. Can I see the flat's importance in all of this?

Dorrian says why don't I stay in her cottage for the two months? What a lovely idea. Except I want to be alone. With my breaking heart. Hazel is gone. She's the man in the moon. And so I say goodbye to the Karoo and my friend and stand in the main road with my suitcase and fan to be ready for the car that's lifting me to Cape Town. Marko can't fetch me from the drop-off point, he is waiting tables. Oscar's all that's left.

It's a surreal drive in our silence. I see a map book in the car and it dawns on me that he's been renting out my car. Hence the hundreds of kilometres added and the empty petrol tank every time he brought the car back from being 'fixed'.

"By the way, Oscar, what's the situation with Marko's car?"

"I bought a Ford Icon with the money. It's going to make Marko a lot of money."

"I want that car to be in his name. In other words, I want it back."

But the papers are with his attorney, who's on leave, out of the country, not back soon.

"I want that Ford Icon."

At home he deftly gets out and proceeds to the cottage.

"Oscar, the keys, please."

His face, it changes as my words penetrate. I take my chance, step forward and take the keys from his hand.

"Thank you."

"I just filled it. You owe me a full tank."

"Oh, sorry, I don't have money with me." And off I go into the house and he to the cottage.

THE PLAN IS to settle in Dorrian's cottage and then join her for Christmas in Bain's Kloof.

On I glide in the green thing right into her driveway, hugging the pole to the right to allow space for another car. The cottage is rather dismal. An enormous living room cum seminar space with a whiteboard is divided from the bedroom by a rickety wooden thing. The ensemble sports a lot of mismatched burglar-bars, but it's spacious and the cottage-pane doors open onto the garden with its dirty fishpond and nice lawn. All in all it's great.

I settle in nicely and even stay calm when I discover the car won't move and that I'll thus be spending this here Christmas Day and tomorrow, my birthday, alone. I'm in a Zen-like space. I'm at one with the world. My phone rings.

It's a lover from decades back. He sounds uncharacteristically calm. And yes, I'll have Christmas lunch with him. He turns out to be completely changed. He doesn't get my hackles up, no, he meets me in my Zen space. We have a lukewarm lunch and decide I'll go to Botswana, where he lives, for a few days. It's all working out. I'll be back in time to run the training crowd's office. They need someone for six weeks, or three months, or maybe more, or less. Don't they need a permanent person? Yes. So? Hello, how am I black? But I'll stick it out. There'll be some income. Until what? God knows, there's no plan anymore.

※

Yes, the Botswana thing, it's done. And the man is okay and also not. But he's going to help me with the car, he's going to take the whole lot over, all the worry as well, and fix everything. He has a special, honest mechanic. And he understands how I can't be a rock for Marko anymore. I'm also going to have a relationship with him, I've decided this. It was a big moment there in the veld with wild animals trotting around. I won't live with him, I'll just fly to Botswana on and off and live here in a place he's going to buy. But I won't be dependent. Or no, I'm going to live in my flat, the one I'm waiting for. Whichever. His mechanic has just phoned and he's going to tow the hated green thing away so hallelujah, only Oscar has now bailed out of our fifth meeting in which he was going to give me the car and he doesn't answer his phone anymore. But on the brighter side, I'm going with Dorrian, safely in her car, to Bain's Kloof and I'm going to float in the river and feel the sun before I come back and head the training office, although I'm not black.

And what do I do? I climb out of the river, walk up the bank and phone the training crowd and tell them I am mortally ill and can't drive out of Bain's Kloof. I lie through my teeth and shudder a bit, but suppress the work ethic which states that never, under any circumstances, do you not turn up. I feel odd, but get back into the river and float there with uncomfortable Hilette – she of the ever-present presence.

Admit it! You have it against those who walk around tenderly nursing their wounds. So bloody wounded.

Not at all! I have it against all who are a certain way.

Yes, you have a blanket dislike for a certain kind of people you can't describe. These people you have it against (have what against?) – who exactly are they? You can't say. You never stopped to think. And then you took all of them and created a Hilette. Who is now the embodiment of people you can't describe.

They are the unquestioning ones. People for whom there is no grey – only their absolute truth, a one-dimensional black and white. Who deny their fallibility, and live behind a lie. And so create the norm.

So?

Maskless me doesn't. And as a result I stand out like a bloody antenna through whom they are confronted by what lies underneath their 'goodness'. Yes, the righteous and their judgement. They fuck you over while they sing hallelujah.

So? So, I live in a kind of separateness, as protection somehow.

Marko is here in Dorrian's kitchen, very at home. He's cooked up a storm for the three of us. He thinks he may not have accommodation with Oscar anymore. Yes, I say, we have to accept he's a crook. I spoke to his ex-business partner and he says Oscar is a crook. A very clever one. He's scammed many people. His car business extends beyond Cape Town, onto the internet and into Europe. He sells cars, collects the money and doesn't deliver. Somehow all the paper trails go back to the partner. He, Oscar Junghaenel, is innocent like the baby's bottom.

Mother and son have now taken to the grass beside the fishpond. They stare into the distance.

"Is he even a medical student? I trusted him!"

"I phoned UCT, but they weren't helpful. You must ask that girl you met at the salsa club, that pediatrician at the Red Cross. Darling boy, cheer up. This girl, she's nice, hey?"

"We're just friends."

"Like hell you're just friends."

"Well, okay, we're friends with benefits. But we're not involved."

"You two are going to fall in love. I saw it that time you and the rest of Cape Town were in the kitchen. I can spot a love in the making."

"No, Mams, you're wrong."

"Let's see. Listen, perhaps this Oscar disaster is just as well. You're young and you're learning an important lesson. At a relatively cheap price. I had to strike Korea first before I learnt to be suspicious of people and before I lost my disastrous innocence. Also, one must not trust people when it comes to business. One must have contracts and such things."

"At least the BMW is an investment."

"The BMW has not been accruing profit. It's making a loss."

Mother and son. There's not a fish to be seen in the dirty pond.

"You can't be without a car again, Mams. I'm okay, but it's not right for you. Perhaps the BMW will still turn out okay."

"Let's see what this new mechanic says. Yes, you definitely can't stay with Oscar next year now he's not answering calls.

"I'll find something."

"No, man, it's impossible. It's already too late. And what if you can't? Hey, move into my flat! You and Mangaliso. It's ideal for you. You can both take the train. Your new job at that architect isn't far from the station."

"But what about you?"

"I'll be between Cape Town and Botswana, although I won't be dependent. I'll only live in his place. Or something."

"No, it's too risky."

"Nonsense."

"Everything has been so strange since you went to Korea. I feel I resist you. It's like I don't know myself."

"Well, I changed so much how must you know how to relate to me. And perhaps you're having a delayed adolescence. You were a pretty mild teenager. And you're still young, you haven't grown up yet. At this age you're supposed to feel like this. And listen, you did everything so willingly – all those times you had to go to the bank to sort out my problems. And fetch me from the airport and drive me all over. At this age sons don't want to do a thing for their mothers. And just think: you kept everything here going. My boxes, the non-built building, all the tenants and their demands. You made sure the house was clean and ready for a new lot. And you did all the repairs. You looked after our whole little empire. You were the person I could phone up. I can still phone up."

"I feel so bad about the car."

"Why? You even tried to get me to shop around."

"I introduced him to you. He was my friend. And now I'm taking your flat."

"It's a brilliant idea. Listen, you can't be the way you are without me being the way I am – whatever these ways are. Dorrian says we're locked in co-dependency."

"How do we break it?"

"I have no idea."

My phone rings. It's the man's honest mechanic. The BMW news is dire. Everything is wrong with it. And it's been in an accident. The story of the old lady and her pampered car is bullshit. The mechanic's mechanic will buy it, but for far less than I paid, and never mind the double I spent on the non-repaired repairs. So I make a dire loss. Plus of course the loss of an entire other car. Gone. I signed it off.

Admit! You can't deny anymore. You hate Hilette because she's wounded.

It's absurd!

Well, it is just so.

✻

Things are moving fast. The new tenants, who want an unfurnished house, are on their way. Marko has to clean up and throw out his mess in the garage. It's sad, in a way. It's the end of an era. I'm moving out of my house. Marko is moving out of his house.

Marko takes the cleaning too literally. He even paid the refuse guys to drive away my Scandinavian couch. Anyhow, while we're at it, whatever he doesn't want for his new flat must go.

Various poor people have accumulated around us on the lawn.

Marko, do you want this bed and that bed and that bed? No. Straight they go to one of the accumulated poor persons. This table, that lamp, this pillow? No. Out they go. This thing, that thing.

In a blink I have stripped myself of most of my remaining possessions, the best having been previously lost to Adel's thieves.

I've kept a few things for myself like the coffee table from before the marriage, a bookcase, Persian carpet and so on. Marko will have a flat full of mostly good stuff. And I'll have some stuff. Though by now I can't be too sure what's where. I've got boxes stashed all over Cape Town. And, I discover, someone, probably Oscar, has stolen the boxes I kept in the house.

I've borrowed a bakkie. First I'll deliver Marko's stuff to Simon's Town and then my stuff to Dorrian's. After that I'll make another trip. I'm fitting out Dorrian's new house with the rest of the furniture. She let herself be persuaded by immoral agents to buy a sorry-looking house in a sorry area to let to students.

And now the man has come from Botswana. This man I'm going to live with, yet not live with. In between my confusion of just what the hell I am doing, he manages to fracture the atmosphere. I don't quite know how he does it, or even what he does, but he riles you for the pleasure of seeing your anger, or discomfort, or loss of control. As an end in itself.

We've settled ourselves in an Indian restaurant. I take out a university magazine I brought along with hilarious pieces Korean students wrote. I want to read them to him, but it will have to wait. The restaurant has a bewildering array of choices. Though they don't mind bringing samples. And here they come, but he's not tasting, he's trying to convince me of my wrong ways: I should, *should* take money from him. Take your money? Never! That's my problem, I should accept his money, be more womanly.

He proceeds to tell me how much he earns.

He wants to buy me?

No, I should let him help me. It's so ludicrous I don't respond.

The waitress brings more tastings.

But what now? I do this on purpose, he hisses. What? Be so talkative with the waitress. And just there I see what he does. He sticks to a point, or often just a sentence, and repeats it over and over no matter what's said to him. Or, if you refuse to react, he goes on and on until your refusal becomes what he focuses on. Dorrian says there's something very wrong with him.

I let him drone on about my being too talkative with the waitress. And then, when he gets no reaction, suddenly, he mimics the way I sit, hold my head, my hand. And I erupt. I get up. I take my shawl and I calmly thank him for the time we had. I walk out.

I'm going to have to walk through three suburbs plus past dark, derelict buildings. But I come from Voortrekkers. If they could get over the Drakensberg and that without shoes, I can walk these miles to Dorrian's. I'm distracted from this marathon by those pieces the students wrote in the university magazine.

"We don't have any system which cinfirm a persons capability except an academic background. In Korea, American doctor's degree and SNU's degree speak not an individual. And also if universities rank system doesn't be destroyed, suffering will continue. The graduates who graduate a school that is situated in Seoul are profitable to be employed than local university graduates. We have been agonised by an entrance examination since we were middle and high school studen. A statistic tells us that after graduating, there is a difference between them relative to graduated school, and is shows gloomy academic clique reality."

And what the teenagers wrote: "My sister is spitting image of parents. I am not spitting parents. My father drink a fish. I worry about that."

Yes, and I worry that I am spitting spitting fed up mad berserk with every fucking absolutely fucking thing. First these Cambodian shoes must go, they have no give in them, there, chuck them away, every fed-up thing. The man's phoning, I'm not engaging anymore. Here comes his car, let him drive off into oblivion. The tar on the pavement is rougher than the tar in the street, here I am, thank God Dorrian isn't here. I cannot live with people and I especially can't have them do things for me. I explode with unease.

Victoria! I'll go and live in her garage. I'll build a kennel for their dogs; the dogs don't need a full garage to themselves. I'll put a ceiling in, run electricity from her house, dig a hole for a toilet, shower under the hose. And I'll be alone. I won't have to talk and be thankful.

Squatters are amenable, they make themselves as small as possible, blend with the background, they wipe the last trace of themselves out of themselves, they stay light, says my Pearl. "I am Maria I am light light on the wall I don't know what you came to do but I came to praise the Lord." Wasn't it Hilette who recited sentences? It was Pearl? But Pearl *and* Hilette disintegrated. It's a book about the process of disintegration under dire circumstances, much like those I'm so deftly creating for myself. A maze of one inappropriate decision after another. Pearl and I may have more in common than is healthy. Pearl and I?! She lived with this one, that one, she was Maria, she was light on the wall. My grip is no longer firm, my hand is pulling free, I must hold on, I must do something other than I'm doing, I can't trust a thing I do, this is clear, I should go back to the man, but also be on my own, I should not go back to the man, because I can't trust a thing I do. He has parked outside in the street. He'll just have to bugger off. I'm going to sleep.

I FLEW TO Botswana. I flew back.

Victoria said she spoke to her husband, who said I most definitely can't stay in their garage in the township. They will, Victoria and her husband, move out of their bedroom and into the other bedroom, together with the other seven people in the house. I can have their bedroom.

Thank you, it won't work, I need to be alone.

I borrowed Dorrian's cell and phoned Oscar, but he put the phone down when he heard it was me. Never mind, I've taken a clear, decisive step.

I'm at the police station. A clever, dedicated man, Constable Jones, takes my case. I explain the whole car saga and also show him Oscar's speeding fines with the BMW, which are now coming in fast and furious. I hand over the pages of sums I worked out and an in-depth summary of the entire saga, all the undertakings and non-deliveries. There's a criminal case, says Jones, definitely, but what can they do? Oscar's nowhere to be seen.

Marko and I, and Karen, the friend with benefits from the Red Cross, have concocted a plan. She's in on the plan since Oscar's taken the money for a quarter of a car from her and didn't deliver the goods, only a clapped-out rental thing which is broken. The plan is brilliant: she'll phone Oscar and ask him to meet her at the salsa club. Then, as soon as Oscar arrives, Marko, who'll be hiding behind something, will phone me. Constable Jones will wait for my call to confirm that Oscar's definitely arrived. And then he'll let the police grab him.

The only snag is that Marko, Karen and I feel terrible about setting a trap. But never mind this now. Karen is phoning Oscar and we all hold our breath. Presto! So besotted is Oscar with Karen that the date and the time – Friday, 11 pm – have been set.

We are nervous. It's 10 pm and our cell phones ring back and forth. Oscar's not there yet. But Marko's behind his pillar, ready, and Karen is sweetly sitting in a chair facing the entrance, feeling dreadful. Should we go ahead with this? It's a horrible thing to do. What will happen to him once they throw him into the cells? How will a Swiss guy manage in a South African prison? It's very cruel of us.

I'm with Dorrian in her lounge. She's waiting up with me. Do I want some whiskey? No. Tea? No, thanks. I feel sick.

Marko calls. His phone goes dead. I feel sicker. I pace up and down. What are we doing? The phone rings again. Marko is whispering: "Call Jones. Oscar's here."

"Constable Jones," I whisper, "Oscar's there."

Such a long wait. Nothing's happening, although Jones sounded very strong, a man in control. But am I sure? Perhaps that's just his daily voice. Bloody hell, accept now. We're doing the right thing.

Dorrian gives me a whiskey. She assures me it'll be good for me. Why did we decide to do this? Perhaps Oscar's escaped and they're chasing after him. By now he's probably dead in a ditch. This is South Africa. If the police didn't get him the gangsters would have.

A call comes through. Marko sounds a hundred years old.

"Mams, it's done." He's on the brink of crying. "Karen is crying. It was horrible. Three uniformed, and armed, police came in. People stopped dancing. Oscar was caught between me and them and he wanted to run. I put my hand on his arm and told him to stay. It would be worse trying to escape. He looked like a caught bird, he was so scared. We feel awful."

"What did Jones say?"

"His men came."

I flop down onto the chair, and down the whiskey.

"It's done."

But, says Constable Jones, he's talked to Oscar all weekend long – hauled him out of the cells – and he strongly advises me to take the car but let the money go. We have to clinch this deal before Monday morning when Oscar will have to be charged in court. Then it's lawyers, Oscar may disappear again and the thing will drag on forever.

And off I go to the police station. It would be better if this lover/mad man cum very distant ex-boyfriend driving me to the police station would shut up. But nothing can rock me. Instead of feeling sick with tension I have gone beyond that, deep into myself – quiet, right there where the steel in me is. Steel, as I go into the charge office and through, to a small room.

Oscar is brought in. He sits. I sit. There is a small round table between us with a light blue table-cloth and two plastic flowers in a vase. Behind us is a window. The mad man storms into the room. He's got Oscar by the scruff. Oscar's feet dangle. He makes an attempt to dislodge the hands clutching his collar. The police storm in. The man's escorted out. What am I involved in? Never mind, concentrate on the task at hand. Oscar is whiter than before. My breathing's gone all over the show. But I compose myself. I have learnt somewhere along the line that in negotiations the one to talk first loses. I am a pillar of silence. Oscar tells me how I'm ruining him. He's going to call his attorney. Pillar of silence, although now I'm frantic about the attorney. I'm afraid of the law.

I'll destroy him. Do I know this? He shakes his head. He can't give me a car. I remain stoic. Now both parties are silent. I clutch my thumbs. It's a leftover from infancy. I stare in Oscar's direction.

"Oscar, I'm going to walk out of here. You're going down to the cells."

And voilà!

Constable Jones comes in. He and Oscar talk. Oscar has to call so and so – the man who's renting the car from him. The car he bought with the sale of my car. The car he's going to give me. Another man, too, has to be called. He's the one Oscar's temporarily staying with. Oscar takes the phone. He explains to his landlord where to find the file with the car papers. The man's not willing; he doesn't really know Oscar. Jones now takes the phone. He is the law. The man has to bring the file. Jones leaves. Dear good God, more silence. My thumbs are numb in their finger encasings. I breathe, I go hard again. Yes, this is how I soldier on through life when it's all too impossible: I clench my jaw, my eyes go dead and I steam ahead.

Jones comes to the rescue. I may leave the room. I go to a corner in the charge office and lean against the counter. A man comes in with a thick file. He's not happy. This is a Sunday afternoon, and he doesn't really know Oscar. Jones is now more of a star. He tells the man to wait. In his strong voice. The man shuts up. I don't look at him. I just lean there in my corner.

Now another man comes. Younger than the file man. Jones calmly explains that yes, the man has paid months of rental for the car, but the man must understand that it is a stolen car and he'll have to lose his money. He's terribly unhappy, but I can see he is a loser like I am: he's already accepted that he's been fucked over. I can't look him in the eye, I just take the keys. Which car is it? The white one there. But the door panel comes undone when you close the door, he tells me. It has good sound. Do the windows work? Yes, they are manual.

Jones comes out with a signed form: the car is in my name. Two other people have joined the car man. It's come out that there are more unfortunates like me. They, too, have been scammed and they know of more who are going to crawl out of the woodwork.

I look at Jones and feel I'm going to cry. I mumble something and leave. Outside the mad man starts telling me how I should have handled the whole thing. I walk past him.

I have a car! A tasteless car, but a car and that's all right. And because I can, because I'm independent, I stop at a Woolworths store, where I bump into an acquaintance. Congratulations. My book's been nominated for an award. It's on the shortlist of three. And JM Coetzee is one of the two judges. Oh, I didn't know. Yes, did the publishers not tell me?

My God, I have a car and I've been nominated!

Now I can go and find a ditch. Drive into that Karoo and settle in nicely.

Nonsense thoughts! Pearl walked into the heat of the Karoo and disappeared. Did I envisage a ditch for her? Am I still living my own life or am I following in the footsteps of my characters? The one disappeared, the other disintegrated.

Don't be ridiculous. Authors write from what came before, they don't enact what they have written. Even though I wrenched this book from beyond the known or remembered.

IT'S THE MAN. He'll be coming over tonight. He'll be bringing money. I have to accept. I have to be practical. I have next to nothing left.

But I remember that time – not too long ago either – when I went to Botswana for the second and last time. When suddenly he jumped up from the bed, moving from horizontal to vertical in the flick of a wrist.

And flicking that wrist at me with pointed finger, no less. Two steps with that tall frame and he's in the bathroom. He's a vertical inferno. He's back again. Ageing is unflattering. Everything dangles, ungainly. What happened? He is incomprehensible. He shouts. I draw the sheet over my head. I lose all motion while the inferno rages between bathroom and edge of bed.

He's managed to cover his face in shaving cream. He'll be in the bathroom now for longer than at the edge of the bed. I get up, walk to the downstairs toilet, open the heavy door without a lock, close it behind me and perch on the loo. He'll go to the kitchen, make coffee and bugger off. I'm okay.

Yes, he's making coffee. Cups clatter. He throws the toilet door open. He rants and raves from that height up there right down to the woman down here. I try to close the door, but he's too strong. I deftly slip past him, out the glass doors. But what was human is now a shouting lunatic on the lawn. The percolator excretes its last ounce of water. He's back in the kitchen.

He's quiet. He must be drinking. I wait. Footsteps, yes, he's leaving. I go inside, pour coffee and wonder what the hell just happened. But my God, he's coming back in again. It starts all over. He's up close to me. I smell shaving cream. Such a loud voice, such long arms. He's right here in my face.

I gently tip the last mouthful of coffee onto his shoulder. We both freeze.

"Now I'll have to change my shirt." He's rational.

"Yes, you'll have to."

He turns around, goes to the bedroom. There are sounds as he changes. And he leaves.

I stand in the kitchen, hoist myself onto the counter top. Is this what I want for my life?

No man, ever, shouts at me. No man, ever, shouts at me.

I pack my bags. I open the electric garage door. It shuts behind me. Now I shall walk around and find someone to take me to the airport. I do exactly this. I fly home.

Yet I, I walked right back into the chaos. I am a stranger to myself. But how can I allow middle age to overwhelm me? If I keep myself filled with wildness, with speeding through every moment, sedentary middle age would have come and gone without my knowing it was even there. And I'd be right into comfortable old age. This ugly cup would have passed me by.

First, he says on the phone, and I'm frozen back into the present, I must accept his money and I must organise my life.

I'll start with selling my dead mother's shares, because I'm in overdraft. I have never been here. Those who live in overdraft lose their footing, like Hilette. God alone knows how you sell a share.

I don't know what I came to do, said Pearl. I came to praise the Lord.

I came to fix the room. The chair here, the table there, the carpet in the middle. This is what I came to do, and sell the shares.

Going, going, gone, go the shares.

And off to the hardware store to get stuff to make hanging space, also curtain rails. A beautiful space I'm making. Isn't it rather useless? I'm moving out. God, I'm a goner. All my nerves going in all directions. No, that was Hilette's nerves in all directions. Hilette and Pearl, Karin their creator. It's a disconcerting book. Disintegration. I'm a goner. Shut up, I'm not a goner, I'm fixing this space, I'm so tired, up and down to the hardware store, no food, I have no food in my fridge. Of course I'm not a goner.

Here comes the man, walking past the fishpond.

What? Must I wear the see-through silk top without

underwear, and the high-heeled sandals?

He wants whiskey, and I haven't eaten today. So much whiskey down two throats. I tell him we have to go and eat, but he's doing his repetition thing: he literally repeats the same sentence over and over – that I must take the money. He repeats it right over my sentence of declining the money.

I sit on the coffee table with the top and no bra, no panties, legs dangling. He's on about something. Living arrangements. It's to do with how appropriate Dorrian's place is. He says without saying it, how, in fact, he can't buy a place in Cape Town. But also, it's temporary. Whichever, that leaves me having to spend inordinate amounts of time with him in Botswana, or stay here. I need a place of my own. I need to be alone. I'm on constant display. I feel like a naked, live corpse in an open casket.

Now he's got a long story going. I listen, what is he getting at? I've learnt that he's not straight and will slip in what he really wants to say by concealing it with other info. I don't do well with concealment. Tell me straight, or I'll feel my good faith to be abused. He gives me the money. There sits the amount of what is a quarter of my rental income in fifty and twenty rand notes, on the table, next to the woman with dangling legs. Where is his story going? Yes! His story has wound its way to include me. It illustrates how I am.

"The Chinese are whores," he says.

Meaning: I am a whore. There are fifty and twenty rand notes on the table, next to dangling tits and legs.

"Take your bloody money. Here."

He refuses.

"I'll shove it in your pocket then. Get the hell out. And all your crap you've been storing here." There goes a shoe, a shirt, another shoe, out onto the lawn.

"I did not really mean you're a whore. The Chinese are."

"Where do you get that from, the Chinese are whores!"

"Here, here's the money. I'm helping you. You don't have enough money. Here, put it in your purse."

He thinks I'm softening, the deal's going his way: the notes are back on the table.

"Get the fuck out!"

He won't take the money.

Out onto the lawn goes the money. There go the notes, they travel through the air, they waft down into the fishpond, the stinking pond. "Take your money and leave."

He's so drunk he's staggering on the lawn. Friends don't let friends drive drunk, said the ad. He'll kill the first driver on the road.

"First sober up, then I'll give you the keys."

He turns back. There is murder on his face. I lock the cottage-pane doors. He's outside, next to the money in the pond. I'm inside in see-through silk. He bangs on the doors, kicks them. I sit down at my computer. I'm writing emails. I am calm impersonated. My hands are shaking.

He has long arms. He gets them through the glass in the doors, with blood on the glass, on the floor. The wood's giving way. He's creating a hole to climb through. Sense returns. Off go the clothes. On comes sensible stuff.

"Brian, phone the police! The man's breaking in. Phone now!"

Which he does. The garden alights with a squadron of police. They're over the high walls. They have surrounded the man. He's talking wildly, his arms fly backwards towards me. But the evidence of broken glass, splinters of wood and blood is against him. He tries to rescue himself by inviting the police to help themselves to the money. There's a healthy bending and scooping up by policemen. Armfuls of the stuff. The head man steps in. He orders them to bring the money into the cottage. He asks me what the problem is while his men line the sodden notes in a straight row on the carpet.

The man barges in. He wants his money back, that which the police haven't taken. No, says the head man, who is going to pay to fix this mess? I feel justified and also sickened by my righteousness. Would any of this have happened had I not taken his keys?

Now the security men are also over the wall. It's mayhem, but the man has calmed down and is chatting up the police. He's a racist, I offer, and again cringe at myself. He turns around and shouts at me. He shouts and shouts.

I hand the keys over to the head man. "You decide," I say dramatically. And indeed he decides: they escort the man out, park his car and himself outside the gate and take the keys.

No man, ever, shouts at me.

Way beyond the pond are trees and plants around the lawn. What a lovely lawn. The lawn-less years in Korea.

This is a case of domestic violence. I was involved in domestic violence.

My cell phone rings. It's a very upset Dorrian phoning from Bain's Kloof. Security has phoned her about the destruction of her property.

"It won't happen again," I hear myself say.

It won't happen again.

To which depths of shame have I sunk?

It won't happen again.

It.

I turn around. It's ending *now*. In fact, it has ended. That something without name that's caused me to be unbearable to myself, to turn away from myself in shame. Now I shall write that '*It*' out of myself.

I take in hand one of Dorrian's white-board markers with felt-tipped ink and move towards my table. It is *my* table and I am going to write down onto it, *into* it, what I need to say to stop my compliance and weakness. It's an absorbent table, my words are immortalised. These won't be obliterated by bad publishers, by fearful readers, by ignorance, by silence, by the bowing and swallowing years of Korea. I say to everyone what I have to say. I say how I saw the world before it was obliterated, and how I see it now. This is head-on, cruel, honest.

The table is covered, I take to my bookcase. It too is absorbent and now I'm onto Dorrian's white-board, *it's ending right now*, there's dance-like rhythm in a thick pen and big letters, I'm not done yet, onto the walls, it's all ending, I dance on the walls, I write what I want, I write myself out of compliance. The walls are covered. *It* hasn't ended yet, I must put a full stop to *It*. I walk to the kitchen, there is a pair of scissors, I shall strip myself of compromise. There goes the hair all around the head, I cut it off. When you come to the scalp there lies the true being. Nothing concealed. When Hilette cut off her hair the ravaged dog was there draped on her scalp. On mine is the glistening me – my strength – which I have crippled for too long. I am done with adapting, fitting in, with making myself small for the world. I am no longer English Teacher, nor the amenable author, the compliant squatter, the queen bee, the victim of Oscar. I am Karin. Unrestrained. I go to bed. Tomorrow I'll know what to do.

Tomorrow comes. I can no longer cope in this world I have created. On a practical level: I have nowhere to stay. I am mortally exhausted, and shall, like Hilette, take myself off to sleep therapy. I do not have money for a private joint. I have extreme genes, therefore I shall have my sleep therapy on the state's expense. I shall go to Valkenberg. Like Pearl?! Like many, many people do.

First I have to recover the remaining money from the fishpond. Dorrian will need money to paint away my words and fix the doors, wipe away the blood. The fishpond is slimy, I am waist deep, I retrieve sodden notes with my toes. The pile is growing nicely, I lay all the notes out to dry. I can do no more than the very least. I'm going to sleep in Valkenberg. It is the most rational and calculated thing I have done in some years.

The matriarch sends an SMS of congratulations on my nomination. I am also done with niceties. I write back: you gave me to two spoilt, indulged and clueless children. I trusted the publishing of my book to you. You broke my trust.

I bathe, I brush my teeth. I put on panties and an almost dress-length long shirt. I don a straw hat, fill my bag with CDs and take my toothbrush.

I phone my friend who is a psychiatrist at Valkenberg.

"Robert, I'm coming to your neck of the woods."

He's on leave, he says, but I'm welcome. He'll let them know. He knows not to sound alarmed. Neither am I at this extreme move. As I pull out of the property the matriarch arrives. She has brought her husband for support. They will take me to Valkenberg.

I am done talking. I sit in the back of the car and feel relieved. What can they bring me? Nothing, except a player for my CDs. We arrive in silence. Forms are to be filled in. The matriarch takes over. Sign here, she says. It says I'm here of my own free will.

"I've come for sleep therapy," I tell the receptionist. "Make sure it's understood."

I turn around and with toothbrush in hand, straw hat on head and handbag in hand, I leave.

A swiped card; a punched-in code; a steel door opens and closes.

DEAR FUCK, I'M in hell.

In front is the nurses' station and behind this what looks like a glass cage filled with desperate people. One has her head against the glass, some shout out to the nurses.

"Excuse me, someone's trying to get your attention."

But the nurse remains with her back to the glass.

"Am I going in there?!"

I'm taken to the linen room where I slide down a wall to the floor.

"I've come for sleep therapy."

"We don't do sleep therapy here," says a nurse kindly and gives me two crimplene dresses. One is to sleep in and the other to be worn in the day over the night one, if I understand her correctly.

"You'll have to hand me your handbag. All your possessions."

"But I've brought CDs."

"You won't have use for them."

It is a new building and everything is very, very clean and inviting. Down the passage is the dormitory, where not a single personal possession is permitted. My bed is a concrete slab with a good mattress, one sheet, pillow and a blanket. I slip my toothbrush under the pillow.

In a room with a small round table and two lounge chairs a psychiatrist is waiting. He starts with name, date of birth, date of today, how come I'm here?

"I'm done talking. I said what I wanted to say. I've come for sleep therapy."

"We'll give you something to sleep tonight."

"This is not how I envisaged it. Sleep therapy means one's attached to a drip, which drips an assortment of knock-out chemicals into one's blood. For days on end. I have come for this."

But to no avail. He's called away. In the meantime I must join the new cohorts in the glass cage, which is really a spacious room with two glass walls that open onto a piece of densely fenced lawn. My new compatriots are either in the cage or outside. Many are plagued by Jesus. They cry out in his name; they sing in his name; some are his name. One woman stares into the distance.

"She's had shock treatment," says an obviously sane woman. Jesus, like my Pearl!

"What are you doing here?"

She's here on the court's orders. She offers no explanation. I quickly understand that social niceties are obsolete. It suits me just fine.

"You are in High Security."

"Why?"

"It's admission policy. You'll get used to it."

"I need to lie down."

I am no longer a primate. My upper body won't stay up. My forehead has dropped. It sags down, over my eyes, which won't stay open. Such a pressure on them. Like Hilette towards the end.

"I really need to lie down."

But this is not allowed. You either sit with your two crimplene dresses in the glass cage or you join the rest outside who call out to the forgotten world out there.

It is shocking beyond words. And the steel door has closed and the psychiatrist departed. I can knock on the glass to get the nurses' attention and be ignored like the rest. Or I can stay right here, next to the court woman.

"One really has little choice," I say amidst the incomprehensible shouts and murmurs and songs.

"Little choice."

I'm called to see another psychiatrist who starts with name, date of birth, date of today, how come I'm here. He urges me to go to Ward 6 where there's a new voluntary six-week programme. I'd have group therapy.

"I'm done talking. I said what I wanted to say. I'm not going there." He is called away. I, meanwhile, feel terribly nauseous and try to make a dash for a toilet. All I have are my crimplene dresses. There I stand with my offering, and am briskly escorted away. When I come outside again I spot Dorrian walking furiously past High Security with its mountainous fence. I call her. She hisses through the wire that she wants my car keys. My car is blocking her driveway because it's miles from the pole. Alas, she'll have to go to reception. They'll know where my bag is. I can't get out of here. There's a steel door between me and her. And off she fumes.

I'm shaken. A Jesus-singer takes my hand and sings her song. She could not possibly have comprehended, but there's compassion buried beneath the psychosis.

And so it's the next morning and we've been marched out of our dormitories, cattled through the shortest shower, into our two dresses, swallowed breakfast and into the cage. Jesus, what have I done to myself? But luckily I'm taken to the spot where psychiatrist number three is waiting.

"Okay, it's clear I have to get out of here. But I'm not going to Ward 6 with its new programme and group therapy. I'm done talking."

As a compromise, he says, I can go to Ward 3, although I should not be there. When people here get better, meaning get down from their psychotic highs, they graduate to Ward 2. When they get even better they go to Ward 3, from where they are eventually discharged. I'll have to wait for a transfer. It may take time.

The transfer takes the entire day and night and into the next morning. By now I have enough clarity to see that Valkenberg is nothing close to the place I'd imagined Pearl went to: dark passages, hidden rooms, moaning behind locked doors. So much for fiction and for the stereotype of a mental institution. But it's far more disturbing to be part of it than I thought.

I sit inside, waiting, or in the small outside, next to the court woman. By now she has revealed that the court thinks she murdered her husband and she needs to be observed. She did not kill him and there is nothing wrong with her. I suppose that's why she's in full make-up and plays mother to the deranged. She is a model of sanity. If only she could speak to her boyfriend. He came after the husband's death.

But her speech is cut short.

I'm called inside. My transfer has come through! And here

I go to Ward 3 with straw hat, shirt and toothbrush hidden in sleeve. It's a short walk away from the cage, but I'm outside and it's good enough.

Ward 3 is a haven, compared. There's a big outside with a low fence and a gate. Beyond this are wards in similar looking houses dotted around with lots of ground between. Inside are personal belongings next to beds, an upright cupboard for each and even a basin per dormitory. All very clean and neat. Still only one sheet with a blanket and pillow. But there's some form of freedom. You can move freely around the big grounds, which are truly lovely, although you have to walk in twos and not alone. In my circumstances you have to appreciate the smallest thing. Coming to think of it, losing your freedom is no small thing.

Ward 3 is a mix of mental states. Here there is no intense psychosis with Jesus-calling, but some are dreadfully insular, walking as if in a trance. The nurses say they're on heavy meds, but on their way to recovery. The rest, with not many really fully alert, are plagued by where they're going to stay once they're released. Yes, my Pearl's problem too. There are no halfway houses, or very few.

The better off will be fetched by a mother and a father or husband and taken to a nice bedroom, with three meals included. There's one, a married woman with the blackest hair, who desperately needs to be home. Her husband put her here and he's going to leave her here, because he wants their children and he's going to use Valkenberg against her. There's nothing wrong with her and by way of example she explains the stars and their meaning, and interaction of galaxies with little bobbing people on them. She is intelligent and quite erudite. In the outside world she'd probably be just a little on the far side of New Age.

There's also the grossest, heaviest woman who sits a hole through the earth. She dismisses everything and doesn't have a shred of sensitivity. She's got hanging on her lips the finest of the lot: an intelligent, decent girl who wants to do ballet, who wants to make something of her life, who realises how difficult it is, and who has nowhere to stay. She's going to move in with the bulldozer.

"You can't, that's the last place you can go to!"

With her sad eyes she looks out into the sky. She understands, but she has nowhere to go and so little money. The alternative is her boyfriend, but the relationship is too new. And off she goes, talking about the ballet classes she'll never take. She has a dream, but this will in due time be wiped out by survival. Reality destroys everything in its path.

Here too you can be exactly as you wish. No one blinks an eye at the hat and hairless head and shirt. But it's a very tedious place. Gone is the intensity of the really loony. There are just hours and hours to fill, sitting on upright, mismatched chairs with soapies blaring on the TV. By now my body lies on my thighs, my head dropped between my knees. But I discover the kitchen with an urn on the constant boil, though you are not to use this. I'm a horse in bridle, I can't decide the simplest thing for myself.

But oh, it's my lucky first day here in Ward 3. My goods have arrived. Every item is meticulously noted in a book, also to the cent the contents of my purse, and I must sign for them. It's almost dinnertime, but before I can be off I must be issued with a pair of pants. I can't go through Valkenberg wearing a shirt only.

After dinner I'm given a variety of pills and sleep like a bomb. The next day dawns and I feel kind of indescribable. Drugged by exhaustion, but I manage to make my way to the bathroom. Here we cannot shower, but must bathe. More time is allotted for this than at my previous lodgings. There's one tap to open the warm water and you have to wait for the tap to make its rounds. No one seems to find this strange. After the bath we have to go for a walk or do exercises on our piece of lawn. Walk done and dusted and now it's breakfast. We start with a prayer and have to wait for a spontaneous soul to recite something. At last the shortest prayer is mumbled. Amen, and we tuck into porridge followed by tea. Now we wait, neatly on our chairs for our names to be called out. When your name is called, up you go to the nurse and hold out your hand for your meds, palm up, and swallow, right there where the nurse can see the pills going down your throat.

I get nothing. Stone cold sober, chemical free, I'm going to go through Valkenberg.

But I have discovered a wall outside to sit against. I have been forced into standstill and reflection. It's been precisely a year since I came back from Korea. It's not been a pretty time. There was the frantic accommodation problem – there still is that problem – and the car business, the book disaster and the refusal to settle down in the cemented reality of middle age. And then there was the loss of Hazel. Adel too, to some extent, with her strange withdrawal.

And the sickness of the man. In a period of only six weeks I went against every grain in my being. Though what did I have to guide me? The premise on which I had based my life had evaporated and had left me with the loss of its security. It added to my life a deep distrust of myself. Plus, central to all is my being so changed that I don't connect with people, and they aren't able to share in the life-changing experience I had. As if time stood still here in Africa.

I was going to come back home to love. Yet I am as alienated and lonely here as I was in Korea. But the most devastating is the loss of solitude. Always living to someone else's rhythm. And in deadening reality. Here it's as good as it's ever going to get. The moments aren't filled with the vibrancy of possible new experience. No, buckle down, accept that keen hope withers. And why ever did I go away? I *have* to try to keep Rilke's poem alive.

> To know serenity the dove must fly
> far from its dovecote, its trajectory
> informs it, distance, fear, the racing sky
> are only understood in the return.
>
> The one that stayed at home, never tested
> the boundaries of loss, remained secure,
> only those who win back are ever free
> to contemplate a newer, surer flight.

Will I win back? I destroyed so much, there's no path left that leads to the past. But I should not forget that if you keep yourself to the keenest in you where the flame originates, you are truly awake, but you risk your life falling apart. This is the rule of the universe: one extreme will be followed by its opposite. On and on in my head, I'm out the front door. The grounds are endless and there are big trees with birds. It's peaceful, bar, of course, the misery inside.

Here's High Security with the Jesus-callers, the shock treatment woman in the same position as yesterday and the court woman still looking sane. She's spotted me. Can I phone her boyfriend? She's not allowed to use the phone inside. Is it legal? It's one thing writing your philosophy on someone's walls, the law is quite another. I press the phone to her ear through the wire.

Back at the ward and I'm to see a psychiatrist. She's a friend of Anna's and she's asked her to come and see how I'm doing. Instead of starting with today's date, she talks to me.

"You must find accommodation, that's your first step."

"I'm now in something like the tenth place in one year. I should not have given the flat to my son."

"He must find other accommodation. You are in greater need than he is."

"I phoned, but he and his friend have now settled in. He has to think of the friend as well, he said. Had it only been his accommodation he would have moved out. He was as cold as a stone."

She wants to know whether I'm sorry that I cut off my hair. Well, I now sit with the consequences. But no, I'm not sorry. This and the wall writing were the strongest and most decisive actions I had taken in years.

"High Security must have been a shock."

"Beyond description. Who were all those psychiatrists I saw? Not one stayed for the whole story."

"They're interns and their programme is full. Think about it: you should not be here. You'd be better off in Ward 6."

"I'm done talking. I said what I had to say. I'm not going there."

I take to the wall outside again, where it's soul-searching, soul-searching, and why do I drag reasons from my innards that may not be true?

I hated that bloody Hilette. I don't anymore. I don't know why and I certainly don't need to invent reasons. Bottom line: my novel now works.

No! Here lies the unwanted. What do I not want to know?

There's nothing to know.
Yes!
It has to do with me, me. And I don't know what.

Thank God, I'm called inside. I have guests. Suddenly I'm a busy little bee. The matriarch has brought a towel, pyjamas, panties, a hairbrush and a CD player. It's not pleasant seeing her. Perhaps I'm ashamed. She wants to know how the sleep therapy is going. Where *did* I get this from? Does it even exist? Another friend brings a T-shirt, moisturiser and tea. And also pen and paper. Write down, she tells me. Here lies a next book. Write down?! What I should write down is the dreaded word 'accommodation' and steps to get it. But all I can think about is how to slip into the kitchen to make tea and where next to sit before five o'clock comes and that sliding door is locked with us bizarre lot steaming inside. But at least there's no Good Samaritan to be thankful to and no making small as a ping-pong ball a whole full human being.

Another psychiatrist whose case I officially am comes. First things first: I have to find accommodation. He's given me a pass and written it into some book. It says I may come and go as I please. So I secure my hat and calmly stroll past security and out the gate. I'm going to get my car.

Dorrian's here, so the gods are not with me. She's fearfully articulate in her anger. Point one to many. My insides cringe, but I weather it. Who am I to judge? I don't even know someone who'd write on someone's walls and destroy the property.

En route back to Valkenberg I think I could easily have coffee somewhere. Back at the gate I deftly say: "Ward 3." Not an eyebrow is lifted. I may as well be a doctor, except for the hat. But I'm an inmate, an inmate. Who parks her car under a tree, next to her ward. Now eyebrows are raised. The nurses like this not one bit, but it's written in the book: in and out as I wish.

If only I could lie down.

I phone Marko instead. He is still a stone. He'll bring my stuff. Dorrian wants it out of her house.

HE'S IN THE visiting room.

"Marko!"

He hands me my camera and suitcase with jewels and silk.

"I'm so glad to see you."

He says he's talked to Mangaliso and they're not moving. If he could he would have reversed the situation. Only two sentences. He's out the door. The mother with hair in tufts and clumps.

Wail-like shouts. I fold forward, clutch my stomach. Nurses rush in. I see Marko's borrowed car, next to mine under the tree, I see his back. He drives off.

It is a death all of its own. Of comfort in what came before; of instinctual trust; of the entirety of a person.

My son has been erased, and replaced.

A nurse takes my camera. I take my suitcase to the dormitory.

I'm shocked into action. I phone and phone, but accommodation is not going to be found on the phone. I'm going to have to drive out to Simon's Town and look around. I figure Simon's Town, where I once spent a year writing, is the answer for a middle-aged woman. Since all else will fail and since I'm at the end of the lusty road of life, I'll at least have the sea and the mountains.

I don my hat and drive out of the gates. I leave one reality behind and enter a very different one. My exodus yields nothing. I go back and sit.

The days come and go.

Piet-my-vrou. Karin! Where did Hilette's abuse come from? She is an injured woman. If she is in me, it's being wounded I share with her.

It's fiction!

Yes, but you are the creator of it. Can one create out of thin air? I don't know. I don't want to know what this pain is I can't name. I don't want to know Hilette anymore. She and her pulverised body and shady past must disappear from my life.

At least in reality, here, I've become a celebrity of sorts. As we were doing our morning exercises in our haphazard circle, I showed them how to stretch and release their shoulders and necks. This was a real hit. A meal prayer also contributed to this new status. I had had enough of waiting for the empty mumble up to the Lord and said a prayer. I thanked, first of all, the state for sponsoring Valkenberg, without which we'd have no care. Then I thanked the good nurses and doctors who nurse us back to health. We owe them our lives. A spontaneous hand-clapping followed.

And though I started from defiance I believed every word. Just where would all these people be without the good and dedicated care of Valkenberg?

Five o'clock has come and the doors are shut. We're in the steam bath. I can't sleep with a sticky body and since the baths and single tap are out of bounds at night I get rid of my shirt and Valkenberg's pants and wash in the basin in the dormitory. I suppose my nakedness is inappropriate, but I'm in a loony bin after all. And sure, no one notices. Now I know how millions of people have to clean themselves.

The upside of night-time is wandering to the nurses when all is asleep, and I can't sleep, what with being chemical free. There's a sense of expanded space and the nurses are kind. I want to know if I can make tea at Ward 6 at free will. Oh yes, it's much different there.

It's the next day and I spot the psychiatrist who decreed I'm to come and go as I please. I'm ready for Ward 6, I say, but: do I have to sit out the entire six weeks?

No, you can leave as the fancy takes you.

But I'll have to wait for a transfer, and transfers to Ward 6 happen only twice a week on specific days.

The first specific day comes and goes. I wait patiently, sitting on this chair, on that one outside, on the ground against the wall, increasingly feeling the plight of these people. Their courage breaks my heart. I see their slow process of recovery and their tenacity to get better.

The wheels of transfer grind slowly. I'm now into week two. I spot the psychiatrist again – actually, I've been looking out for him, single-mindedly. Please, will you check what's happening? The system's forgotten me. You're my only hope.

And voilà! He's gone and meddled in other people's systems and my transfer comes through. Here I go with suitcase and hat across the grass, accompanied by a lively nurse. I look back and there's the woman with blackest hair now with whitest hair. But onwards to greener pastures. There's no fence around this ward and we enter what looks very much like the previous ward. I'm full of expectancy. Up we go to the nurses' station and slap-bang into sullenness. First things first: I have to hand in my cell phone. I can have it at night. And I have to hand in my car keys. No leaving the grounds. They have it in for me. It's written all over her.

I have a quick look. There are two taps per bath, but still only one sheet per bed.

Ward 3 was alive with struggle, with nurses rooting for their patients in their various stages of recovery, with dedication. Here, well, your very presence is an imposition to the staff, who create this wretched atmosphere.

The place is a morgue. Most of us loonies sit squeezed together out of the wind on decrepit chairs in a courtyard outside the kitchen with bins and drains as decoration. There are many troubles. Accommodation problems rank high and also an intern psychiatrist who stops medication without explanation, though the person complaining about this doesn't seem entirely together. It can't be true. The head nurse, specifically, is much hated. She of the brusque, sulking nature.

This new programme seems to be a failure, though there is a small group of younger people who keep to themselves and who are nearing the end of their six week stay here. They have benefited, they say. But for the rest, people aren't suitably occupied. There are scheduled sessions, but not all materialise. The only sure thing is a specific weekly gathering everyone fears. Here you have to tell another person what you don't like about him or her, but there is no follow-up afterwards. It creates great anxiety and people fret about this for days before.

The person leading this is a shiny new mint fresh from a psychology department. Today is our weekly dread. We file into a room and sit on new chairs around the walls. All very clean. To our mint's chagrin I can't keep my mouth shut. These sessions create anxiety, I say. And what exactly is the objective? Insulting someone can hardly bring more understanding of yourself. As for the poor insulted, what must that person do – without follow-up – with the barrage of negativity?

No, it's straight and simple. But there's no one I have a problem with. I don't know these people, how can I dislike?

What obsesses me is in which box, in which house, I will find clothes. It's not as simple as it sounds. At this point I don't know what I possess.

No, the new mint says, my contribution is not spot on. This is not about the individual, it's about the group. I capitulate and pick a guy who talks a lot. Well, then, that one. Sorry, what's your name? Sorry, I hardly know you. We have now all forced a dislike out of ourselves and everyone leaves the room in great distress.

But worst is to come. We're gathered again. This time in the lounge. Our esteemed leader is at the helm. We're in a circle on upright chairs and one after another – moving around the circle – we have to introduce ourselves and come up with a good suggestion for the group. Mine is that we should get a ball. At least then we'd run and jump and get off our chairs there next to the drains and bins.

And so we hobble around the circle. At last it's the turn of a fear-stricken soul. He can't get a word out, not even his name. He's seized up. This is what happens to him. Our leader has deemed it fit to wait while the poor man starts sweating. He's gone red and the sinews in his neck are ropes. He forces his mouth open, but not a word comes out. We sit, we wait. The longer we wait, the worse he becomes. It's become unbearable and nothing short of cruel. To see someone in such a state and watch wordlessly – it is inhumane. He tries again. He opens his mouth, this time wider. But still not a word. The tension has now spread to everyone in the room. Some look down at their laps, or stare past him. Others fidget, some hold their breath. My breath has come out of my mouth and I make a lot of sound: I don't see the point of this. He is clearly in such a state of anxiety that he's not going to utter a word. This is humiliating and counter-productive.

I should not take over the session, do I understand? We finish the session, still without a word from him.

Outside, and Helena, who is in Cape Town for business, is here. She's brought me a sheet and a lot of airtime. I have a horrible feeling, I tell her, that they're going to throw me out. I don't have accommodation yet and it's by far not the end of the month.

But I have taken decisive control. In the mornings I pretend to hand in my phone. I need the thing to phone around to try and find accommodation. And phone I do, standing in a wind-swept corner in front where no one goes. But it's useless. I can't go out and look at places. And yes, they *are* going to throw me out. I can see a bad moon rising.

Marko has phoned, still rather icy. He found a flat, but the agent won't give me the contract in absentia. He knows what's on the market – he's been through every possible flat – and this one is by far the best. I'm so touched. I didn't know he was looking. That he was making sure I'd be fine. A child should not have to take on a parental role. My poor boy must be eaten raw by the internal conflict all this has been creating in him.

It's now well into week three. Each one has a turn to appear in front of a panel led by the head psychiatrist. I just know they're going to throw me out and I'm right. In the kindest way the head tells me that my problems are situated in the world, they are not interpersonal. I'd be better off outside. I thank the panel and leave. The head joins me outside the room and asks how I am.

I'm very fortunate. I now know what mental illness is and I've been spared a lot. It can befall anyone, at any time, he says. And to make light I say I can look at it in two ways. I'm being thrown out of Valkenberg because I'm too sane, or that not even Valkenberg wants me. We laugh a bit. He's really a kind man. When I pack I realise that my camera didn't make it to Ward 6. Back at Ward 3, and there's no camera and nothing signed in where it should have been. Theft has followed me here in South Africa like a slinking dog.

In the clear light of afterwards I stand baffled: why could I not see clearly? Why did I guide myself so disastrously?

Yes, one person entered Korea. Another left it.

For the few days until the end of the month when I can move into the flat that Marko found, I've come to the Karoo. I'm in the same house and same town I always go to. I've driven way out of town and park at my usual spot and start walking into the veld. I stop at the bottom of the hill where I saw Pearl walk out of a tin house and into the scorching veld to disappear forever. And here, that's where Hilette with her court shoes and skirt got lost in the veld. I was so tired and that's when Hilette's sleep therapy came to me. Halfway up this hill I was overcome by the impossibility of what I was attempting to write. I turned around, clenched my teeth and went back and wrote.

Walking at the bottom of this hill, between nothing to the left and nothing to the right, our hard earth crunches under my feet. I can feel the vastness of life and I know Dae-ho and Hye-mi and Sam and Mae will not share a Karoo veld with me. And I know the loss of them. And the gain.

Since I don't have a cup, spoon, plate, sheet, pillow, or anything for that matter – Dorrian's tenants even vanished with my furniture – Marko's stuff has to be split. The girl from the Red Cross, who is now definitely more than a friend with benefits, opens his door and calls him. It's very uncomfortable. There we stand in the entrance hall. There is no familiarity between us. And I can't believe it, but I do say to him that he and Mangaliso have to pay me the deposit I paid for the flat. I reckon if we're going to be two separate individuals then this is necessary. Sure thing, he will. Just how will he manage to do it since he gets so little from his intern job? That's not my concern, he says, still in his icy voice. It's bloody horrible, though he's generous in giving me back my stuff. Still, he has to live too and we both end up with less than we need.

The last item needs to be negotiated. It's the most beloved, one-of-its-kind, never-to-be-seen-on-the-shelves-again garlic press. There it lies, on the kitchen counter. Am I going to succumb to motherly sacrifice and give it to him?

I look at this man in front of me. This is my boy with his blond curls. This is my child! My hand goes to the garlic press.

I don't pull it back.

I HAVE CLEANED the windows of my flat and stand back. Does the sea get rough here? Or have I moved into the Bay of Remembrance? Quiet thoughts, quiet sorrows for the me that's passed into bygone time, that I cut loose, sorrow for this harsh violation. Can you start again, so, without anchor?

But I should not forget. This is also the time for the still point. From which all can arise and all can pass.

The sea, the distant mountains, the high sky, and when it is low you are held in clouds, or just a film through which the setting sun shines. The colours, strong, at times soft, but always wrenching and at night, the moon, the stars, the sea all glitter. And the ancient stone of tombs among the green trees, right in front. The beauty is unbearable. It is so intense you feel your DNA change but then, of course, nothing changes. You are not able to absorb the beauty, etch it into forever. It passes away as if it had never existed.

Oh, how I long for Hazel. How the two of us sat on her veranda and looked out over the sea.

Hazel, where are you?

There's a spasm between my shoulders. There where a crater is, hollowed with the weight of sorrow and loss. Mine heaves, as mighty as the sea in front, and my voice wails pitifully: I want Hazel. Hazie, where are you?

And sure as sure, Hazel comes. But she floats up, away from me, she's going to the very far north, her arm is stretched out backwards, my arm is not long enough, I try, heaven knows I try. Her slender hand is in front of me, just not near enough, see, there she goes, back to the north of dead land. Dead, deadest land.

I wail, it's pitiful. Orpheus played and played his lyre, but Eurydice could not come back. Look! There goes Hazie, float away, Hazie and old Mister Plod, my Jasper barks, it is soundless, I scream: Hazel, I want you! You can't erase twenty years of friendship, cut it out of my heart. My bedrock friend. My crater heaves so violently, I'm down on the floor, please, I cannot without you.

And sure as sure, Hazel is right here next to my shoulder, with her silk dress. My hartjie, my hartjie, I will stay here, right here with you. See, my dress is shiny and it is green, you can't miss it, you will hear it as it makes its sounds, even when you sleep.

Hazel has not gone to dead land, merged into the nebulous energies in the air, no, she has a form, and she is right here.

What does it matter that I know this not to be so? I shall make the positive philosophical choice and believe Hazel to be in her selfsame shape, right here with me.

Yes, it's best not to be too complacent in the current good moment and therefore trusting in the continuation of this: seismic shifts can occur in the blink of an eye and all the good feelings so softly cuddled and frantically guarded can disappear, and be replaced by the deeply known, semi-misery of daily life.

I have received an email, shocking in itself, but also comical. It's from our Buddhists, sent to me in error. It's a long back-and-forth between Adel and the one at whose house the meditation was. It notes in detail how wrong I am, and bad; the despicable liaison with the man; a Valkenberg case to boot, not to be associated with. How I need to be cleansed, the root of all evil banished from me. And just how unacceptable what I did to Dorrian was.

I write back. Just how the fuck did I harm you?

It's in solidarity with Dorrian, comes the reply. I can't imagine Dorrian needs or wants their solidarity, but there you go – she has a little group rooting for her that feels terribly aggrieved on her behalf.

I have a sensible reply for them: you hardly know Dorrian. I ask you again: how did I harm you?

No, I haven't, comes the next reply. But they've been worried sick. I phone around and yes, the Buddhists have united in a cabal with the spearhead, Adel, recruiting under my friends. She's got Dearie in the bag. Other friends won't follow, they're suspicious of harmful childishness. But the cabal of three has judged and I've been found lacking. They profess one thing and practise another. I wonder where their compassion is. That compassion that turns their faces into comic earnestness?

Of course I'm angry, but most of all I'm shocked. How tenuous is the illusion that we are safe in a structure bigger than ourselves and shielded from extinction by our friendships, because our friends, and therefore us, have a place in the world.

It's unthinkable not to have Adel in my life. And impossible to admit she betrayed our friendship. Although, did I not also betray her when I broke away to Korea, and so destroyed our dependencies and the roles we played for each other? Oh, my dearest friend, how sad I am for the loss of you.

To add insult to injury: news has travelled from Cape Town all the way up to Joburg and back again. The fat publisher with his various pretentions says one can't book oneself into Valkenberg. I must have been committed. Of course, where's the juice in the gossip if you admit yourself? It has to be a deranged woman forced into captivity.

Well, Fat Publisher, as testament to my admitting myself I am now faced with a steep bill. I could have gone to a private joint and probably got my elusive sleep therapy. This is their system: you are admitted against your will – you don't pay; you admit yourself – you pay. Publisher, let this word be spread as enthusiastically.

Not so bad, the bill, considering.

The court woman from High Security was found guilty of murder.

It's a time of sobriety, and so I write to Dorrian.

An apology is not what is owed you. I have done so and no urgent and increasing apologies will undo what I have done.

As I see it the writing on the walls is not the real harm. Nor is the inconvenience of the time you had to spend to deal with the debris of my actions.

I shattered your trust. And for this I am really, truly sorry. When you feel the heartbeat of another, you should tread with caution.

I am not going to urge you to see what happened as a breakdown and so be blameless. It was a breakthrough, strong and liberating. As you no doubt know, it is from our shadow that we draw the strongest energy, which can lead to real, fundamental change: for the good or for the bad. It unleashed itself in me, that night. I was a force stronger than myself; I was defenceless against it, yet I was it. In the face of something life-changing control is not on offer, neither is reason. I was a force beyond reason and you were the accidental casualty of it. The gods smiled cruelly on me that night. But they smiled and I am the richer for it.

I shan't sketch how the years and eventually the months, days and hours ticked off to ground zero. When you phoned, after the whole miserable lot with the man had happened, I was standing in the garden. By the way, I was not drunk. But I was drunk with fury at suppressing myself in Korea, and the year back here; at trying to fit in, at silencing myself. I was drunk with the force of the energy that had kept me submissive.

That energy had finally erupted.

Then you phoned. I heard myself say: "It won't happen again." My shame at what I had become flooded me and with that the strongest will to change it. At that stage I still had reason, and wrote on what was mine – the table. I wanted my words engraved *into* that wood. But I had not purged myself fully by the time my table was full, so I started on your whiteboard. And there everything changed.

I tell you from the coalface: I could neither stop myself, nor reason. I, my whole body, had become the very momentum of the writing. Writing is a re-creation – what I'm doing now. But then I was the movement of writing itself. There was no split-second gap between the thought – and the expression of it. There was only the *being* of it. When I finally wrote, "My God, I'm desecrating Dorrian's walls" that gap had come between me and what I was doing. But then it was too late. All was over.

That night did not end there. What needed to come to

an end had not yet come. And I cut off my hair. I spent ten years creating a character who did exactly this. It goes without saying that it is indeed symbolic of something very strong.

With this I had exorcised the weakness I had become. I had finally let my strength through in all its force, which also meant its destructiveness. It doesn't mean the misery of my weakness won't overcome me again, a sliding back into smallness. But it does mean I am on a different path.

I do not wish to excuse myself. I am so terribly sorry for its harming our friendship. I was as stunned by what I had done as you were.

It seems I unleashed everyone's dark side. We are all acting in unknown ways. We are at the mercy of ourselves. This is not such a bad thing. We are all too clever for our own good; too safe in our firm beliefs; too much in control. To the point that we become automatons repetitively living in small, safe parts.

It is not incidental that my female support base has collapsed at just this time in my life. I'm moving out of the folds of the eternal mother's breast. Here lies the crux: when I came back from Korea I did not endear myself to them through shared weakness. I carried my struggles on my own. I was a concern to others. To very few a burden. At least in Korea I had learnt to suffer myself. And I am paying the price for that now.

There are some friendships I'm willing to sacrifice for this cardinal shift. I risk, of course, not having any fold to run back to. Women are harsh and will not easily forgive the breaking of the pact of dependency. I don't see you as part of a female fold.

Oh Dorrian, I am not going to go gentle into that good night of middle age. I am too extreme – for God's sake, I'm now even a Valkenberg case! How will I ever live this down? No, I am too restless with life force, too heedless of common sense, which can stand one in good stead, but which can also prevent one living fully.

You asked: what are you doing with your beautiful life? I'm *living* it. It means being thoroughly dead, equally alive; weak and strong; wild, free and just as caged in. All my flaws are exposed, and therefore my shame as well. But this simply means being me.

We are both aware enough and I pray that if our beastly selves lock horns one of us will retain our hard-won consciousness and bring sanity.

My dreams are exhausting, fraught with persecution, escape and confrontation. A while ago there was Hitler! I am grappling and grappling. But I shall not cower. I'll face my battles head-on.

Yes, yes, I lost it. I got lost in that vast space inside. You know that space where you try to stay super-calm, and all your energy goes into that. And then it starts feeling like you're inside an echo. And your foundation is echoed away and too late you realise you're in a space from where you can't be retrieved, and you just go deeper and then you realise it's all a fuck-up. And you don't know how to get back.

But you forced me out of it. You forced me into my shame. In the end *this* was where I had to sink to before I could rise.

"It won't happen again", that exquisitely shameful sentence. That was the lowest point, the most deeply shameful point of my life.

Look what has become of you, I told myself. And I shuddered as I felt that whatever had grown so big in me that I could humiliate myself to the point of utter lack of self-respect, that that concoction of emotion was still alive and well.

And I knew: It. Has. To. End.

To cut off your carefully cultivated hair – highlights and all – means no return. There is a way of being before you expose your scalp, and there is a distinctly different way after.

What shone on my scalp was the end of what I had become. It was a dramatic transformation, and sudden in its announcement. God, I was resolute. There was going to be an end to the shameful mass of body tissue and bones and mucus I had become.

And from this I have to rise.

Oh yes: it's quite disturbing to be the perpetrator. Gone are righteous indignation and the pain of the long-suffering just. I can tell you this.

Dearest Dorrian, Love

Dearest piet-my-vrou. Karin!
　Wake up!
　Where did you get Hilette's abuse from?
　I don't know. I don't know. I don't know.

It is award night. I have dressed myself to the nines. The matriarch gave me money for clothes for the event. Did she think there was a need? God forbid not. Or was she just kind? I took the whole substantial lot and bought high-heeled Kurt Geiger boots.

My hair has grown again and gossip is losing its serpentine tail. Dorrian has wished me luck and Marko has sent an sms.

It's a lavish affair. My 'publishers' are here, though they have closed shop and the books aren't really available. No surprise in this. Never mind.

Never mind anything, there I totter on the Kurt Geigers up to the stage. My God, what do you know? I've won the award.
　JM Coetzee!

My brother-in-law died yesterday.
　Jan!

Piet-my-vrou.
　Boetie and Piet.
　I don't know. I don't know. I don't know.

MARKO HAS JUST been for dinner. I had good wine and a leg of lamb, the way he likes it. At first we smiled uncomfortably, and then we hugged and laughed. And we both knew we had cut the cord, God, this excruciating thing, oh, my boy, you have no idea what it took. To tear away from your child, to let him go, free him of yourself. There are many sacrifices, and are they bearable? But shot through is a love that comes from the marrow of you, and a protectiveness that will destroy anything in its path. Yourself included. Because your child is more your being than you are. But then comes the point you have to stop being your being and shatter the self you are.

And my boy? To give answer to his biggest life task – to launch himself into the torrents of life – he had to break free from his mother whose life was overwhelming his.

In how much agony he must have been. This man who is imbued with love, who moulds his soul so fully with another. Tearing away is a violent act. My Marko boy, you with your blond curls, which aren't so blond and curly anymore, you have grown tall, a man, and I have grown wiser and together we'll be mother and son, independently.

It is very quiet. I stand between the dishes, greasy wine glasses and the faint smell of food. How warm and happy is this sight. A testament to the fullness of life. I'll leave this till tomorrow, and prolong our togetherness.

I'm aware of a spreading silence in me. Have I been sufficiently prepared to live in the absolute of this? Where will it take me? If I could fetch the future for a while and fill its ear, would it say Marko has finished his studies; he is an architect, or perhaps not – who knows what he will do? But if – then – Karin has the audacity to criticise his designs. She harps on about 'dead space', which Marko assures her is not in his designs, but is a result of her inability to read plans. He is a little condescending and Karin isn't sure that she dislikes this all together. After all, it is a sign that he is in full command of his profession; that he is no longer a student, but a grown man, one who speaks with authority.

Marko is married to Karen, the friend with benefits from the Red Cross with whom Karin is besotted. She is kind and warm with enormous eyes and the softest skin. They have a little girl, or a little boy, who has their mother's big eyes and father's wide smile and is a joy, a joy.

What is also a joy – a blessing! – is that Karin has not, to her surprise, seen the end of carnal pleasure yet. The cut-off date is still due.

But dream as I may the silence comes like a mist and the images go. They are not important and can't give substance to a woman who is here looking down on a happy sight and wonders:

Who is here in this silence, standing, looking? Who asks what happens when the door opened and you took more courage than you had; stepped through; realise that the you that was born before is now behind. Will there be new births and new deaths? Or, without the pressure to survive, might you stop breathing and give yourself to the effortlessness of non-being? Might you?

No!

I, creator and destroyer of Hilette Barend, professor of anthropology, I shall clench my teeth, sit down at my desk and let the fear in the silence overwhelm me. And I shall write myself back into existence. I shall stand in awe as a new me is born, or as no me is born. But I shall write.

All was; is; and all awaits.

Acknowledgements

I have been blessed with big-hearted people in my life who have made the completion of this book possible.

I thank Fiona Moodie for her generosity, as always. My gratitude to the Gavin Relly Educational Trust for sponsorship, as well as the National Arts Council. Thanks to Jane Taylor for her endorsement for funding.

I thank Inge and Mauritz van Aarde, as well as Gerry Maré and Thembisa Waetjen for their houses in Prins Albert, which are pretty much heaven. All the people involved in the Karoo Boekehuis Hantam in Calvinia who once again helped make wonders happen. My writer friend, Donvé Lee who understands our shared writing world so well, and Marika Joubert for endless Korean translations. And of course Marko Coetzee who seems unable to lose faith in his mother.

But there were dark times as well. Gerrit Olivier read an unimpressive, raw draft and managed to see the value in it. I clung to his insightful and encouraging report which carried me through times of despair. Thanks to Hanni Allan and Hettie Scholtz who also managed to sound upbeat, or at least, not too shocked, after a first reading.

I wish to thank my editor, Alison Lowry. It is rare to have complete faith in someone, but I do in her. She is the most humane and insightful editor a writer can ever hope for.

I'm thankful to Gretchen van der Byl who created the gorgeous cover design. Janine Daniel, of JDoubleD Publicity, who will help carry this book into the world, is a joy. I thank Anna Strebel and Andy Thesen for their meticulous reading.

And Colleen Higgs, my publisher, and her assistant Aimee-Claire Smith, who carry all of us safely in their hands.

And to all those who helped me create this story by living it with me, a big thank you.

www.ingramcontent.com/pod-product-compliance
Lightning Source LLC
Chambersburg PA
CBHW010833230426
43671CB00018BA/2948